MADAM ATATÜRK

MADAM ATATÜRK

A Biography

İpek Çalışlar

Translated from Turkish by Feyza Howell

SAQI

First published in hardback in 2013 by Saqi Books
This edition published 2019

Copyright © İpek Çalışlar 2013
Translation © Feyza Howell 2013

İpek Çalışlar has asserted her right under the Copyright, Designs
and Patents Act, 1988, to be identified as the author of this work.

First published in Turkish as *Latife Hanim*
in 2006 by Doğan Egmont Publishing

ISBN 978 0 86356 335 5
eISBN 978 0 86356 847 3

A full CIP record for this book is available from the British Library.

Printed by Bell & Bain Limited, Glasgow G46 7UQ.

Saqi Books
26 Westbourne Grove
London W2 5RH
www.saqibooks.com

Contents

Introduction

Chance helped me identify my next project when I left my newspaper job: Madam Atatürk. She had for so long been brushed aside as plain, spoiled and impertinent that I, like many others, believed it all. The moment I discovered she had demanded Atatürk change the law to enable her to stand for parliament, I knew I had found the woman whose biography beckoned. The journalist in me kicked into action with an urgency that led me to the shelves to read every single book about her published eight decades earlier and every history magazine I could lay my hands on.

Despite her extraordinary intelligence and outstanding education, Latife Hanım, as she is better known in her native Turkey, has always been portrayed as an accident that somehow happened to Mustafa Kemal Atatürk. At a time when Bertrand Russell was standing as a candidate for women's suffrage, Latife attended Tudor Hall School (then in Chislehurst, near London) prior to reading law at the Sorbonne.

Latife 'Ouschaki', who hailed from afar, from the Ottoman Empire, spoke English well enough to surprise her teachers. She had acquired her flawless command of the language years earlier from her English governess.

She shot to international stardom at the age of twenty-four when she married Mustafa Kemal, who delivered her country from occupation. Old Tudorians must have been thrilled to see her picture in the *Illustrated London News*. Now, ninety years on, their grandchildren can read the story of this first lady from Izmir who was a school friend of their grandmothers.

The spoiled woman label affixed to Latife was a conservative retort to her demand for equality. The history books that ignore women relished accounts of her petulance, but completely neglected to credit her love of freedom, her contributions to the steps taken in the early years of the republic or her status as Atatürk's assistant.

All you needed to discover her secrets was to look with a woman's eye.

Latife surprised me when I began scanning through newspapers from the 1920s. Her fame had spread around the globe as the unveiled wife of Mustafa Kemal and a defender of women's rights. She was hailed as the harbinger of Turkey's transformation and a celebrity. Her name topped the list of potential successors after Mustafa Kemal's heart attack. Yet none of those comments published in the world press made it into Turkey.

Mustafa Kemal emerged as an exemplary husband, a man who delighted in his wife's accomplishments in every field and who enjoyed exchanging views with her, disregarding the disapproval of his close circle.

Was this a love match? I have included all the clues I could find. The brevity of their marriage caused much pain to both of them.

Latife may have kept her silence until her dying day, but she had no intention of vanishing altogether. She wrote her memoirs hoping for eventual recognition and guarded all documents she valued in bank safes for disclosure in the future. These documents entrusted to the Turkish History Society are sadly destined to remain secret for some time yet. That being said, such a vivid portrait of Latife Hanım revealed itself as I wrote her biography that I stopped wondering a long time ago what they contained.

İpek Çalışlar
Galata, Istanbul 2012

Translator's Note

Atatürk was known as Gazi Mustafa Kemal Paşa until he took his surname in 1934, nine years after he and Latife Hanım divorced. Throughout their marriage, his wife was addressed as Latife Gazi Mustafa Kemal, and to this day, all of Turkey refers to Madam Atatürk as *Latife Hanım*, the Lady Latife.

We have adhered to modern Turkish spelling for proper nouns and standard British spelling in the interest of consistency.

Turkish is phonetic, with a single sound assigned to most letters. A circumflex accent [^] either elongates the vowel upon which it rests or 'thins' the k or l preceding it.

The consonants pronounced differently from English are:
c = English j in *jack*
ç = English ch in *chat*
ğ = 'soft g' is silent; it merely lengthens the vowel preceding it
j = French j in *jour*
r = English r in *read*; at end of syllables closest to the Welsh, as in *mawr*
ş = English sh in *shine*
y = English y in *yellow*

The vowels are equally straightforward:
a = shorter than the English a in *father*
e = English e in *bed* (never as in *me*)
ı = schwa; the second syllable in *higher*
i = English i in *bin* (never as in *I* or *eye*)
ö and ü = like the corresponding German umlaut sounds

Given names are usually accented on the final syllable, so *Lah-ti-FEH*, *Mus-ta-FAH Ke-MAL*, etc.

Abbreviations

CUP	Committee of Union and Progress
FRP	Free Republican Party
PP	People's Party
PRP	Progressive Republican Party

Feyza Howell
London, 2013

Glossary

Bey: honorific title meaning 'sir', 'lord'; usually follows the first name

Çarşaf: 'sheet'; Turkish for chador, 'a baggy, black cloak'

Efendi: honorific title meaning 'esquire'; usually follows the first name

Gazi: 'war veteran', 'victorious military leader'; a title frequently used to address Mustafa Kemal Paşa

Hacı: a person who has carried out a pilgrimage.

Hanım: honorific title meaning 'lady', 'madam'; usually follows the first name

Hanımefendi: 'noble lady'

Jandarma: the fourth armed force in Turkey, acting as military/provincial police

Kadı: an Ottoman judge with additional administrative duties

Müftü: a Muslim scholar, responsible for religious affairs of a county or district

Padişah: an Ottoman sultan regnant

Paşa: 'pasha', 'general', 'high-ranking statesman'

Şeyh: 'sheikh'; in Turkish, strictly limited to religious leaders

ud and *kanun*: also known as oud and qanun (from al oud in Arabic); stringed instruments

Usta: 'master'; a term of respect

Zeybek: a folk dance of the Aegean region

Zılgıt: 'ululation'; Turkish for zaghareed.

I

Meeting

It was an autumn evening in 1919 when a smartly dressed Frenchman alighted before the White Mansion in Izmir's Göztepe district.

The blockade sentry strode threateningly towards the gate, where the closed phaeton flying the tricolour had come to a stop. His determination to bar the visitor's path only earned him a rebuke:

'I am the French Consul, here to play bridge with Muammer Bey.'

Although the soldier spoke no French, he drew his rifle to one side: the documents the diplomat pulled from his pocket impressed him enough to make him retreat.

Izmir's Turks had been suffering untold hardship under Greek occupation since 15 May. Yet, mused the consul, gazing at the house wistfully as he walked down the rose garden, he had singularly failed to convince his friend to hoist the French flag. Why couldn't he have followed the example of Turks from Damascus? *They* raised the tricolour, and *they* were spared Greek harassment.

The door opened before he reached the bell: Izmir's celebrated merchant Muammer Uşşakizade, smartly turned out in his customary crisp white jacket, greeted his friend at the door, and the two men embraced. Spotting the suitcases as his feet followed the familiar route to the reception room, the consul knew the family were ready.

Prominent Turks had been under pressure to collaborate with the occupation, and Muammer was the most influential merchant in all Izmir. He had confided the last time they spoke freely, 'They're insisting I become mayor; neither does a day pass but that I don't receive death threats.'

Both men were freemasons, and their friendship, which had begun at the Bridge Club, predated the occupation by some time. The White Mansion in Göztepe was something of a second home for the consul.

He was genuinely terrified at the risk of death Muammer faced, and had repeatedly urged expediency, adding how he had already assisted some of his Turkish friends to escape from Izmir.

All being well, Muammer and his family would leave for Marseilles on a boat sailing that night. The consul had arranged for tickets and passports for the entire family; these documents were hidden in a secret compartment of the case in his hand.

'Is Makbule Hanım coming? What have you decided?'

'No,' replied Muammer, 'my mother begs to stay behind: she says she is too old to travel. Travel is more risky for her than staying in Göztepe.'

'The passports are ready. Here: Latife, Adeviye, İsmail, Ömer, Münci, Rukiye, Vecihe and yours ... Here's one for your mother, too; she might still change her mind, don't you think?'

Adeviye entered, a glum-looking Latife beside her.

'Please don't sulk, Latife; these Greeks are only here temporarily,' mumbled Muammer.

'My grandmother,' explained Latife, 'she won't come along. It's not easy leaving her behind.'

The consul tried to placate her. 'But we are here right beside her. Should anything go wrong, you could be back in three days. This curfew can't last for ever, and the resistance is spreading ... Everyone has great confidence in Kemal Paşa. He's certainly impressed our lot; they refer to him as a military genius.'

The bridge table was set in the garden, as usual. İsmail and Latife joined in to make up the four. Talk was loud, as usual, and Latife had a good run of aces and kings. The bridge party went on until nightfall. A sumptuous dining table had been laid, again as usual. The servants busied themselves with their tasks, as the household followed routine. Adeviye gathered a few more items that had been overlooked and checked Münci's medicines. Their youngest son had contracted polio; how he would cope with the journey was a real worry.

The family boarded the phaeton in the dark, careful not to be spotted by the sentries. Latife was the first to leave the house, followed by the rest as Muammer took leave of his friend. Makbule came out, a crystal pitcher in hand, and poured water at the roots of the old wisteria, honouring an ancient custom that bids travellers a smooth journey and a speedy return.

The phaeton was not big, so the younger boys had to lie on the suitcases and one of the girls sat on the other's lap. They followed the last few passengers boarding the French ship when they reached the port. Once through passport control safely, they all gazed at Izmir one last time from the deck.

The consul sank into a book he had drawn at random after the departure of the fugitives; he would read all night, the mansion ablaze with lights. The Greek soldiers were accustomed to all night long bridge parties at the White Mansion.

He was whistling as he left in the morning, again as usual, albeit a little tense on this occasion, and walked out between the unsuspecting sentries. He had rescued his dear friend Muammer and his family.

Three years later

Latife was standing on the deck of the boat leaving Marseilles, her gaze fixed on the deep blue sea. She was on her way back to Izmir, then still under Greek occupation. Their worst fears had come true, and bad news did travel fast: her grandmother Makbule was ailing. The young woman stopped her father, who was preparing to return:

'Father, they'd kill you; it's best I return instead.'

Once she made her mind up, that was that. Muammer's influence proved invaluable once more, and a French passport duly arrived, bearing a note: 'Under special protection.'

The Greeks were losing to the Nationalists on all fronts. Latife had been following news of the resistance and trusted Mustafa Kemal to liberate Izmir. She was wearing his portrait – cut from a newspaper – in a locket for good luck.

The boat was destined for Istanbul, where she would spend a day before making her way to Izmir. Three years earlier, she had, in fact, been actively engaged in the resistance; this time, she had some papers to collect in Istanbul.

She had planned her every move during the passage. Collecting the documents at the address she had been given proved no problem at all; she boarded the Izmir boat without opening her case. Unusually for her, she was dressed in a *çarşaf* this time, taking special pains to avoid a search. Her passport might identify her as a French citizen, but she still was the daughter of a prominent Izmir family well known to the occupation.

She arrived in Izmir on 17 June 1922, as Mustafa Kemal met his mother in Adapazarı, an event witnessed by an emotional crowd. The general had taken the opportunity of a visit with a diplomat to arrange to meet Zübeyde Hanım. He knew he had been neglecting her, rushing from one battlefront to the next; the time had come to take her to live close to him.

In a strange coincidence, Mustafa Kemal and his mother had also spent three years apart. Chance would throw these people together a few months later.

It was Latife's twenty-third birthday. Returning to her birthplace was not as straightforward as entering Istanbul had been. Suspicious of this Turkish girl travelling on a French passport, Greek officials wanted to search her. She was defiant: how could they search a Muslim woman? Haughtily she denied them permission to even touch her *çarşaf*, when, all the while, resistance documents were concealed in her undergarments.

The soldiers gave up on this covered girl and flung her into a cell instead.

'No food or water' was the order.

News spread instantly: the celebrated businessman Uşşakizade Muammer Bey's daughter had returned. Yet there was no sign of her. The French had provided entrance documents, but could do little through diplomatic channels now. What if they compromised their earlier role in the entire family's escape? So they took the next best course of action: making sure people learned of her arrival and immediate incarceration. It was not long before the entire city knew: 'Uşşakizade Latife has returned, but is in custody.'

Her maternal uncle Ragıp Paşa had been warned before her departure. When she failed to turn up, he reached out to his influential contacts amongst the occupying forces. The solitary confinement of a Muslim girl increased the tension. Risk of an even greater reaction ultimately forced their hand, and the Greeks had no choice but to release her on the third day. Latife had indeed made it to her grandmother's bedside within the week.

Sadly, their troubles were not yet over. An inflamatory letter she had written to a leading Izmir official in the early days of the occupation ('The enemy might well have occupied these lands, but the time will come when Mustafa Kemal will liberate the country, and we will all be free') had fallen into Greek hands, sparking her next ordeal. Now marked as a troublemaker, she was placed under house arrest.[1]

The brace of sentries posted at the Uşşakizade gate checked up on her hourly. To spite them, she frequently covered up in a *çarşaf*, pretending to be the ironing woman, going out and coming back as she pleased. Oppressed by the occupation, she had confided in a friend, 'You know what I'm going to do? I'm going to marry the commander who liberates Izmir.' Liberating commanders graced the dreams of many an Izmir girl.

Latife said much later, 'It was an interminable nightmare; they could have executed me at any point. I never once considered escape; I was so convinced of our ultimate liberation.' And encouraging news did indeed trickle in from the front.

She vowed to host Mustafa Kemal Paşa – whose valour she had found awe-inspiring – at her home, were he to enter Izmir victoriously.

As the Nationalist forces liberated the Aegean region step by step, Greek propaganda persisted in promising imminent victory. The truth was very different, however. Not even the Allies harboured any delusions of the Greeks' ability to last one more winter in Izmir.

In spite of the war raging in the interior, life in Izmir had been curiously unaffected, even carefree, until the last days of August 1922. The city was the centre of the nation's commercial and agricultural life, and although trade with the interior was diminished, the harbour bustled with traffic.

In season, baskets of rose petals lined the streets [...] In some streets the smell of freshly baked bread overpowered the roses. [...]

The markets testified to an abundant harvest [...] grapes, fresh figs, apricots, melons, cherries, pomegranates.[2]

On 26 August, news of the collapse of the Greek front at Afyonkara-hisar reached Izmir. The Greeks and Armenians wanted to believe the Turkish advance to be of a temporary nature. The British Consulate, concerned at the turn of events, alerted its subjects to be on their guard. English clubs in Buca and Bornova buzzed with comments on the news coming from the front, and wealthy Greeks and Armenians would mention, in passing, impromptu plans for a short break abroad. All would become clearer within a few days, in any case.

Latife followed the reports in the local press and recounted tales from the front – spread by word of mouth – to her grandmother. Encouraged by the turn of events, Makbule Hanım brightened up visibly. Afyonkarahisar was retaken on the 29 August. The Greek army was surrounded in Dumlupınar on the following day. In Izmir's attics, young women secretly embroidered crescents and stars in pearls on crimson fabrics, preparing to adorn the entire city come liberation day.

It was on this first day of September, too, that the Greek wounded began arriving. [...]

Civilian refugees from the interior began to flood the city next – Americans estimated that by 5 September they were arriving at the rate of thirty thousand a day. Most came on foot with their children, their draft animals, and all the household goods they were able to carry. Some were taken in by relatives and friends, some by strangers, but the streets were massed with them [...]. They [...] stormed the foreign consulates pleading for visas. [...] Within days the panic spread to the local Greeks and Armenians as well.[3]

On 7 September, General Hajianestis – commander of the Greek forces – departed, accompanied by a group of officers, and so ended the occupation of Izmir.

The sentries vanish

Latife arose early that morning and looked out of the window. She climbed up the terraced garden to the upper road: the sentries had vanished.

She was shouting, 'Grandma, they've gone! We're free! Mustafa Kemal Paşa will be here any time now!' Makbule Hanım went out into the garden to offer a prayer of thanks. The two women hugged each other: Latife was finally free; the house arrest had ended.

The Nationalists entered Izmir on 9 September. Cheers from the Turkish quarters mingled with the retreating army's yells of disarray. Yet Izmir was not entirely safe. Warships lay at anchor in the port, their guns facing the city, and gunshots were heard from a number of neighbourhoods. Troops running away from the front and minority Christians clamoured to get to the boats; the streets were strewn with furniture.

Mustafa Kemal Paşa entered Izmir on the 10th. A deliriously happy Latife and a few of her girlfriends joined the crowds flocking to greet the victorious commander.

He knew the end of the war had come. But what of the tension in Izmir? The next few days would be crucial – of this he was convinced. Staying on the waterfront whilst British and French guns faced the city would hardly be expedient. A house overlooking the bay but well outside the range of the warships, that was what he needed. There were not many houses that fit the bill; Muammer Uşşakizade's residence was one of the few that did. Since he himself was out of town and the house occupied only by his mother and daughter, a letter of invitation was sought.

Osman Efendi, one of the clerks working for Muammer Bey, knocked on the Uşşakizades' door on the morning of the 11th.

'Madam, we've received a call from the headquarters of Mustafa Kemal Paşa. They would like a letter of invitation from you. They might consider using your house as a residence.'

Just what Latife had in mind! She ran to the desk, reaching for paper and her pen.

She handed Osman the letter that pleaded, '... would Mustafa Kemal honour us by considering our Göztepe house as residence, and indeed, not deny a Turkish family this distinction?'

Mustafa Kemal had spent his first night at the İplikçizade mansion on Karşıyaka's seafront,[4] but that house was in gunboat range. Hillside houses, on the other hand, offered a safer distance, but the finest belonged to the English. Hence Latife's addition of 'Turkish family' to the invitation.

She fetched her phaeton, as much to check her daydreaming as to fulfil her pledge to hand out cigarettes, Turkish delight, bandages and medicines to the troops entering the city. Settling on the bench, 'Come on,' she called out to the horse and started driving. On that day, many Izmir ladies were similarly occupied with gifts of tobacco, cigarettes, bandages and soup.

Latife returned along Hatay Road, drawing up by the upper gate, her usual route when she went out in the phaeton. Opening the gate, she went down the terraces and arrived at the front garden to find an unfamiliar crowd standing around. Armed men in strange outfits had surrounded her home. This was, in fact, Mustafa Kemal's guard detail, his Black Sea braves, but she could not have known that.

'Halt! No entry!'

Entrance to the house in which she had been confined for three months under house arrest was now denied her!

Speechless, she stared at these ragged men. Young, tall and handsome, each and every one carried a rifle on his shoulder and wore a cartridge belt across his chest.

All she could think to say was, 'But this is my home!'

Mustafa Kemal in her home

As Latife argued with the guards, word reached Mustafa Kemal: the lady of the house had arrived.

She spotted the handsome man sitting in a chair, legs crossed, a kalpak on his head, looking very much the master of the house. She had expected a reply to that morning's invitation, but he had simply turned up instead. She had left the house briefly, and the commander she was so eager to host was there to greet her on her return.

Mustafa Kemal was smoking his cigarette, staring into the distance. Suddenly aware of her presence, he turned towards her. He got to his feet and descended the stairs; the September sun sparkled on his fair hair and blue eyes when he removed his kalpak in a gallant greeting. Latife saw the hand stretched out towards her.

'Welcome, Paşam. Let me kiss your hand.'

Mustafa Kemal replied, 'You're welcome in your own home, young lady; let me kiss *your* hand.'

Latife could not stop thanking him. During this very short first chat, Mustafa Kemal had learned of her return to Izmir and how she carried his portrait in a locket. Her enthusiasm impressed him.

The house was suitable for his headquarters.

'It's a fine house. Would you allow me to stay here?'

'Nothing would honour us more, Paşam,' replied Latife. 'Please give us a little time so that my grandmother and I can move out.'

Latife: all they could talk about

A few hours later Mustafa Kemal Paşa was telling Halide Edib, the writer and Nationalist fighter, of the young lady he had met. Latife was the talk of the evening: how she had suddenly left France, where she had been reading law.

'The young lady knows you and speaks of you as her teacher.' This might have been merely a title of courtesy, Halide Edib thought at first. Much later, she would learn that Latife had for a year attended the preparatory department of the American College for Girls, where the two women had indeed met.

The writer continued to relate Mustafa Kemal Paşa's account:

'She carried a locket around her neck with my picture in it. She came near me, and showing the locket said to me, "Do you mind?" Why should I mind?' He chuckled delightedly. He was already imagining her in love with him. But at the moment all the Turkish women could have carried his picture in a locket around their necks without being in love with him at all. However, I thought, this was the best thing which could have happened to him at the moment. It would have a humanising effect on him, and keep him out of mischief.[5]

The novelist in Halide Edib described the young lady who had so captivated Mustafa Kemal:

She wore a black veil over her hair and her face was very pleasing in its sombre frame. The face was round and plump, so was the little body. Although the tight and thin lips indicated an unusual force and willpower, not very feminine, her eyes were most beautiful, grave and lustrous and dominated by intelligence. I can think of their colour now, a fascinating brown and grey mixed, scintillating with a curious light.[6]

As for Latife, she wrote to her dear uncle Halit Ziya (later, Uşaklıgil) of her emotions at meeting Mustafa Kemal, 'I met a pair of beautiful blue eyes.'[7]

'The girl who turned up at headquarters'

'Although I had never met Mustafa Kemal, I invited him to be our guest during his stay in Izmir. I admired his courage, patriotism and leadership,'[8] she would later tell journalists when asked about how they met.

Yes, she had invited Mustafa Kemal to stay. But the manner of this invitation was nothing like the myth that lingered for eight decades! A chic, unveiled young lady rides to headquarters, insists on speaking to Mustafa Kemal, enters his study and invites him to her home ...

Where she had arrived was, in fact, her own home, converted into headquarters in half an hour. The letter of invitation had been written upon request. Behind it all was Mustafa Kemal's courteous nod to the conventions of the era.

It might have been Latife's unmistakable air of independence that gave rise to the myth of 'the girl who turned up at headquarters'.

Latife's Family

Who was this young lady who had so enchanted Mustafa Kemal in one brief meeting? What was her background?

Her mother, Adeviye, was the daughter of Havva Refika Hanım and Daniş Bey, of the Sadullah Efendizades, meaning 'noblemen's sons', a leading wealthy family of Izmir. The family were known by the cognomens of 'Despatchers', and later, 'the Postmen'. One branch of Adeviye's family that hailed from Crete was known as the Giritlizades: 'sons of the Cretans'.

Her father, Muammer, was the only son of a wealthy family originally from Uşak county, thus the family cognomen of Uşşakizade, 'son of those from Uşak'. The family had been engaged in trade for the past three generations.[1]

Muammer's father, Sadık, had begun trading in Izmir, his seed capital a mere three prayer rugs given to him by his own father, the carpet merchant Hacı Ali Bey. Sadık soon surpassed his father.

The great-grandfather Hacı Ali Bey

Tall and well built, Hacı Ali Bey looked even more imposing in his lightweight trousers, a fine silk kerchief wound round his fez and a loose jacket over his shirt.

That Latife's disposition and demeanour took after her great-grandfather became more apparent as she grew up into a dominating personality commanding respect and obeisance.

Hacı Ali employed Greek clerks, Armenian stewards and traders of Jewish or Levantine origin. He had forged great relationships with Christian bank managers and non-Muslim merchants, who controlled the market in Izmir.

Aristocratic and prominent guests would gather in his reception room of an evening, chairs would be lined up, sometimes overflowing into neighbouring rooms, and the young Halit Ziya, then a bubbly thirteen- or fourteen-year-old, would be summoned as 'reader', his grandfather's 'Halit the Parakeet'. These sessions would last for a couple of hours. Steward Kevork collected the books ordered in Istanbul: Turkish and translated novels, some in instalments, *The Red Mill*, *The Count of Monte Cristo*, and many more ... Young people's taste in books fascinated Hacı Ali.

He held no truck with fanaticism. Constant learning was his principle, and he took pains to raise his family accordingly.

Education was an Uşşakizade family tradition. Tutors in Arabic, Farsi and French as well as the sciences, poetry and literature frequented Hacı Ali's home. Yusuf, one of his sons, had published a small anthology of poems in his early twenties.

Izmir in the late nineteenth century was truly polyglottic: the upper classes spoke French amongst themselves, Greek to the servants and haggled in Italian in the shops. Commerce was conducted in Italian or French. English was relatively unpopular.

It was a time of great discovery and invention. Precious goods and innovations were presented to the entire world at expositions held in Paris and London. Uşşakizade carpets woven at the family workshops in Uşak were shown at the 1869 Paris Exposition and won a gold medal. Emperor Napoleon III presented the prize-winning carpet to his wife, the Empress Eugénie.

Sultan Abdülaziz (r. 1861–1876) attended these expositions on his European visit, the first such tour undertaken by an Ottoman sultan to develop commercial links with London and Paris. Upon his return, he placed an order with the Uşşakizade workshop for a carpet to be presented to Empress Eugénie, who was scheduled to pay the Ottoman Empire a return visit.

The grandfather Sadık Bey

Hacı Ali had made a fortune from the handwoven carpets he marketed worldwide. But when a newly founded foreign business named the Orient Carpet Company took over the market in 1907, his son Sadık rightly predicted a great future for the transport business. Forming a massive 2,000-camel caravan, Sadık soon dominated the transport of figs, sultanas, wheat and barley from Aydın to Izmir. He wanted shares in the new company that was constructing a railway between the two, but when he was rebuffed by the British, he vowed to establish a camel train long enough to form an unbroken line between Aydın and Izmir. And so he did. When his cheaper camel train proved more attractive to trade, the railway company had no choice but to concede.[2]

Sadık was a commercial genius, the first Turkish member of the New York Cotton Exchange. His son Muammer later carried on the membership.

Half the population of Izmir, the most commercially dynamic city of the empire, was Turkish. The other half included Greeks, Armenians, Jews and Levantines. Each community lived in its own neighbourhood. Foreign visitors frequently commented on the high proportion of Greeks, and with good reason: after the formation of an independent Greece in 1821, the Greeks, who had hitherto been Ottoman subjects, were given a choice, and some did take on Greek nationality.

The Armenians were the closest to the Turks in lifestyle and traditions. They spoke unaccented Turkish, stayed out of politics and lived quietly.[3]

The Jews, similarly, were quite insular, uninterested in politics or any controversy with the ruling classes. They enjoyed good relations with the Turks and the Armenians.

Foreigners and Levantines had the least contact with the Turks. Most were subject to their own laws, implemented by their missions. They lived in elegant quarters known as the Frankish Neighbourhood, led a life of pleasure and were exempted from taxes.

Izmir presented the image of a city of concentric circles.

In 1908, there were fifty-three mosques, fifty-one *mescid*s – Muslim chapels – thirty-five churches and seventeen synagogues.[4] The city was laid out along religious divisions. Some neighbourhoods even had walls and gates that shut at night-time.

The Armenian quarter was at the site of today's Fuar ('showground'). The Jews lived to the south of the showground, and the Turks to the south of the Jews; the Greeks lived to the north, whilst the Kordon, the waterfront promenade, was home to mostly foreigners. The Uşşakizade family had first settled in Basmane; that first house today is a hotel. The second stop for the family was Soğukkuyu in Karşıyaka. This was the house where Zübeyde Hanım would later be cared for during her final days.[5] Sadık's third Izmir house was the famous White Mansion in Göztepe, which Mustafa Kemal would later use as headquarters.

Following the custom of the day, Sadık picked the airiest part of town, ordering offal to be hung in various locations around the city to determine the site where the meat stayed fresh longest. One thousand steps led up to the two-storey house perfumed by the variegated honeysuckle; a fine terrace greeted the visitor, with huge wisteria framing the veranda.

The neighbourhood is known as Sadık Bey even today. Two bus stops, one named after Daniş Sadullah Bey, father of Adeviye, and the other after Sadık, continue to commemorate the Uşşakizade family in Izmir.

On a visit to Istanbul, Sadık fell in love at first sight with a Circassian concubine. He married the beautiful Makbule; the marriage proved to be a lifelong loving success. As open to western culture as he was, Sadık also cared passionately for his own culture. Makbule had a wonderful voice and was an expert *ud* and *kanun* player. Sadık, too, was accomplished on the *kanun*, and husband and wife made music together.

Their first child died in infancy. They named their second child, born in 1872, Muammer.

The boy was tutored at home first, learning English and French; later he went to the school his father had founded to educate the neighbourhood children.

When he turned sixteen, his father placed him at the Ottoman Bank as an apprentice clerk. Not for him a son to lord over the family business: the young man had to learn how to work for others first.

In the following year, the family sent Muammer and his cousin Halit Ziya on a long trip with the ultimate aim of vising the 1889 Paris Exposition Universelle. The two young men sailed to Piraeus in what was to become a delightful trip up and down every historic site, palace and beauty spot around Athens, and later, Italy. The last stop was the Place de l'Opéra in Paris. The exposition was so vast, and so impressive, that the two young men found little opportunity to visit the rest of the city. Halit Ziya published his account of the tour in *Hizmet*. By then great friends, they called each other uncle and nephew rather than cousins.[6]

Having started work at the Ottoman Bank, Muammer eventually took over his father's export business. It was time for him to marry, and he chose Adeviye, a legendary beauty like a classical painting.[7]

Sadullah Bey wanted to make his daughter a woman of independent means. So he put one of his properties on the market – the historic Kızlarağası Hanı in Kemeraltı – to provide her with a dowry as well as a lifetime income. Adeviye was truly blessed: the purchaser turned out to be none other than her father-in-law, Sadık. The two fathers had acted in tandem to give the young woman a great wedding present: Latife came from a family that valued its women.

Adeviye was well educated, privately tutored in Arabic and French, and Muammer was an only son. Sadık expected a handful of grandchildren, and the young couple did not disappoint. Adeviye and Muammer had a total of ten children, of whom the youngest six survived. The first was Latife, born on 17 June 1899.[8] Possibly as an evocation of divine intercession for her to be allowed to live, she was given the middle name Fatma, after the prophet's beloved daughter (and wife of Ali). Two boys followed: İsmail and Ömer. Then came two more girls and another boy: Vecihe, Rukiye and Münci.

The family faced west, but preserved eastern values.

Muammer, a leading Izmir businessman by the time he was in his twenties, was a partner in the British Portsmouth Agency, which conducted sea trade between Britain and the United States. Few Turks were involved with exports in those years of Abdülhamid's reign. Not content with trading with Britain, Muammer reached out to America, obtaining in 1900 his own seat at the Tobacco Exchange as its first Turkish member. His father, Sadık, had earlier earned a seat at the New York Cotton Exchange, which he had later transferred to his son. Muammer had visited the United States four times in those years, missing the birth of his middle daughter, Vecihe, in 1907: he was in New Orleans at the time, according to an article in İş Bank magazine from November 1988.

The Uşşakizade children were brought up to be independent. Adeviye never had to raise her voice, it is said, but directed her six children with a look. Muammer, in contrast, was an indulgent father. Vecihe's grandson Muammer Erboy says, 'He wouldn't suffer disrespect gladly, though.' He then adds, 'However respectful they might have been towards each other, tales of Great-grandpa Muammer's womanising did reach our ears from time to time.'

Latife

Latife grew up in a household of governesses, cooks, maids and gardeners. A child who looked people in the eye, there was no timidity in her.

Until the birth of her sister Vecihe, she shared the world of her brothers. Surrounded by boys' toys and games, she learned to be assertive. She had little time to play with dolls.

Muammer, with such close ties to the outside world, placed great importance on his children's foreign language education. Conscious of the ascendancy of English, he engaged an English governess for his first child, Latife. Treating his daughter differently from his sons was never an option. Latife began English lessons at the age of three or four; French, German and Latin followed soon after. Muammer engaged teachers from Britain, France and Germany. Muammer Erboy says:

> Engaging so many teachers for one child alone would have been sinfully profligate in his view; so he commissioned a chalet-type building with eaves, below today's Izmir Independent Turkish College. He designated this building a tutorial hall. Bright children of the neighbourhood, whose families could ill afford

a decent education, came here for lessons. Every day. Just like a school. He had around twenty children so educated alongside his own. There were teachers from every nation and speaking every mother tongue.

Muammer and Adeviye were far ahead of their time in that they educated their daughters as equally well as their sons. Aware that his devotion to his daughters was unusual in his time and place, Muammer was known to remark on how it would be a couple of generations before suitable Turkish husbands for girls as well educated as them would come along.[9]

Educating girls was considered superfluous in the first quarter of the twentieth century; most families tended not to educate their daughters 'too well to find husbands'.

Seventy-odd years earlier, the educational needs of Izmir's Turks had been as neglected as everywhere else in the empire. The explorer Rollestone states that there were only eighteen Turkish schools in Izmir in the second half of the nineteenth century, attended exclusively by boys.

Turkish children had little opportunity to access education other than via the mosque schools, which primarily taught religion and a little bit of mathematics. Wealthy Turkish families educated their children privately. The 1900 Izmir city guide indicates a total of 707 pupils in eight boys' schools and 436 pupils in five girls' schools.[10]

By 1917, there were eleven Turkish schools, eleven foreign, twelve Armenian and nineteen Jewish. The Greek population ran one male teacher institute, two female teacher institutes, and five secondary and seventy-one primary schools.[11]

Tevfik Fikret and Halit Ziya

Once competent in foreign languages, Latife needed to improve her Turkish, Farsi and Arabic. Her uncle Halit Ziya, whose reputation as a *littérateur* had grown after his move to Istanbul, was the natural choice. He was the son of Hacı Halil Bey, Latife's grandfather Sadık's brother.

This was the ideal solution: Latife would lodge with Halit Ziya in

Yeşilköy. He had spent his childhood and adolescence years in Izmir, developing a close bond with Latife's father, Muammer. Since his move to Istanbul in 1893, he had served two sultans: chamberlain to Abdülhamid and chief chancery clerk to Mehmed Reşad, these positions having given him access to a large and influential circle.

Latife was fourteen when she arrived in Istanbul. Halit Ziya's masterful pen impressed her hugely, kindling a love of literature. He tutored her in Arabic, and she studied Turkish and Farsi with Tevfik Fikret, another celebrated writer and poet of the time. Muammer Erboy says that his great-aunt was able to translate with equal mastery between these languages.

Halit Ziya supervised Latife's progress in Turkish, French and general knowledge. She, in turn, became great friends with his son Vedad.[12]

We also know that she attended the preparatory department of the American College for Girls in the same year.

What the fortune teller said

An interesting episode from Latife's younger years concerns a fortune teller.

She may have been thirteen or fourteen at the time. A flower seller–cum–fortune teller spotted Latife and her nanny as the two were walking down the street. The Izmir gypsy wanted to read Latife's hand, but the nanny objected: 'Hold on. This is Muammer Bey's daughter.' The fortune teller insisted: something inexplicable had compelled her. Her enthusiasm excited Latife, so the nanny gave in.

The gypsy took one look at Latife's fate line and gulped, as if she really had foreseen the future: 'Happiness and joy for you, the greatest ecstasy and devastation all at the same time. The cause of all this will be blonde and blue-eyed. Your destiny is a blonde, blue-eyed man. None other shall there be!'

In a strange coincidence, Joséphine, later the wife of Napoleon, had heard a similar reading during her younger days on Martinique. Both women lived to see these predictions come true; there were baffling parallels in their lives. Fortune tellers may well predict similar destinies for daughters of rich men around the world, but Latife never forgot what she heard.

She was said to take after her grandmother Makbule in looks, with a clear Circassian complexion and black hair. In stature, she took after her tiny maternal grandmother, Havva Refika Hanım. She laughed and glowered with her eyes. She spoke Turkish with a melodic intonation, now joyful, now haughty. Her demeanour demanded attention.

In *Grey Wolf*, Armstrong describes how she might have appeared to Mustafa Kemal: 'She had a quiet air of authority, as one used to being obeyed, and she looked him straight in the eye as man to man, and not with the veiled-sex looks of the women to whom he was accustomed.'[13]

As the eldest daughter, Latife frequently supervised the dining table arrangements. The renown of the delicious fare offered on precious china at the Uşşakizade table had spread far and wide.

She was particularly talented in the arts, literature and music. Her grandfather Salih had brought a piano for her from London. The pianist Anna Grosser-Rilke, niece to the famous Austrian poet Rilke, gave her piano lessons for three years. She mentions Latife in her memoirs, entitled *Nie verwehte Klänge* (*Never Forgotten Melodies*):

Latife Muammer was the most remarkable Turkish woman I ever knew. She was but fifteen years old when I first met her, the eldest daughter of a millionaire Izmir merchant. They lived in a house decorated in the English style, and they lived like the English. This was how they had learned foreign languages so well. They spent a few months each year in London or Paris. Despite fewer visits to Germany, Latife adored all things German: the language, literature, arts, and in particular, music. She had beautiful and intelligent eyes and an expressive mouth. She impressed me the very instant we met. Her mother was one of the most beautiful Turkish women I have ever known. She looked like a Murillo Madonna. Latife interpreted for her mother. The purpose of their visit was to request I give Latife piano lessons. I asked her to play something for me. My astonishment doubled when she began to play the delightful Adagio from Beethoven's *Moonlight Sonata*.

There were certain technical flaws in her playing, but her grasp of the piece was surprisingly good. I was delighted to have met such a talented student. I truly enjoyed the lessons I gave her until 1918. She spoke flawless German, and passionately admired the great German writers. She could recite the first section of Faust by heart. She was the most talented of all my students, and she will remain the most interesting always.[14]

The children frequently entertained their parents, just like in the days of Hacı Ali, displaying their talents and most recent accomplishments. Muammer engaged a companion for each of his daughters when they turned fifteen. Latife's companion was an Izmir Greek girl named Kalyopi; the two would stay together all their lives.

The Ottoman Empire had enjoyed three decades of peace, Abdülhamid's despotic rule notwithstanding. The sultan's determined efforts to create a middle class had paid off: commerce and industry were in the ascendancy, and families with an appreciation of music, literature and painting had begun to appear on the social scene. The Second Constitutional Era had altered the nation's lifestyle visibly.

The blue-eyed young man who died in Gallipoli

Latife reached adolescence at the start of the Great War. The Gallipoli campaign would alter the course of her life. A blonde, blue-eyed young man she was fond of at the time went to Gallipoli, never to return. Death had brought her first romantic attachment to a sad close, just as the fortune teller had predicted.

Latife was passionate about poetry and literature. She had an extensive library and was particularly fond of German literature, knowing quite a few books by heart. Fluency in Arabic, Farsi, Latin, English, French, German, Italian and Greek gave her access to the entire world.

She followed world events avidly. Many members of the family had welcomed the prevailing ideas of the time, with virtually every single philosophical or political movement in the empire having found an adherent or two: royalists, Young Turks, Union and Progress Party sympathisers, and even socialists. This wide range of views and open minds further broadened Latife's horizons.

By 1916 Latife was reading all she could get her hands on regarding women's issues, following women's magazines published in Turkey, researching into women's status and taking copious notes. She had studied women's role in prehistoric times as well as in the Islamic societal order and was heard telling her mother, 'Women may have a secondary place in the family, but they still have the capacity to rule their husbands by the power of their personality.' The issues of polygamy and divorce occupied her thoughts. An ardent supporter of women's rights, she would warn heiresses who intended to bequeath their own assets to their husbands not to do so.

She was a good rider and had named her horse Cici ('Sweetie'). Also a good shot, though one who hated hunting as the sight of blood repelled her, Latife was energetic and vivacious; Anna Grosser-Rilke, her music teacher, describes her as a romantic ...

A massive political upheaval raged in neighbouring Russia in 1917: the Tsarist régime was overthrown and the Bolshevists took over.

3

The Occupation of Izmir, Latife's Hometown

Izmir was a small-scale Paris of the Orient with its hotels and cabarets, fine houses, and well-lit, wide roads. Two-storey houses stood on the Kordon, the waterfront road and promenade. The streets behind it, however, were wide enough to allow only a single carriage to pass.

The 1915 deportation of Armenians had little impact on Izmir. Of the population of a quarter million in the early twentieth century, 55,000 were Greek, 21,000 Jewish, 10,000 Armenian and around 50,000 foreign nationals. The rest were Muslim Turks.[1] Some researchers note that the Greek population doubled prior to the war, reducing the Turks to a minority.[2]

The Turkish district was located at the highest part of the city, by the foothills of the ancient Byzantine fortress, where pergolas shaded narrow alleys and a multitude of fountains cooled the air.

Until the end of the nineteenth century, social clubs were the exclusive domain of Europeans and Levantines. Changes to admission rules enabled Greeks and Armenians to join and caused some members to snort, 'What! Admit a man who only a few years since wore a kalpak and long robes?'

Few Turks joined any of these clubs. Latife's father, Muammer, was an exception, being a member of the Sporting Club, whose fine gardens and sherbets had inspired a news item in *The Times* in 1905.

Cabarets, clubs, theatres and music played a major part in the life of the city, mandolins and guitars strumming Greek tunes on the streets. Cafés would fill with elegant patrons of an evening. Bands specially invited from Vienna, Budapest and Athens would play Viennese waltzes, tzigane tunes and *hasapikos*, Greek folk songs for Kordon cabaret dancers to perform to.

Shops, inns and taverns lined the Taverna Street by the Aya Fotini

Church, enticing patrons with mezes, fish and alcoholic drinks: a few taverns in the Karantina district had obtained licences near the end of the nineteenth century.

The Odeon Theatre and the Key and Pathé cinemas stood on today's Republic Square. Further back, to the rear of the Efes Hotel, rose the Italianate Izmir Theatre. Opera performances and concerts took place frequently; tickets to prestigious touring company shows sold out.

The first theatre building had opened in 1775 and had been staging regular performances since then. Others had arisen in time, turning the city into a major centre of attraction. Gustave Flaubert had visited Izmir in 1850 and mentioned two plays he had attended in his journals.

Yet women were barred from the theatre. Complaining of the lack of a single member of parliament to defend women's rights, a reader named Ayşe İsmet from Izmir wrote to the Salonica magazine *Kadın* (*Woman*) in 1909:

> Our sisters were subjected to attack last week in Izmir, and thousands of people gathered to forcefully ban Muslim women from going to the theatre, yet neither the forces of law nor government officials did anything more than watch this bigoted attack.[3]

Swimming in the sea was a male-only activity. There was a 'sea bath' in Alsancak. Bathers waded in wearing lightweight towels in Karataş, Salhane and Göztepe; some *yalı*s, 'seafront villas', had bathing machines for women. Girls of İnciraltı and Narlıdere swam surreptitiously, away from prying eyes.

Segregation of the sexes forced medical doctors to grow beards so that they might be identified as physicians and make professional calls on Turkish households with little hassle.

A number of cafés were frequently accused by the press of hosting prostitution on the upper floors.

When moving pictures came to Izmir on the heels of the Constitutional Monarchy in 1896, youngsters demonstrated, asking for Turkish subtitles. Women-only screenings began in 1914: the National Library cinema held women-only showings on Monday afternoons.

The women of Izmir

The degree of face covering was a clue to a woman's ethnicity. Greek and Levantine women left their faces entirely uncovered, whilst Jews and Armenians covered half their faces. Turkish women tended to cover their faces completely.

Footwear was another clue: Turks wore yellow, Armenians red, Greeks black and Jews blue.[4]

The promenades Kazızade Hüseyin Rıfat took in Göztepe in 1909 with his silk-cloaked wife on his arm had caused tongues to wag for a long time.

The most elegant women of Izmir were the Levantines and the Greeks. The latter had thrown off the yoke of seclusion in the nineteenth century, and their beauty captivated countless foreign travellers. As for Turkish women, we do know that despite having to wear an overcloak of some description, as well as a veil covering the face, they did experiment with fashionable bobs and distinctive trouser and coat styles.

By the second half of the nineteenth century, Izmir's Turkish women had rejected the older style of heavy facial veil, preferring brightly patterned silk dresses, ankle-high yellow boots and a sheer piece of fabric on the face. The *Hizmet* newspaper complained of women parading skimpily clad on the Kordon and in Göztepe in 1889; it would later lambast threateningly the latest fad for highly elegant ladies promenading in yellow cloaks.

Despite calls for police intervention, segregation on public transport was no longer enforceable.

Izmir's women had clearly grown out of oppressive seclusion practices, especially in their clothing. Nor did they respect restrictions on their right to go outside the house.

The *Hizmet* newspaper claimed, in January 1890, that women had been flaunting themselves in outfits that defied the rules of hijab:

It has been observed in our city of late that certain women have been shunning the çarşaf in favour of European-style coats, and these coats, as known to all, are of such tight proportions as to reveal the entire figure of the person within, and moreover, by flicking the veil back over the head, neither do these women comply with the rule to cover the face.[5]

Newspapers in Turkish had been launched in 1869 in Izmir, and their numbers grew on the heels of the announcement of the Second Constitutional Monarchy. By the end of the nineteenth century, there were three Greek and four French dailies in Izmir. The Jews published two weeklies. Of the seventeen printers in the city, five published in Greek, three in French, three in Ladino, one in Armenian and five could handle any language.[6]

Muammer becomes mayor

Muammer's involvement with the Izmir city council began in 1908. The Tilkilik District Progress and Union Club, which he served as chairman, had formed a committee named the House of Altruism. They used the City Club as their headquarters.

The most liberal election in the history of the Constitutional Monarchy took place in 1909; this was a city council by-election. Muammer won the mayor's seat for a city council whose coffers were completely empty.

The Izmir Metropolitan Council web site of the 2000s introduces the businessman:

> Uşşakizade Muammer Bey (1876–1951), who has served Izmir twice as mayor, was the father of Latife Hanım, Atatürk's wife. It was he who brought the first motorcar and ferryboat to the city, and who established the gasworks.

Muammer issued a Council Improvement Declaration as soon as he took office: he prioritised the widening of roads to serve the city, followed closely by the development of public gardens, a power plant to expand electrification and an extension to the tramline from Kokaryalı through to Narlıdere. There was so much to do, but no money with which to do anything. The new mayor prepared a fifteen-item reform package to restart the faltering Izmir Council. This package included proposals for increasing council income as well as modernising the city's lifestyle entirely; the County Council passed the proposals, albeit in a significantly truncated form. Work began on the items that were approved.

Inspections were carried out on scales and measures in the shops, the cleanliness of bakeries and the quality of the bread. The streets were cleaned regularly and carriage drivers regulated. Stonecutters and sweepers were put to work, and dressed paving stones were ordered to improve street furniture. Three wide boulevards were in the plans, as well as a public garden, clubs, theatres and a library. Support for the city council was strong in the press.

When the city council took over the management of the ferryboat company, citing corrupt practices, foreign companies initiated powerful opposition. Unable to raise new taxes, the city council found itself in trouble.

The newly appointed governor of Izmir County, Muhtar Paşa, took up arms against the city council from the start. Muammer's first term as mayor did not last long.

The occupation of Izmir

It took newspapers two days to report that Izmir had been occupied on 15 May 1919. Newspapers that defied the censorship were slapped with a further twenty-four-hour closure. But the news went round anyway, by word of mouth or in print:

> The Greek military occupation began with a big massacre yesterday morning. Troop carriers sailed into Izmir Bay at seven thirty; the first groups of soldiers disembarked at 8:40 …

Governor İzzet Bey was marched out of the County Hall, along with his staff, and forced to shout, *'Zito Venizelos!'*[7] Ottoman officials were frogmarched along the harbour side, their clothes and fezzes torn, as jubilant local Greek girls in blue and white outfits walked alongside Greek soldiers. Armed bands of local Greeks brought up the rear; a single handgun shot was heard as soon as the line began to pass the barracks.

Ordered by corps commander Ali Nadir Paşa to refrain from resisting, Turkish soldiers had withdrawn to their barracks. Greek soldiers attacked the Turkish troops immediately after the gunshot. Bayonets at the ready, Greek detachments marched their captives along the Kordon and imprisoned them in the holds. Martial law was declared soon after.

Countless Turks were killed on the day of the occupation and many more arrested.

The city where Latife was born and had grown up was no longer the same. Halide Edib wrote of the first week of the occupation in her memoirs:

> The waters near the shore were pink, according to the Izmir people, and this spectacle of human slaughter by torture was calmly watched by the allied warships, which were near enough to the shore to perceive the details of the show. Whilst this jubilee went on in front of the fleets, the Greek soldiers and some native Christians were entering the Turkish houses in the back streets, robbing and killing the men and violating the women. In a week this celebration by murder, robbery and rape went farther into Izmir regions.[8]

Mustafa Kemal's departure from Istanbul coincided with the occupation of Izmir, which proved to be the final straw for the Turks and thus sparked the resistance. This newly appointed inspector of the Ninth Army sailed on the *Bandırma* on 16 May towards the Black Sea.

The demonstrators at the university gardens in Istanbul heard from a female student: 'We are as aggrieved as you, possibly even more so. We wholeheartedly join in your effort and wish to make this one fact very clear: who says a woman is a small creature? A woman may well be the greatest creature.'

On 24 May, Halide Edib gave her famous speech at Sultanahmet Square to a crowd of thousands, many of whom were women. One hundred thousand Istanbul citizens pledged to resist the occupation.

The resistance had begun by 30 May, when the invaders set fire to the city of Aydın. Female faces were featured on the handbills inviting Anatolia to join the resistance.

To the victors go the spoils: the three major powers held all of Izmir's economic power throughout the occupation.

> Of the two great railway lines that branched north and east from the city, one was owned by the British and the other by the French [...] the tramway lines were French concessions. The important liquorice and tobacco interests were American, as were the oil depots standing on the north end of the shoreline that curved to face the city. The carpet, grain, mineral and dried fruit businesses were largely run by British firms.[9]

4

Love Springs from the Ashes of the Great Fire

The Uşşakizades in Europe

The Uşşakizade family spread across Europe after their perilous escape in the autumn of 1919. Muammer and Adeviye settled in France with their young son Münci – who was suffering from polio at the time. The house was in Biarritz, close to the Spanish border, and was called the Villa Stella Maris.

The parents looked for a suitable girls' school for Latife. Tudor Hall School in Chislehurst, founded in 1850, seemed ideal. This pioneering girls' boarding school offered an extensively varied education, making every effort to develop and train the natural gifts of each individual pupil. Culture and linguistics topped the thorough and comprehensive academic curriculum that included arithmetic, mathematics, geography, ancient and modern history, botany, astronomy, chemistry, literature, Latin, French, German, arts, calligraphy and gymnastics, all taught by highly qualified staff. Dancing and piano lessons, a riding facility and six tennis courts made the school even more attractive to Latife.

Eminent lecturers and musicians regularly visited Tudor Hall School. Frequent debates were held on such fascinating topics as the suffragettes, freedom of the press or the need for a Channel tunnel – one ultimately opened in 1994! The school organised regular outings to art galleries, museums and landmarks in London, which was not that far. The pupils staged their own shows, opera included, for the benefit of disadvantaged communities nearby.

Residential facilities for eleven- to eighteen-year-olds were well advanced for the time, with hot and cold running water in the bathrooms; prettily appointed bedrooms had landscape views both back and front over the parkland towards the woods. The school reached a size of fifty-four pupils in 1917.[1]

The Uşşakizades lived in Biarritz, but they also had a place in Paris. When Latife was ready for further study and old enough to look after herself, the family decided she ought to go to university in Paris.

So Latife found herself in the midst of Paris in its heyday, the pioneering heart of every artistic movement imaginable. In the years immediately following the Great War, Paris was the single destination many intellectuals flocked to, with Americans leading the way: Gertrude Stein, Alice B. Toklas, Henry Miller, Ernest Hemingway, F. Scott Fitzgerald, and even Cole Porter. The females-only parties of novelist Colette scandalised Paris as Mata Hari was dancing in private halls. Renoir and Modigliani had only recently died. Joan Miró, Matisse, Braque and Picasso were painting their immortal works in Paris, the heartbeat of world art. Prestigious exhibitions competed with one another; Paris nourished the entire world. Latife went to the theatre and the opera and visited exhibitions, breathing in the culture-infused air.

She continued to foster her interest in music and improved her piano skills. When she was invited to give a concert, however, Muammer Bey objected, 'No daughter of mine performs in a music hall.'[2]

Latife enrolled at the Sorbonne to read law, although her real passion was literature. She began to make plans for the future: she could practise law as a solicitor, or teach, or work at an embassy. The conditions that had prevented women from working were changing in her own country as well as the rest of the world.

Her family had no cause to worry over Latife. Living in Paris was an education in itself. The opportunity to get to know both London and Paris as intimately as she did, studying in these ancient cities, must have influenced her view of the world. First England, the country that had limited the sovereign's powers 700 years previously and so embraced a parliamentary revolution, then the city that ignited the French Revolution. These credentials taught her about class struggle and the process of earning civil rights.

Her sisters, Vecihe and Rukiye, went to the Pensionnat Hubie, a girls' school in Lausanne. Her brothers İsmail and Ömer also finished secondary school in Switzerland, before graduating to the École Spéciale Militaire de Saint-Cyr, the foremost French military academy, steeped in tradition.

The entire family followed news of the Turkish resistance, both in the foreign press and in letters from close friends still in Turkey. Any item offering hope caused elation, sparking plans for their return in the not too distant future. The family got together at the Villa Stella Maris on special occasions and holidays. They spent three years in total in Europe, and Latife was the first to return.

In occupied Izmir

The occupation had weighed heavily on Izmir. What Latife had to contend with since her return had been enough to fill a lifetime; her wildest dreams had come true in the past week. She was freed from prison, Izmir was liberated and she had met Mustafa Kemal Paşa, who needed headquarters. She wore her lucky locket at all times as she occupied herself happily with the preparations for a base suitable for Mustafa Kemal Paşa.

Izmir descended into chaos in the four days following 9 September. Some were celebrating their deliverance, whilst the vanquished sought shelter, terrified. The death penalty awaited any soldier found mistreating civilians; this announcement might have allayed the terrors of the first couple of days. That the Turks might seek revenge for the crimes of the occupation still gave rise to apprehension; the war was not over yet.

Halide Edib believed 'the number of queer, suspicious-looking individuals increased in the streets. The inhabitants were mostly keeping to their houses. I heard that there was a lot of looting going on. I believed that it was possible to prevent it. It may not have been, however.'³

The great fire started around noon on Wednesday, 13 September. In her memoirs, Halide Edib records the flames reaching out to the heavens:

Three long days the fire lasted. After the first few hours it became impossible to approach it. The dynamite and the explosives hoarded by the Greeks under the churches of Aya Triada and Fotini, as well as in a number of private houses, were exploding. The sight and noise of it all was ominous. The crimson days in Izmir evoked other crimson scenes over other fair cities. When would the ordeal by fire and sword of every people cease? When will the peoples prevent their politicians from gambling with their lives and homes?[4]

As crowds escaping the fire huddled ashore, they could hear the naval band on board the British flagship playing their scheduled afternoon concert.

Mustafa Kemal kept his composure as the fire approached his quarters. It was his aides-de-camp who finally moved him, rounding up a lorry full of soldiers and a few motorcars. His car was an open-top, a present from the people of Izmir. The lorry forced its way through the crowds, and the motorcars followed in its wake. As Izmir disappeared under a dense cloud of smoke, the convoy made for the house in Göztepe, to the south of the bay, the house where he had met Latife two days previously. The Uşşakizade home was in the most secure location possible for a headquarters.

Latife's beloved birth city continued to burn like a torch; it was 14 September.

'Your gracious arrival in Izmir has delivered the Turkish nation. You have honoured my home, and my dreams have come true. Welcome, Paşam! Welcome, generals, welcome! I am so grateful to you all, and I will never forget this night for the rest of my days.'

Mustafa Kemal was pleasantly surprised.

He turned to İsmet and Fevzi accompanying him, and said, 'Let's go in.'

Entering the house in the big garden, Mustafa Kemal said to his young chatelaine, 'You have a very fine house, Latife Hanım. Everything is in its place. I thank you for making me such a good headquarters.'[5]

The cook earned his wings that first night. 'The food was so delicious that the likes of us, who had just come out of the privations of war, could scarcely envisage anything better,' says aide-de-camp Salih Bozok. Mustafa Kemal's orderly Ali Metin talks of those days in Izmir:

The mansion Latife Hanım had prepared for Atatürk and his retinue was very fine, and well kept. Those of us who came from barracks appreciated the uniform beds and mattresses in particular. What better offering for us, who had not seen beds for days? In any case, everything was perfect.[6]

Salih never forgot the first meal laid on at the White Mansion:

The Gazi invited Fevzi and İsmet Paşas to the table, along with me, Muzaffer and our hostess, Latife Hanım. We cheerfully filled our tumblers, except for Fevzi Paşa. The mezes were varied and delicious. Despite not drinking alcohol, Fevzi Paşa was refilling his plate with stacks of calamari, saying, 'How I've missed this calamari of Izmir's; it's the best,' eating with relish as he did so. In short, everyone was thoroughly satisfied with the meal and the night that was just beginning. Ruşen Eşref told us just then that some journalist friends of his arrived from Istanbul. So Asım [Us] of the *Vakit* newspaper, Falih Rıfkı [Atay] of *Akşam* and Yakup Kadri [Karaosmanoğlu] were all invited to join the party.[7]

Upon the arrival of the new guests, Latife got to her feet and made for the kitchen. Mustafa Kemal intervened. 'Please sit down, young lady. You are no longer the owner of the mansion. Seeing to the guests is my duty now.' Then, turning to Salih, he added, 'Salih, go check the kitchen; see if the cook requires anything.'

Salih noted in his memoirs how Latife had blushed like a poppy, pure light beaming from her eyes at Mustafa Kemal.

Latife and Mustafa Kemal were left on their own on the terrace overlooking the sea. Latife was talking of her parents, and of what she had done to date. In turn, Mustafa Kemal spoke of the Battle of Dumlupınar. The fire was raging on unabated; flames had engulfed the area that today is the Fuar district, and the Kordon. The two aides stood at a respectful distance, but close enough to hear the conversation. Mustafa Kemal asked:

'Do you think the fire destroyed any of your property?'

'A significant portion is in the area burning now,' she replied, and then added emotionally: 'Paşam, let it all burn. So long as you are safe. Who cares for property, now we've seen these happy days? The country is delivered. We will rebuild it by and by, and better than ever before.'

Her response pleased him.

'Yes!' he said. 'Let it all crash and burn. It can all be rebuilt.'

Yet Salih heard weeping from behind a closed door as he wandered around the house. It was Latife's grandmother who was crying.

Why did Izmir burn?

Was it really the Greeks who set Izmir on fire, as is alleged today?

Whilst it is not unreasonable to expect the vanquished to start the destruction, there still remain a good many conflicting reports. The *New York Times* of 15 September asserted it was the Turks who set fire to Izmir, although many other publications accused the Greeks. The celebrated journalist – and a visitor to the White Mansion at the time – Falih Rıfkı holds Nurettin Paşa accountable:

> Infidel Izmir burned in bright flames by night and smouldered by day. Was it really Armenian arsonists who had started the fire, as we were told at the time? I believe that but for Nurettin Paşa, known as a thorough fanatic and a rabble-rousing demagogue, this tragedy would never have run its course. [...] As it is my intention to write down what I know sincerely, I wish to note here a page from my notes taken at the time: Why were we burning down Izmir? Were we afraid that if seafront villas, hotels and restaurants stayed in place, we would never be free of the minorities? When the Armenians were deported in the Great War, this same fear made us burn down all the neighbourhoods fit to live in, in Anatolian towns. This did not derive from a simple urge to destroy. A feeling of inferiority had a part in it. It was as if anywhere that resembled Europe was destined to remain Christian and foreign and to be denied to us.[8]

İsmet Paşa, for his part, states he did not know 'where it started, and by whom':

> My saddest memory of those days when we entered Izmir is the fire. The cause of these fires should be sought in the great events of history. Subordinates say they carried out orders; senior figures, that there was a breakdown in discipline.[9]

Nurettin Paşa, who had been promoted to head the First Army in the final push against the Greeks, had also been implicated in the murder of Izmir's Greek archbishop.

Marshal Fevzi Çakmak blames him for two outcomes with tragic results:

> One was the great fire of Izmir, the other, Gazi Kemal's move from his hotel to the sanctuary of Latife Hanım's home in Göztepe, prompted by the fire. The first was partially attributable to Nurettin Paşa's narrow-mindedness; the second owes more to coincidence.[10]

Coming so soon after their liberation, the great fire had aggrieved all of Izmir. İsmet wrote how the elation of the first four days vanished. A dark cloud had settled on the people, as if to say, so what if we had delivered Izmir? Half of Anatolia, and Izmir with it, was razed to the ground. All the same, Mustafa Kemal's liberation of Izmir had convinced all that the great struggle had been won. He was insistent: rebuilding was not going to be an issue. Optimism and visions of a brighter future would soon dispel the gloom of the fire.[11]

Mustafa Kemal despatched a telegram on the fire to Yusuf Kemal Tengirşek, the foreign secretary:

> It is necessary to make the following statement in relation to the fire of Izmir. Our armies took every possible precaution to prevent any mishap prior to their entry into Izmir. But the Greeks and Armenians had been determined to incinerate Izmir and to this end had made prior arrangements. Christosmos's sermons, heard

also by Muslims, shouted out that burning Izmir was a sacred duty. That was the cause of the fire. Any persons intent on attributing the fire to our soldiers, or accusing them of having started it, are invited to visit Izmir personally to observe the situation. Yet, an official investigation is out of the question in this instance. Journalists of all countries currently here already attest to this angle ...

Supreme Commander Mustafa Kemal, 17 September 1922[12]

Latife leaves the White Mansion

Having helped her guests settle in, Latife and her grandmother left for the house in Karşıyaka. Her original intention was to manage the housekeeping from a distance. But news of it all going awry forced her back on the third morning: chaos reigned, the house all but unlivable. She brought in cleaners; and convinced of the impracticality of running a house from a distance, she moved into a cottage in the garden.

> Mustafa Kemal found himself looked after with every care and attention in his new quarters, but the hostess herself remained invisible. Her influence, nevertheless, was continually felt. Everything that might injure his health – and he took very little care of that – was kept away from him.[13]

She learned what foods he liked; Mustafa Kemal's favourite dishes appeared on every menu. When he went for a stroll in the garden, a butler appeared with a cardigan; when the cool set in, his window was shut. Newspapers left in his room featured his portraits, framed with hand-drawn flowers. Every day, a sweetly scented fresh flower was placed in the vase by his bed.

Of the health scare in his Izmir days little is known. Muammer's physician was called in, and diagnosing a coronary spasm, he proscribed alcohol and cigarettes. Latife implemented the doctor's advice at once; she removed all bottles of alcoholic drinks from sight and altered the dining and other house routines. Only two single cigarettes were left on Kemal Paşa's bedside table each night.

Mustafa Kemal displayed a cavalier attitude towards his own health, which is why Latife was so determined to protect her guest from anything that might cause harm.

This invisible housemistress was beginning to intrigue him.

Not one used to having his will thwarted, he objected to these restrictions, although concealing his displeasure, lest he offend Latife. He wanted to get better acquainted with a girl who was so well able to secure implicit obedience from those who served her. They conversed for a long time. Mustafa Kemal found himself impressed by Latife.[14]

The White Mansion became the heart of the Nationalist cause, the outhouses now providing lodging for other commanders who had arrived in Izmir: İsmet Paşa, Premier Rauf Bey Orbay, Ali Fuat Cebesoy and Foreign Secretary Yusuf Kemal all stayed at the Uşşakizade property. The hospitality impressed them all.

Mustafa Kemal's close friend the French writer Mme Berthe Georges-Gaulis says, '[H]e lost no time at all in making good use of this mind he had just discovered,' and adds immediately, 'Latife became his secretary. She spoke many European languages, which transformed her into a priceless interpreter. They exchanged views as they worked.'[15]

Unforgettable night at the White Mansion

On 18 September, Latife invited İsmet and Halide Edib, along with a selection of journalists, to celebrate the Izmir victory. An intricate profusion of ivy, jasmine, wisteria and roses framed the steps leading up to the house, and they commanded a scenic view of the blue waters of the bay; this rambling aspect rendered the house even more attractive.

It was an extraordinary night at the Uşşakizade mansion. As she greeted the arrivals on the veranda, Latife must have known she would be the centre of attention.

Mustafa Kemal had accompanied Halide Edib to the house in

Göztepe. On the way, he waxed lyrical about Latife: how well educated she was, what good manners she had and how, although her father had lost most of his property in the fire, she was patriotic enough not to mind it.

Halide Edib interprets his state of mind at the time by saying, 'It all sounded like the beginning of home building for the hardy soldier at last.'

A very little lady in black stood at the top of the steps and received us. Although she was said to be only twenty-four [actually twenty-three] at the time, she had the quiet manners and the maturer ways of a much older person. Her graceful salaam had both dignity and Old World charm. No movement of hers recalled the cinema-star gestures of the young girl in society.

Mustafa Kemal Paşa disappeared for a little time and came back dressed in white. His colourless fair hair brushed back, his colourless fair eyebrows bristling as they always do, his pale blue eyes gleaming with internal satisfaction, he stood by a table covered with drinks. She sat on the sofa by me and looked at him all the time. She was dazzled by him, and he was frankly in love. So the strong current of human attraction between the two enlivened the evening; otherwise it was boring and dull.[16]

Mustafa Kemal invited Halide Edib, normally not a fan of alcoholic drinks, to have a glass with the rest of the party:

'We are celebrating Izmir – you must drink with us.'

'I have never touched rakı, Paşa – but I will drink champagne to celebrate.'

As he raised his glass, Mustafa Kemal pointed at Halide Edib and said: 'This is the first time I have drunk rakı in the company of this Hanımefendi: we were always a bit uneasy in her presence.'

Halide Edib wondered if Mustafa Kemal's description of her as an ultra-puritanical woman had damped her youthful spirits, but then consoled herself with the thought that Latife was a woman of sober tastes and of a melancholy disposition.

İsmet, Rauf and Halide Edib approved of the chatelaine, so immersed in European culture, and found her a fitting mate for Mustafa Kemal. The party included journalists from Istanbul: Yakup Kadri, Asım and Falih Rıfkı.

İsmet wanted to know Halide Edib's thoughts on Latife. She replied that she had found the young lady very charming.

Halide continues in her memoirs:

Inwardly I was paying tribute to Mustafa Kemal Paşa's taste. I had not been interested in his love affairs so far. Fikriye Hanım and Latife Hanım, the only two women who aroused real feeling in him, were unusually arresting figures. I knew Fikriye Hanım would suffer deeply when she heard of Paşa's new attachment.[17]

Mustafa Kemal danced the zeybek that night and sang Rumeli folk songs before his guests and future wife, inspired the fire of Izmir, according to Fevzi. Both he and Mustafa Kemal were deeply saddened by the fire; both men held Nurettin accountable.[18]

On 19 September, the journalist, explorer and sculptress Clare Sheridan, first cousin to Churchill, paid a visit to the White Mansion. Sheridan had previously stayed in Soviet Russia, sculpting the busts of notable revolutionaries: Lenin, Trotsky and Kamenev, and she wanted Mustafa Kemal to pose for her. Her book *Nuda Veritas* reveals she did meet Latife, and that neither woman took to the other. In 1922, Sheridan was working for the *New York World*.

[...] the villa outside the town where Mustafa Kemal had his temporary headquarters. It stood at the top of a terraced garden overlooking the bay. I came by appointment, and as I followed an aide-de-camp up a thousand steps in between shady trees and a cascading stream I was conscious of a party of people watching me from above. Somewhat hot and out of breath, I reached the summit. There was an intimidating silence as I followed my conductor across the crowded terrace and into the house. The Gazi at my approach had evidently left his party in order to receive me in the salon. His sphinx-like expression and unsmiling ultra-politeness were to me quite unfathomable. I was disconcerted by the fact that having placed me on a sofa he sat on the other side of the room near an open window so that the people on the terrace could overhear us. The distance between us was chilly [...] [19]

She was struck by the simplicity of his uniform, belying the rank of marshal; his fair hair and blue eyes she found particularly unoriental. She noticed he was fingering red coral prayer beads, which made her think she was disturbing him. She wanted to interview him, but he took the wind out of her sails when he stated he had already given a two-hour interview to an American press representative, John Clayton of the *Chicago Daily Tribune*, and that it was therefore useless to reiterate the political situation. Mustafa Kemal had made it clear that he wanted peace. He hoped to get to Istanbul by peaceful means in order to avoid a tragedy similar to that of the burning of Izmir.

A servant then appeared bearing a silver tray on which were beautiful old tankards of water and two dishes of jam. There were spoons but no plates. Sheridan was quite at a loss to know what to do. Noticing her discomfiture, Mustafa Kemal smiled for the first time and helped her.

Clare Sheridan then moves on to describe how she met Latife:

He [...] then rather nervously (very nervously for such a self-possessed man) said he would like to send for the 'lady of the house'. I had no interest whatsoever in meeting the lady of the house, and managed to delay his purpose by producing a little collection of photographs of my work, and asking if he would let me do his bust. [...]

He answered that he would be 'proud and delighted'.

'May I begin tomorrow?' I begged excitedly. He hesitated.

'I have very little time ...'

'But still,' I urged, 'even Julius Caesar managed to find the time, and Alexander the Great, and Napoleon!'

At this juncture we were interrupted by the 'lady of the house', a short, thickset, round-faced, big-eyed woman, young, and yet with the poise of middle age. She sat down and looked at me with such insolent contempt that further conversation, whether journalistic or artistic, was paralysed. Kemal said something to her in Turkish and tried to show her the photographs of my work, but she would not look at them, emitted a scornful chuckle and crossed her arms as if to say, 'I wonder how much longer she will remain.'

I did not know that the lady in question was Kemal's bride-to-be, not that this fact could justify or explain her extreme discourtesy. I got up to go, but I made a last effort to secure the Gazi's head!

'If you would let me ... I will wait in Izmir until you can spare the time ...'

He looked rather hopelessly around the room and said:

'*Madam, je ne suis pas chez moi,*' as if with the encouragement of the 'lady of the house' he might have consented. She remained, however, disdainfully silent and he added conciliatingly:

'I will sit for you in Istanbul.'

'But that's a long way off!' I exclaimed.

'Perhaps not so long,' he replied enigmatically.

[...] Latife Hanım (for it was she) had captured this adamantine Trotsky, so well worth capturing! That she did not succeed in keeping him [...][20]

Latife was renowned as a gracious hostess; why, then, had she given Clare Sheridan the cold shoulder? Sheridan remarks that Mustafa Kemal greeted her with an unsmiling politeness and left the window open so others could overhear their conversation. She may well have been of a touchy disposition herself.

Mustafa Kemal had grave concerns at the time over the ongoing negotiations with the Allies. The statement that he could sit for the sculptress in Istanbul, and that it would not take long, was a clear message to the British: 'Sign the armistice and depart, or I am on my way.' Mustafa Kemal invited Latife to this meeting deliberately. She was no longer simply the lady of the house; having also undertaken the duties of his interpreter and secretary, she had become an indispensable adjutant.

Soon after their meeting, Mustafa Kemal began to address her as *Latif,* both the masculine version of her name and used as an adjective denoting grace, gentle beauty. He also, from time to time, referred to her as 'aide-de-camp'.

The note Latife wrote

The sixty-four foreign vessels still at anchor in Izmir Bay preyed on Mustafa Kemal. He instructed Yusuf Kemal, the foreign secretary: 'Write a note to the British Naval Command. They are to leave Izmir harbour within twenty-four hours. Their presence here is no longer required. We are confronting a vanquished state. We have prevailed, and stand here in the calm of victory. That fleet is superfluous. Should they insist on staying, I shall sink them one by one.'

This note took its time, as Yusuf Kemal wrestled with the finer points of diplomacy. Annoyed at the delay, Mustafa Kemal enquired about progress on a number of occasions.

He grumbled, 'What's the delay: just a four-line message, and it's still not written?'

Latife noticed his tension:

'Paşam, allow me to write it.'

'It's to be written in English; go ahead and write it!'

He took the note she had written:

'Perfect, just as I wanted it. Yusuf Kemal Bey, you've taken so long over a single note, yet to be written; and here, the lady took two minutes to write it. I have expressed my gratitude; you can relax now ...' He then turned to Latife and asked:

'Madam, which pen have you used to write this note?'

When she pointed to the black gold-trim fountain pen in her hand, he reached out. 'Give me that pen,' and he kissed it.[21]

Latife kept this pen all her life.

5

Mustafa Kemal Paşa Proposes

Balmy Izmir nights set the stage as Latife and Mustafa Kemal discovered each other. The more they conversed and debated, the more they enjoyed each other's company. Latife was an attractive young woman, intelligent and lively: an eloquent intellectual who defended her ideas fearlessly. The liberation of her sex was high on her agenda; raising Turkish women to the same level of social and cultural advancement as their European sisters was her dream. She was determined to break down the traditions that had enslaved women for hundreds of years. Her ideas took Mustafa Kemal's fancy.

As for Mustafa Kemal, he told of her his dreams for Turkey, the superstition, prejudice and ignorance he was determined to eradicate. The girl found herself enraptured as she listened. Her position had already surpassed that of secretary or aide-de-camp. Love was waiting in the wings.

Mustafa Kemal's biographer Patrick Kinross would later describe Latife:

> She stimulated his mind with her fluent talk, her arguments, her advice, her ideas born of a wide European culture. Here was a woman to whom he could talk as to few of the men around him. [...] With a lively masculine mind she combined a desirable feminine body.[1]

Vamık Volkan and Norman Itkowitz, joint authors of *The Immortal Atatürk*, claim Mustafa Kemal had identified her as a representation of himself as a young man.[2]

The mansion witnessed all manners of upheaval during those three weeks. Mustafa Kemal was busy on two fronts: bringing the war to a conclusion and courting Latife.

His ever-present companion during his time in Izmir, as he had been everywhere else, was his aide-de-camp Salih, who suddenly had to face the possibility of demotion:

> Latife had overtaken a part of my duty – immediately, and subtly. Last to bed, she was also earliest to get up. She had subscribed to European newspapers. She took all the papers from Istanbul and Europe, scanned them minutely and marked useful items. She then took Mustafa Kemal his morning coffee along with the papers into his room when he awoke.
>
> As the Paşa slowly sipped his coffee, Latife summarised the day's important news, related the commentary and handed him cuttings of items about himself.
>
> This ritual converted the Paşa in no time at all, and became indispensable. One morning he had awoken early and asked for his coffee. It was too early for Latife to be up. I took his coffee in; watching me astonished, he asked:
>
> 'Where did *you* come from? Where is Latif? Arouse her immediately, tell her to bring the papers ...'
>
> I must confess I was upset. I resented very much his asking me one morning where I'd come from, as if taking his coffee from my hand for the first time, after I'd served him this many years.[3]

Salih's explanation that he had brought the coffee as Latife was still asleep did little to appease Mustafa Kemal, who paid little attention to his aide-de-camp's hurt feelings.

His intentions must have become apparent to those who noticed the harmony between them. She spoke of those days to Berthe Georges-Gaulis in 1923, and the French journalist published it in her book entitled *La Nouvelle Turquie*:

> Latife's charms were steadily beginning to captivate Mustafa Kemal, and this he revealed to her. Latife was not indifferent either. But when he made vigorous advances, she resisted and made her position clear in no uncertain terms. So Mustafa Kemal explained

his principles to her: he could marry only after his work had achieved success. Latife countered: her principles were equivalent to his, and she could never compromise them.

She loved him; that much she granted. But she would either be his wife or would never marry. In any case, she would not become his mistress. Her own principles forbade it absolutely.[4]

Intrigued, Mustafa Kemal listened to the girl's principles as she listed them, but as far as he was concerned, he did not see any need to marry before he had delivered the nation.

Latife's sister Vecihe İlmen says, 'Atatürk wasn't that interested in the idea of marriage. But our family would never have tolerated any other option. This they must have discussed.'

Vecihe's account does indicate that the couple must have debated the question of marriage.

Ultimately, with no other alternative, Mustafa Kemal made his decision. This woman had suddenly turned up in his life, and could help him in his work. Setting off on the journey to transform Turkey with such a woman by his side might ease the way on so many counts. Everyone who had met her found her suitable: İsmet, Kâzım Karabekir Paşa, Rauf, Ali Fuat, Salih, Ahmet Emin and Ruşen were all charmed. True, there were obstacles. Fikriye, for one, but he could deal with her. Ankara's tough living conditions, for another, but Latife would have to cope with them. The war was on its last legs, and peace was just around the corner. Mustafa Kemal had an impulsive disposition, and all obstacles to this union dealt with in his mind, he made his move. One night when they were dining alone, he proposed they marry immediately. They had only to walk out and commission the first *müftü* they could find to conduct the wedding. Latife rejected this proposal unequivocally.

Mehmet Sadık Öke, Vecihe's grandson, takes up the tale:

The Paşa leant down for a kiss, hoping to show Latife Hanım the depth of his true love. So Latife Hanım swept out to the big marble table on the terrace, where the vanquished commander Trikoupis's service pistol lay, and shooting three rounds into the air, she told the Paşa that she would shoot herself with the fourth should he insist on pressing his suit in this manner, as he was essential to the deliverance of the country whilst she herself was dispensable.

The Paşa sent away the guards and ADCs – who had rushed to the sound of gunfire – telling them that he had challenged Latife Hanım to display her skills since she was such an accomplished rider and carriage driver, and had boasted of her proficiency with firearms. That they had been testing the idea that with such good shots as Izmir women, the Greeks would have ultimately lost the war anyway. So soothing the guards, he also flattered Latife Hanım at the same time.

When the Paşa asked her in admiration and astonishment, 'Would you really do it?' she replied, 'You are a victorious commander who knows when to advance and when to retreat. You may stop, but I am a mere maiden; if you don't stop, I may not be able to either.' She then added, 'And that would never do for either of us. But I am Latife Uşşaki; I would ultimately stop you, even if at the expense of my own life. I simply couldn't hurt you.'

The Paşa accepted this. 'I believe you, Latif.' Then, more gravely, he added, 'Young Lady, I hereby present this pistol, symbol of Izmir's liberation, to you as a mark of your courage. Use it should your person ever come under threat. But should I ever threaten you in the future, I pray you shoot me, not yourself. I could not bear the thought of your beauty, and intelligence and knowledge, which I am certain will benefit the country greatly in the future, being squandered thus. I may go over to the hereafter, but wherever I go, I shall carry the love I have for you, your black eyes and your black heart with me.' This romantic appeal did find its mark in my aunt Latife's heart; so she confessed that she, too, loved him, but the manner he proposed was unfeasible.[5]

Such a rushed wedding could so easily be misconstrued. In any case, Latife had no intention of marrying without her parents' blessing, so she had to wait for her father's return from Biarritz.

Although determined to stick to her guns – she would not marry in haste – Latife tenderly continued to preside over the domestic arrangements. A pink rose she picked first thing in the morning went into the vase on his bedside table. Vecihe states that Mustafa Kemal Paşa proposed three times during the fortnight he stayed in Izmir.

Lyrical proposal

One morning Mustafa Kemal made a request of Latife as he was leaving:

'My gentle Latife, would you personally tidy my room up today, please?'

'Of course, Paşam,' replied Latife.

She wondered what was going on when she entered his room: it was quite tidy, and the bed had been made.

The only thing out of place was the portrait of Mustafa Kemal that normally hung on the wall: it was lying on the bed. The rose she had freshly picked that morning had been placed over the picture. Latife hung it back up on the wall.

It was either that night, or the following night, when they sat down to a tête-à-tête supper, that Mustafa Kemal asked, 'Latif, did you not notice anything out of the ordinary when you tidied up my room?'

'There was a portrait on the bed. I hung it back up on the wall.'

Mustafa Kemal pressed on, still teasing:

'Would you please fetch that picture?'

He had a mischievous air. Puzzled, Latife went to the room, lifted the portrait off the nail and brought it out.

Mustafa Kemal continued, 'Would you please take a look at the reverse?'

> Take a look at this picture
> And if you still reject me
> I will not ask again![6]

Mehmet Sadık Öke calls this a family legend, frequently retold, but tells a slightly different version.

My aunt Latife saw the portrait and read the writing on the reverse. Since she really wanted to hear him say it out loud, she decided she, too, would play a little game. She hung the picture back up and never said a thing about it all day, feigning ignorance of the Paşa's questioning eyes, inwardly smiling to herself. The Paşa, for his part, dug his heels in and didn't ask a thing all day long. Come evening, knowing he could bear it no longer and would relent, Latife pinned the rose to her collar on the inside so it didn't show and went down to supper. Still seeing no reaction from Latife, the Paşa asked, 'Dear Latif, you did tidy my room up today, didn't you?' 'Yes, Paşam, I did,' she replied. When he asked, 'Did you not notice anything out of the ordinary?' she said impishly, 'Paşam, I saw nothing out of the ordinary, except for the portrait on your bed, and I hung it on the wall.' The Paşa, denied anew, tried one last time, and asked, 'But there was a rose on the picture; what have you done with it?' as he noticed the playful glint in Latife's eyes. So she showed him the rose she had worn on her collar, saying, 'I took it and placed it above my heart.'

The Paşa had to concede. 'All right, Latife, you win. But don't expect me to kneel; I've never knelt before anyone. When we shall get round to marrying, I have no idea. There is so much to do for the country, Ankara, you see.' So my aunt Latife was elated. Kissing his hand, she said, 'I'll wait Paşam, even if I have to wait a hundred years.' The Paşa interjected, 'Oh, child, have a heart! What could I possibly do at that age!' and they both laughed out loud.

Current Opinion ran a feature in January 1924 entitled, 'Mme. Kemal Tells of Her Romantic Marriage to the Turkish President', quoting Latife extensively:

'That evening we were alone, and we talked a great deal – not sentimental talk, but about the future of our country. These conversations continued for four days, and on the fifth evening I was surprised when our great general told me in a very matter-of-fact way that, having a western education, he thought I would make a fitting partner for him, and before I realised what I was doing I had accepted the offer in a real unsentimental, matter-of-fact spirit. But there was nothing said about when the marriage was to take place. I didn't expect it for years.'

This version features a pragmatic young lady accepting Mustafa Kemal's proposal as a natural extension of their existing relationship, rather than a starry-eyed maiden who had just received a proposal.

Time magazine quoted her in 'Divorced' much later, on 24 August 1925: 'Our union was more a joining of minds than anything else.'

As for the portrait of Mustafa Kemal that bears his handwritten proposal on the reverse, Vecihe presented this picture to the Military Museum – which Latife's flat faced – after her death.

Last night alone together

Salih's account of the last day in Izmir begins with the morning as he awaited instructions for dinner. Mustafa Kemal, who was getting ready to depart for the day's work, took one look at his chief ADC and flinging his blue cape over his shoulder, said, 'There will be no guests for dinner tonight. Latif and I shall dine tête-à-tête.'

The chief aide-de-camp knew something was in the air. That night the couple stayed up for a very long time.

Early next morning Mustafa Kemal departed for Fevzi Paşa's headquarters. He had not told Latife they were due to leave Izmir. Hearing that there would be no big dinner that night, and learning of the imminent departure of Mustafa Kemal, Latife became quite upset.

Salih thought it strange for Mustafa Kemal to depart without taking her leave; he wondered *exactly* what had taken place the previous night. He says:

'How the world changes ...' Mustafa Kemal had mused. 'In the old days, men would shy from opening their hearts up to women; nowadays, bless us all, girls feel quite relaxed about telling men about their love! That night we ate, drank and chatted ... Eventually Latif told me she was in love with me. I shouldn't leave her here! I should take her to Ankara, give her something to do and keep her close to me! She'll suffocate if she stays in Izmir! On and on and on … I told her this was impossible. She was very upset.'

Who knows what else took place that night, which the Paşa summarised so cursorily! Not for nothing had Latife Hanım complained in my room on the following day. Add to all this a romantic night, a fresh victory and a maiden's heart in love.[7]

It was impossible for Latife to go to Ankara immediately, whilst Fikriye, Mustafa Kemal's current mistress, was still there. This distant relation of Mustafa Kemal's was a tall and elegant beauty with a dreamy gaze. She had been despatched by their close relations to assist the leader of the National Struggle, and had been the de facto first lady of Çankaya since reaching Ankara in November 1920 after a perilous journey. The presence of the two women at the same time could easily have caused a massive scandal.

The following morning, generals, members of parliament, Izmir's leading citizens and journalists had all gathered at the White Mansion.

Latife said, 'You're going …'

'Yes,' replied Mustafa Kemal, 'I forgot to tell you last night. I'm going.'

Latife asked that the Göztepe house be formally designated as headquarters and be assigned a detachment of guards.

Two teardrops rolled down silently from Latife Hanım's eyes as she stood at the top of the stairs.

'I will worry about you so much! And I suspect I shall continue to worry about you even when you reach Ankara! Oh, how I would love to come to Ankara with you, Paşam; I wish you'd take me along. Do let me come to Ankara …'

Mustafa Kemal refused:

'No, you must stay here! Wait! Let us go back first; if I deem it fitting, I will send for you,' he replied.[8]

A group headed by İsmet set off for Mudanya for the armistice negotiations. A ceasefire agreement was imminent, and they could finally get down to negotiating the terms of peace.

The tables had turned: now it was Mustafa Kemal who would torment his lover. Suddenly uncertain what the future held, Latife found herself quite despondent.

Her mother and sisters returned before their father, who had some loose ends to tie. Latife was impatient for his return so that she might obtain his blessing on the proposed union. She was confused: although the written marriage proposal that she had finally accepted still hung on the wall, there was no word from Mustafa Kemal.

6

Waiting for the Wedding

Mustafa Kemal's departure had left Latife in limbo. Neither she nor Izmir would ever be the same. The city of her birth, the city she had grown up in, was a pile of ashes. A massive black hole in its centre, Izmir was bereft of people. There were countless dead and many more had escaped; the bay continued to expel corpses.

She found herself rattling around in the White Mansion, scouring the newspapers all day long for news of Mustafa Kemal. She had the benefit of a few additional sources: Asım Paşa's wife, now in Izmir, Salih, the aide-de-camp she corresponded with, and the troops stationed at the headquarters all gave her news of Ankara from time to time.

She might have been tormenting herself, as she heard little directly from Mustafa Kemal. But if she could have heard the talk in Çankaya, she would have breathed a sigh of relief, since he took every possible opportunity to sing her praises, talking about the depth and breadth of her knowledge and cultural assets.

The time had come for him to marry, thought those in his closest circle. Mustafa Kemal asked his friends one day, quite frankly, 'What is your opinion of this Latife?' İsmet's reply was unequivocal:

I fully favour Latife Hanım in every possible way. Firstly, she is highly cultured. Not just because she has read in a college, but she is a young lady who has read and assimilated seminal works of our time. She knows the world, and our country. Her knowledge of foreign languages is certain to assist our Paşa in the coming years, as our diplomatic relationships develop. She is the daughter of a noble and wealthy Izmir family ... And, as far as I can ascertain, she worships you, Paşam! Pretty, affectionate, knowledgeable and a noble girl; I don't know how I could add anything more.[1]

Mustafa Kemal replied, 'I see you're all in agreement on knowledge, nobility and beauty. For my part, I'm considering marrying Latife because I don't find her overly beautiful. We seek meaning and depth even in a painted portrait. I sense a meaning and depth in Latife. Should she not alter in the future – as things stand now, this presents an ideal picture.'[2]

His references to Izmir at every meal did not escape Zübeyde Hanım's notice: 'If only you could see her, Mother ... You'd like her, too. She is so insightful.'

Zübeyde Hanım might have continued to treat her son like a young child, but his desire to marry was plain to see. She said, 'I'd better see this Latife then,' a wish that was possibly her last to come true.

Latife receives an invitation to Bursa

As he was leaving, Mustafa Kemal had told Latife, 'Telegrams will suffice; there's little need for letters.' But then none of her telegrams received a reply. Ultimately she had to resort to writing a dejected letter to Salih, the man who had treated her like his own daughter:

> [...] I had been consoling myself by attributing the continued silence of all to being over-occupied. As a matter of fact, I have kept busy by small details of decoration and arrangements of this happy house to better please the beauty-loving eyes of my honourable and sacred guest. I've been waiting for you, my eyes constantly on the road. As you can see, we have not parted in thought. The former hustle and bustle is now gone. Yet although the Headquarters of the Commander-in-Chief be unoccupied, its honour is preserved. The only occupant, however, is this little me, in black from top to toe, sad and lonely, after getting accustomed to company, sentenced to reopen the black pages of my life and suffer the great oppression of countless hideous imaginings.
>
> Uşşakizade Latife
> 19 October 1922[3]

The young woman received a telegram asking her to go to Bursa around then.

> Dear Latife Hanımefendi,
>   The Honourable Gazi is due to pay a visit to Bursa. I hope we shall make it there for the 12th [this must be an error, since the actual date was more likely to be the 22nd].
>   Respectfully yours,
>   Salih, Chief Aide-de-Camp[4]

The wired response to her sad letter made Latife cry tears of joy. She immediately prepared the documents necessary for travel to Bursa. But disappointment followed a day later with an encrypted telegram informing her of the cancellation:

> Dear Latife Hanımefendi,
>   The trip to Bursa is temporarily postponed due to the Honourable Paşa's illness. I beg of you to delay your departure, and extend my deepest respects,
>   Salih, Aide-de-Camp[5]

Believing Mustafa Kemal to be gravely ill, since he normally brushed off minor discomforts, Latife tortured herself, writing a telegram expressing her dismay. But the reason for the last-minute cancellation was not illness; it was Fikriye.

Were Mustafa Kemal and Fikriye married?

In his semi-documentary historical novel *Fikriye*, Hıfzı Topuz offers an entirely new approach to the Mustafa Kemal–Fikriye relationship. He claims they were officially married. The documents would be presented in the case there was any gossip, but unless absolutely essential, this marriage would be kept secret out of deference to the family ties between the two parties. He cites Fikriye's nephew as the source of this information.

Having already invited Latife to Bursa, Mustafa Kemal confided in Salih, 'There is a snag. Fikriye is coming to Bursa.'

Salih replied, 'Oh, Paşam, do not worry; surely we will find a solution.'[6]

Latife telephoned the Anatolian Agency to find out that the Bursa trip, supposedly postponed, had actually taken place. She wrote to Mustafa Kemal and Salih separately to express the sentiments these conflicting telegrams had evoked in her.

My Sacred Paşa,

I had such happy moments. And now I am crushed under a deep grief. The honour you have left with us here blesses the entire family. Yet your lonely subject has one more precious asset. And that is your memory, ever fresh. How else could I have survived all on my own, after the pomp and circumstance? I can see that I follow your august presence with all my being. My only aim is to serve the saviour for ever.

I had asked for a small duty on a number of occasions. This has not been deemed appropriate. [...] I will ever live together, even only in my thoughts, if not physical presence. In effect, all my happiness derives from serving your august presence. My sole desire is to furnish you with a sidearm made out of my loyalty. In any case, how many people could possibly love you so innocently, so free of personal interest?

Hearing of your illness I was exceedingly sad and aggrieved. As you have pressed on with your trip, your good health must have been restored, I imagine. I am content and grateful for the order for me to travel to Bursa. It is an enviable honour for you to have remembered me even if for a brief moment. Thankfully I spent two delighted nights in anticipation. If you could bring yourself to cast your eyes over these sentences that spring from the deepest corner of my heart, you would make me exceedingly happy. Ever waiting on your honourable commands, and kissing both your hands with my deepest respects, my sacred Paşa ...

Latife

Göztepe, 25 October 1922

Fikriye goes to Munich

By the time Mustafa Kemal came to a decision to marry Latife, Fikriye had been ailing for a while. He devised a suitable solution: Fikriye would go to a sanatorium in Munich. The tubercular young woman had acquiesced, but first she wanted to accompany Mustafa Kemal on his Bursa visit. Fikriye knew of the existence of the girl in Izmir; her room in Çankaya was next to that of Zübeyde's, and she had overheard Mustafa Kemal's mother saying, 'Marry that girl before I close my eyes.'

It was Mustafa Kemal's decision to indulge one woman that prompted the cancellation telegram to the other. He and Fikriye went to Bursa in separate cars. Fikriye was due to depart for Munich two days later, accompanied by Mahmut Bey Soydan, MP for Siirt. As Mustafa Kemal was seeing her off, they met Halide Edib.

> 'I am going to Europe to a sanatorium, Halide Hanım – the doctors tell me I will get well,' she said.[7]

Did Latife know about Fikriye? As she followed everything to do with Mustafa Kemal in minute detail, she must have done. The marriage proposal must have meant that the decks had been cleared. On the other hand, it is not unreasonable to suppose that she would have attributed any hitch in *their* own relationship to the existence of Fikriye, concerned as she was at the risk of losing her man.

Zübeyde falls ill

One night Mustafa Kemal told Salih, 'The doctors recommend my mother should be treated in Izmir. Go look for a place for her.' He cautioned, 'Mind, not an abandoned Greek house though!' Salih left for Izmir via Konya, keeping his departure secret. Yet when he arrived at the Izmir station, he found Ahmet Ağa waiting for him, despatched by Latife.

Dressed in black from top to toe, Latife met him at the gate. She explained how she had despatched Ahmet Ağa to the station as soon as she had heard about the departure from Ankara. 'This being your headquarters, how could it possibly be appropriate for you to stay anywhere else? This is now your home.' She then asked him question after question about Mustafa Kemal and Ankara, and Salih did his best to answer.

Evidently the officers at headquarters were a source of news from Ankara.

Salih explained the reason for his visit: he needed to find a home for Zübeyde, who was ill.

Latife laughed, saying, 'I am aware,' and added, 'Having her stay in our Karşıyaka house will be an exceptional pleasure for us.'

As soon as Latife had heard of Zübeyde's illness, she had written to Mustafa Kemal, asking for him to send his mother to Izmir. There Latife would look after her as her own mother.[8]

They went to see the house on the following day. It was ideal: a villa set in a large garden with a profusion of trees and flowers, much more pleasant for a sick person than a sanatorium.

Yet Zübeyde's departure was delayed time after time. This irritated Latife. Fearing the worst, she informed Salih that she had decided to go abroad.

Mustafa Kemal regretted upsetting Latife and immediately despatched some presents: his favourite horse, Sakarya, and several tins of honey. He also instructed Salih to write a letter to appease Latife.[9]

The most crucial political event of the time was the abolition of the monarchy on 1 November. The order was served on Sultan Vahideddin at Yıldız Palace by Refet Paşa. The declaration appointed the Turkish Grand Assembly as the only ruler of the country. The caliphate would continue as a discrete institution for the foreseeable future. Upon Vahideddin's escape to Malta on 17 November, Abdülmecid Efendi, the former heir to the throne, was notified of his appointment as caliph.

Mustafa Kemal was putting his signature on momentous decisions as he prepared to wed Latife.

Muammer objects to the marriage

Latife's family had their doubts about this marriage that appeared to build up steam again. Still in France, Muammer was brooding over these developments. Latife had written of her father's deep admiration for Mustafa Kemal and his delight at their home serving as headquarters.[10]

That he admired Mustafa Kemal Paşa's military genius was indisputable, but the perceptive businessman was not so sure that a veteran commander would make his daughter happy. His concerns had been countered by a firm 'I love him so much' from Latife. Her resolve was unshakeable.[11]

In any case, Zübeyde was on her way.

Muammer's return from France would coincide with Zübeyde's arrival in Izmir.

Zübeyde comes to see the bride-to-be

It was either 12 or 13 December when Salih's telephone rang in the middle of the night.

'Salih?' asked Mustafa Kemal Paşa. 'What are you doing at the moment? Get up immediately ... Get dressed and come over!'

Salih leapt out of bed, got dressed and went up to Çankaya. Mustafa Kemal was troubled. His mother was set on going to Izmir immediately, heeding neither medical advice nor her son's pleas. She might die, yes, but she would rather die in Izmir, she insisted, and so got up and got fully dressed, up to her cloak.

A special train was laid on immediately.

Salih asked for permission to take his wife along, and it was given readily.

He wired Izmir of their imminent departure; they would set off as soon as Zübeyde felt well enough to travel. To Muammer, Mustafa Kemal sent his personal greetings; to Latife, a letter along with the horse. This letter would bring her untold joy.

Mustafa Kemal told his aide, as he saw his mother off at the station:

'Salih, my mother's illness has taken a turn for the worse. I am worried something might happen on the way, but there was no way I'd deny her final wish. Should the worst happen, do this: if you are closer to Ankara, return. If you are closer to Izmir, then continue. My mother should be interred somewhere I can visit easily.'

Zübeyde talked of nothing but Latife all the way.

'In Izmir is a Lütfiye [sic]; my son has found this lass to his liking ... Let me go to see what sort of girl this is. Will she be a good match for my son? Tell me, what is your view now?'[12]

Zübeyde was on her way to meet the girl who would become her son's wife. Though weak and ill she might have been, she would seize any opportunity to prevent Fikriye from applying for the position.

Zübeyde Hanım, the Mother-in-Law

Having lost his father at a young age, Mustafa Kemal was very close to his mother. Whenever separated by war, he took pains to ensure her well-being and financial security.

War, and the dangers her son threw himself into, dictated the course of Zübeyde Hanım's life, ultimately forcing her to leave the land of her birth and live in exile.

Her adopted son, Abdürrahim Tuncak, describes her as 'being very authoritarian and overprotective'.[1] Zübeyde frequently intervened – verbally or otherwise – in her son's private life as well as the tough struggle he had joined.

So who was this Zübeyde who ordered Mustafa Kemal about, this iconic statesman of the twentieth century? What part did she play in Mustafa Kemal's efforts to include women in social life?

Zübeyde was probably born in 1857 in the Salonica province, somewhere close to Albania. Salonica in those years was a city of 70,000, of whom half were Jewish. Turks constituted the second largest ethnic group, with about 15,000. The most westerly of all Ottoman cities, it looked European, though with a very strong Turkish-Muslim heritage. Salonica pioneered a rich variety of ideas.

Her family were known as the Hacısofular. Her mother was called Ayşe, her father, Feyzullah, a farmer from Langaza, near Salonica. Research done on Zübeyde's family records revealed two brothers, Hasan and Hüseyin, with the same parents.[2] Were there no sisters? Rasih Nuri İleri states that Reşat Fuat Baraner, leader of the Turkish Communist Party, was the son of Zübeyde's sister. He also refers to Mustafa Kemal staying with his maternal aunt when he went to the military high school in Salonica.

Zübeyde was a healthy and very beautiful girl in her youth, with fair skin and light blue eyes. She was probably fifteen or sixteen years of age when she married Ali Rıza Efendi, twenty years her senior. She grew into a dynamic woman in bright, shiny frocks and sporting an air of independence, yet pious and traditional at the same time, which gave rise to the nickname Zübeyde Molla. Ali Rıza Efendi was a customs official, whose posting to Çayağzı would be the beginning of hard times for the family.

Zübeyde bore six children: Fatma, Ömer, Ahmet, Mustafa, Makbule and Naciye, of whom only Mustafa and Makbule survived. Mustafa Kemal's family suffered the loss of several infants, just like the Uşşakizades.

Zübeyde was highly intelligent and rational. Some sources state she was lettered, others that she could barely read and write.

It was her wish for Mustafa to begin his schooling in the traditional way, with hymns accompanying the young pupil on his way to the local clerical school. Ali Rıza Efendi, on the other hand, had his heart set on a school with better academic credentials. There was some tension between the husband and wife, but Ali Rıza Efendi resorted to subtlety. Mustafa began the clerical school with the usual ceremony, thus indulging his mother. Soon after, he left to attend Şemsi Efendi's school. Muslim tradition had been followed before the neighbourhood, but Mustafa was ultimately sent to a secular, western-influenced school where the pupils were not caned, where they sat at desks and did gymnastics in the yard.[3] This school would form the foundation of Mustafa Kemal's ideas on secularism.

Ali Rıza Efendi did not live long; one source claims he died in 1888, and another in 1893.[4] In any case, Zübeyde was widowed at a very young age.

She had to move, together with her two children, to a farm near Langaza where her brother Hüseyin worked as watchman. Mustafa and Makbule grew up in the country, but schooling was a problem. Although the neighbourhood was largely Muslim, Mustafa enrolled at the village Greek school; he did not take to the priest-teacher.[5]

Relenting, Zübeyde sent her son to Salonica, to lodge with her sister whilst he attended the military preparatory school.[6] This school was the last thing she wanted, despite the prestige the military enjoyed in the Ottoman Empire. Mustafa Kemal told Ahmet Emin Yalman in 1922,

'Mother was frightened of the military. She opposed my career path violently. I contrived to sit the entrance exam without letting her know. So I had effectively faced my own mother with a fait accompli.'[7]

Zübeyde married for the second time whilst Mustafa was at the military school. Her second husband, Ragıp Bey, was originally from Thessaly and had migrated to Salonica. He was an official at the tobacco monopolies and had two daughters and two sons from a previous marriage. Fikriye, the daughter of his brother Colonel Hüsamettin Bey, would later play a significant part in Mustafa Kemal's life.

Mustafa Kemal enrolled at the military high school in Monastir,[8] from which he graduated. He arrived in Istanbul in 1902 to begin his higher education at the war college.

From Salonica to Istanbul

The Greek occupation of Salonica in 1912 prompted Zübeyde to take her daughter, Makbule, and emigrate to Istanbul. Ragıp did not go along: one account says Zübeyde had divorced her second husband and fled to Turkey with her daughter. Another claims Ragıp sent his own daughter, Rukiye, with them. History books concur, however, that Zübeyde made straight for Istanbul.

After his mother settled in Istanbul, Mustafa Kemal left for the front for the Battle of Bolayır. At first he stayed in his mother's home in Akaretler whenever he returned, but later, he moved out to a flat in Şişli. This arrangement gave him a little more freedom in his private affairs.

He was careful not to neglect his mother, though, accompanying her to parties and weddings.

Countless letters Mustafa Kemal wrote to his mother have found their way into books. We also know that he looked after her financially. He kept close tabs on her well-being, seeking news from close family and friends.

Initially disconcerted about his involvement with the resistance, Zübeyde had little choice but to accept the situation. She witnessed a multitude of meetings held in her home and supported Mustafa Kemal's effort to 'finish what he had started'.

Zübeyde in Çankaya

Mustafa Kemal sent for his mother and sister when he went to Adapazarı to meet with the French writer and diplomat Claude Farrère in June 1922. Standing on the balcony, Zübeyde watched her son with tears in her eyes as he parted large crowds to reach her. She was staying as the guest of Major Baha, the head of the National Service Office.

This was the first meeting for mother and son after his departure for Samsun in May 1919. Mustafa Kemal had brought Fikriye along, whose unofficial status discomfited his mother and his sister. Although their attitude was no secret, Mustafa Kemal had still intended for the entire family to gather in Çankaya. But when Makbule slighted Fikriye, Mustafa Kemal told his sister to return to Istanbul.[9] As for Zübeyde; she would spend the last few months of her life in Çankaya, close to her son. She never got on with Fikriye either.

The Zübeyde Hanım of Çankaya was a venerable presence who chatted with many of Mustafa Kemal's friends and who graciously received filial visits every morning.

Hüsrev Gerede says, 'He always treated his devout, bright-faced mother with great respect. Not even Napoleon could have been such a dutiful son.'

Mother and son took great pains to prepare for their visits. The first rule was that it was always Mustafa Kemal who paid a visit. If he intended to see her that day, he would despatch word as soon as he awakened to beg her permission. Then he would dress as if going to a formal ceremony. Zübeyde, likewise, would prepare herself with a great deal of attention, even on her sickbed. She would have her hair combed, put her embroidered headscarf on, wear her embroidered gauze shift – a remnant of her nubile Macedonian youth – over which she would wear a silk frock. Her Istanbul-style cloak would complete the outfit, and then she would send word back to her son: she was ready to receive him.[10]

8

A Purebred Arabian as an Engagement Present

Zübeyde wore her white cloak, but no veil, on her way to Izmir. Her two adopted children, Abdürrahim and Fatma, accompanied her; Sergeant Ali and infantryman Mustafa made up the guard detail. Her physician Captain Asım, Salih ADC and his wife Pakize, and – upon Mustafa Kemal's wish – Tevfik Rüştü Aras, a close friend of the Uşşakizade family, completed the entourage.

Latife, Asım Paşa – a classmate of Mustafa Kemal's – and Asım's wife were waiting at the station. Latife felt close to Mustafa Kemal's mother from the very first. Having originally hurried back from France to look after her own ailing grandmother, Latife was now making plans to restore Mustafa Kemal's mother to health.

Let us lend an ear to Sergeant Ali Metin, Mustafa Kemal's orderly, as he relates the meeting of the two women:

The people of Izmir welcomed Zübeyde Hanım with open arms. She was suffering from bad knees. As she had difficulty walking, she was carried on a wicker chair. She received the first wave of the welcoming committee in her carriage. She was enervated and tired by the high number of visitors; now she could barely see around her. So she failed to pick out Latife in that crowd. I could sense her curiosity. At one point there were only a few ladies left in the carriage. Zübeyde Hanım took this opportunity and told the guests she needed to be left alone on a private matter for a while. The carriage emptied. I went out and made sure Latife Hanım brought Zübeyde Hanım a drink of water.[1]

Salih took this opportunity to say, 'Look, dear mother, this lass is Latife,' and she replied, 'Salih, my son, our lass is very pretty indeed.'

All Latife could manage was, 'You flatter me, My Lady; let me kiss your hand.'

Zübeyde drank the water Latife gave her, looked her up and down and returned the glass, the younger woman's hand still in her own.

'Bless you, child, you are much prettier in person. I do hope we've not made you wait too long.'

'Please don't mention it, My Lady, the anticipation was all. You, too, are far more beautiful in person than photographs depict you ...'

Zübeyde said, 'Let me give you a little secret, into your ear now,' and winking at her, she whispered: 'The more you gaze at beauty, the more beautiful *you* become.'[2]

Cares like a nurse

There is little in anyone's memoirs on the contents of the letter Mustafa Kemal asked Salih to deliver to Latife Hanım. The letter that caused her such joy must have heralded their engagement.

Zübeyde was pleased with the villa that had been prepared for her. Latife had ordered a wheelchair for the house and removed all the doorsteps. This little detail, which gave Zübeyde access to all parts of the house, met with her approval.

She spoke in her charming Rumeli accent, entertaining all present. All the servants did their best to please her, the butler, cooks and maids.

Latife spared no effort to ensure Zübeyde's comfort, doing all she could to alleviate the elderly woman's suffering. Poultices were applied, injections meticulously monitored, and Latife personally administered her medicines.

Asım Gündüz says, 'Latife Hanım had engaged a doctor, a nurse and a carer. She went to visit her guest daily, dressed in white, like a nurse, and occupied herself with the lady's meals and care.'[3]

Zübeyde might have been delighted with the care she received, but some people heard rumours of her criticising Latife to the servants, 'quite plain really, and so short,' behind her back.

The two women were poles apart. It was Mustafa Kemal who brought them together. Latife had met Mustafa Kemal and fallen in love. As for Zübeyde, her Mustafa, her beloved son, came before everything. Zübeyde assessed her Mustafa's bride-to-be minutely, offering advice framed in proverbs. She spoke of her son's childhood, character and the life of a soldier; she spoke at length of the Mustafa she herself knew well to better prepare Latife for married life. It is also said that Zübeyde and Muammer got along very well, holding long and amiable conversations.

Zübeyde had come for the engagement and brought presents. According to Ali Metin, Mustafa Kemal had made his preparations and then sent his mother along to conduct the engagement. The entire city knew the purpose of her visit, but the family would not advertise it.[4]

Sakarya, the most valuable gift of all

The gift was Sakarya, the horse that had been despatched several days earlier. This purebred Arabian horse with white markings on three legs, a pastern, a sock and a stocking, had been Mustafa Kemal's constant companion throughout the National Struggle. Salih says of that day, 'On a fine early afternoon, after her arrival at the Karşıyaka villa [there is a note that says, 'on the second day'] Zübeyde Hanım presented Latife with the horse, her son's gift. The younger woman was delighted with Sakarya, this historic horse that had borne Mustafa Kemal to victory.'[5]

Evidently Zübeyde had not clarified whether this was an engagement gift or the customary houseguest's present to her hostess.[6]

Mustafa Kemal's gifts were the talk of the town in Ankara. Grace Ellison, the explorer-journalist who was visiting Ankara at the time, found them befitting a commander's glory:

The originality of his gifts to the bride recalls the Prophet of Islam. Mahomet gave his daughter a Koran, a prayer-carpet, and a coffee-mill; Mustafa Kemal has given his wife-to-be General Tricoupis's revolver and an Arab horse! She is an excellent rider, sitting astride, with the veil only confining her hair.[7]

Mustafa Kemal: I'm getting married

As Zübeyde settled in Izmir, the talk of the town in Ankara was Kemal Paşa's imminent wedding.

Ambassador İbrahim Abilov, one of the unforgettable names of the National Struggle, was hosting a New Year's banquet for twenty or so guests on 4 January 1923. The Azeri embassy in Cebeci was an old wooden mansion. Platefuls of black caviar covered the table. Musicians had been engaged to play Azeri tunes. Although Mustafa Kemal Paşa had sent his regrets, everyone still expected him to turn up. And arrive he did, albeit quite late. İsmail Habib Sevük, then a fledgling columnist, was present as a guest of Yunus Nadi. Sevük wrote of this particular night in *Cumhuriyet* immediately after Atatürk's death in 1938:

The Gazi began with an important disclosure. All eyes fixed upon him, all ears wide open. His news was a surprise indeed:

'I'm getting married!'

Everyone was astounded ...

'Seriously, Paşam?'

'Seriously, sir; seriously, definitely and decidedly: I'm getting married.'

It might have been Ağaoğlu who asked:

'Who is this happy person who conquered the heart of the Conqueror of Izmir?'

'A girl from Izmir.'

He went on to speak for the first time, and for a long time, of this marriage.

Speaking as one who cared less for physical beauty in his intended than the spiritual, he said:

'No oil painting. But she is so intelligent, and speaks so sincerely ... the entire family had pledged to host me in their mansion if I were to retake Izmir ...'

She can read minds!

Mustafa Kemal's voice was full of admiration as he summarised his time in Izmir. He explained frankly how he accepted the offer of lodgings and how Latife played the piano and spoke four or five languages:

'Her greatest asset is an astuteness that has the capacity to discover what's in your mind. For instance, one day, after we had settled in her family's mansion, I found myself missing İsmet Paşa. It was a fair step from his place to ours. Even if I sent word, he couldn't possibly make it here anytime soon. But how I wanted to talk to him just then! Suddenly there was a knock on the door. I called out, "Enter!"

"'Ooo! İsmet Paşa! Well done you; I've been missing you!"

'İsmet Paşa was taken aback.

"'But I received a call, your command for me to come!"

"'Who made the call?"

'The girl enters and says, "I took the liberty of calling, thinking you'd be pleased to see İsmet Paşa."

'See how she knows what's going through my mind?'

He talked and talked and invited others to talk ...

The host drew the curtains apart. Astonishingly, it was bright daylight.[8]

Mustafa Kemal had explained that night why he wanted to marry: 'I'm not treating this marriage business lightly. I must set an example in order to create a new family life standard in our country. Too long have women remained like bogeymen!'[9]

During an interview with Grace Ellison, the conversation came to the topic of women, and Mustafa Kemal made his views very clear. 'This time next year, woman must be free. She must uncover her face and mix with men.' Ellison then continues:

Taking my courage in both hands, I ventured to mention the fear his friends had expressed to me, of his marrying a princess.

'That will never happen,' he replied. 'I have already chosen an educated woman of my own people, with character enough to be "equal partner" in all my work. There can be no happiness in union for only half one's character and one's life. But I stand for democracy ...'[10]

İsmet wires his congratulations

It is thanks to İsmet's telegram from Lausanne that we know precisely when Latife and Mustafa Kemal were engaged: three days before the death of Zübeyde.

> To His Excellency Gazi Mustafa Kemal Paşa
> The glad tidings of your engagement have caused me great joy. You will be happy, by the grace of God Most High. I congratulate both you, and us.
> İsmet [13 January 1923][11]

Theirs was an engagement party with no ceremony, rings or even bride-groom: Latife was holding vigil at Zübeyde's bedside, whilst Mustafa Kemal was on a tour of western Anatolia. Trunk calls being all but unheard of at the time, they must have got engaged by telegram. They must have wanted to spare Zübeyde any more anguish as she lay on her sickbed.

Zübeyde Hanım's death

Izmir's heart gladdened at the sight of Zübeyde enjoying the sun in the gardens of the Karşıyaka house: so long as she was there, her son might soon return.

When Mustafa Kemal telegraphed his orderly Sergeant Ali, summoning him to Ankara, Salih said to Latife, 'He might be on his way to see his mother.' Sadly, Mustafa Kemal did not make it to Izmir in time. He despatched Esat Bey, the photography officer, to his mother for some portraits – which turned out to be her last.

She is thought to have dictated a second will in her final hours, with

Latife in attendance. Zübeyde died on the evening of 15 January 1923.

The first person Latife informed of Zübeyde's death was Abdülhalik Bey, governor of Izmir.

Almost all of Izmir turned out for the funeral. The procession was nearly a kilometre long. Latife wanted to join in the march in her black coat and veil, but facing objections from her family and the clerics, she had to concede and follow in a closed phaeton instead. The dictum was unanimous: women did not participate in Muslim funerals.[12]

Zübeyde had been particularly devout. A will made when she lived in Akaretler had detailed all that was to be done after her death. They included interment at the Yahya Efendi Cemetery in Beşiktaş, a prayer supper to be held on the third day after her interment, five sacrificial sheep to be distributed and a drinking fountain to be erected. Since she had died in Izmir, however, she could not be buried at the designated cemetery, as Muslim funerals traditionally take place within a day of death.

Latife had hundreds of silver coins distributed to the poor at the cemetery and engaged thirty-three of Izmir's top Koran reciters on the first night to have the entire Koran read until the morning. She also had prayers read for three days, and a *mevlid* (the prayer for the dead) on the fortieth. In addition, she distributed Noah's pudding to the poor on the fifty-second and commissioned a complete recitation of the Koran once more.

Mustafa Kemal sent Latife a telegram of gratitude: the young woman had far exceeded her mother-in-law's wishes.

> To the Lady Latife,
>
> I am utterly convinced that you shall participate in my grief with all your heart. Your compassionate attention and care shown to my mother in her final hours console me. I am deeply grateful.
>
> My paternal aunt and my sister joined me in İzmit for one night upon hearing the news of her demise, and Halide Hanım [Edib Adıvar], who is here for a meeting; they all kiss you on the eyes. I shall depart for Bursa tomorrow evening. I shall then move to Balıkesir after approximately two days.
>
> Gazi Mustafa Kemal [19 January 1923][13]

9

'Get ready; we're getting married!'

Mustafa Kemal arrived in Karşıyaka on the morning of 27 January. All the top commanders were in Izmir, with the exception of İsmet, who was representing Turkey at the Lausanne peace conference.

Mustafa Kemal had missed his mother's funeral. He would take her leave first, and then go to the other woman who was waiting for him: Latife. The time had come to face the nation no longer as a bachelor commander running between fronts but as a man whose wife heralded change.

Izmir had been inundated with journalists. Members of the foreign press, in particular, were on starting blocks. They might have ostensibly come along to follow the Gazi's Izmir visit, but their real purpose was to witness a wedding.

Latife was not amongst the crowds waiting to greet him in Karşıyaka. She might have wanted to welcome him, but that would have scandalised the prevailing social conditions. Her father, Muammer, waited at the station in her stead, in his customary whites from top to toe.

Salih says:

Mustafa Kemal's train finally pulled in. Latife Hanım's father was in the front of the welcoming committee. Mustafa Kemal beckoned me before disembarking. And he asked for some information on Latife Hanım. 'I've made my mind up to marry Latife. Is her father here now?' Hearing that indeed he was, Mustafa Kemal said this in full confidence: 'Then go now, and inform him of my decision. And add that he is not to tell anyone!'[1]

Izmir greeted Mustafa Kemal with a rapturous welcome as he stepped down to the platform. Military commanders, ministers and deputies stood alongside them. Governor Abdülhalik introduced Mustafa Kemal and Muammer.

A large crowd followed Mustafa Kemal's flower-bedecked car as he went to visit his mother's grave. Explaining his grief at her death, he spoke sincerely and emotionally of how she had lived under constant *padişah* and government oppression and torture, and how she had suffered a stroke due to the anguish of thinking the death sentence on him had been executed. His voice trembled as he spoke of how Zübeyde lost her eyesight from crying day and night, and he pleaded for her forgiveness. He had neglected her in his struggle to save the country.

The White Mansion in Göztepe played host to yet another memorable day. The family welcomed Mustafa Kemal at the garden gate. Muammer had left the entourage and returned home earlier.

After the ceremony of introductions, Mustafa Kemal expressed his gratitude for the care and attention shown his mother during her illness.

The reply was, 'This was our most holy duty.'

They had their coffees. Mustafa Kemal asked Muammer's permission by saying, 'If you will permit me, I have something to say to your daughter,' and taking Latife by the hand, he left.

Those in the drawing room knew what this meant.

'Get ready,' he said to Latife, 'I'm summoning the *kadı*.'

Latife objected to this attack order of a decision to marry. 'But, Paşam, in two hours?'

He insisted, 'Orders are orders. You have to obey!'

But Latife held her ground. 'I must invite a couple of close friends.'

So Mustafa Kemal went to see Muammer.

'You have a very headstrong daughter, Muammer Bey!' he said.

Mustafa Kemal had to concede the point in the face of Latife's resistance.

'All right, two days then,' he announced, settling the matter amicably.[2]

A banquet table was laid out, to which Kâzım Karabekir and Fevzi Paşas also were invited.

Muammer: *'Latife, please reconsider!'*

However uneasy Muammer was, the last thing he would do was dampen his elated daughter's spirits. Wedding preparations were under way, everyone in the house flitting to and fro. Bracing himself for one final talk, he summoned her. Father and daughter sat side by side; Latife knew what was coming, but waited in silence. Gathering his inner strength, he began:

'You still have time. Please reconsider, Latife,' he said. 'It's hard to build a home atop a garrison. If you are frightened of saying no, I would take full responsibility.' Latife objected violently. She was well aware of the difficulties that awaited her, yet she still wanted to marry. Father and daughter debated for a long time.

'Papa, I love him so much. Please do not interfere in my life,' Latife implored eventually.

He had rarely stood in her way until that day. And yet here he was, pleading on his knees with his daughter. He also knew just how obstinate she could be. Seeing her resolve, he had only one more thing to say. 'Should this marriage ever come to an end and you return to my home, never talk to me of him, or of marriage!' And so ended the discussion.

Mustafa Kemal advances the wedding by a day

On the morning of 29 January, Asım Gündüz went to the White Mansion by car, taking Marshal Fevzi Çakmak and Kâzım Karabekir Paşa along. Governor Abdülhalik and Kâzım Özalp Paşa had arrived earlier. Asım says, 'We chatted for about an hour in the drawing room, Latife included. But something extraordinary was clearly in the air. Just then there was a knock at the door; the *müftü* had arrived.'

The Uşşakizades had thrown a party to celebrate the liberation of Izmir, inviting military commanders as well as close family and friends. Latife's hard won two-day reprieve was due to end on Tuesday. But Mustafa Kemal deftly succeeded in converting this event into a wedding party, presenting her with a fait accompli. Few had noticed this turn of events, and so there is little mention of it in the various memoirs; Latife, however, later spoke to a journalist:

One day my father gave a reception to forty or fifty friends in celebration of Izmir's recapture by our armies. I had no intimation that my future husband would take advantage of this occasion and turn this into a wedding party. The visitors had all come, and I was administering to the preparation of food in the kitchen when Kemal Paşa came to the door and motioned me to come to him. With a smile on his lips he asked me if I would object to utilising this occasion for the wedding. I asked him if he had spoken to my father. He said, 'We will.' Then he sent for my father, who, on being told of the plans, said smilingly that if it was agreeable to us both it was agreeable to him. You can imagine my excitement and embarrassment. [...] I was perhaps the first Turkish girl who was wedded to her future husband in his presence. One of the visitors was a registrar, and he performed the ceremony. It was a true western wedding.[3]

Mustafa Kemal had asked of Fevzi, 'Paşam, if you would be kind enough to become my witness, and Abdülhalik Bey would act as Latife's, and we addressed the matters of immediate and deferred settlements, we could conduct the marriage ceremony here and now.'

The marshal was taken aback. 'Oh! Paşam, we had no idea. This is quite sudden,' he muttered. As this conversation carried on, Latife left the drawing room to fetch a scarf, having noted the *müftü*'s arrival.

The Uşşakizades were sitting in the room to the right of the entrance, and the Gazi and his friends to the left. Latife's brothers and sisters were busy entertaining the guests.

They settled on the dining room on the ground floor for the marriage ceremony.

She wore little make-up

Rather unsurprisingly given the conditions of the time, the wedding dress ordered for Latife had not yet arrived. Instead of wearing her own mother's wedding dress, Latife chose a pink Lanvin dress with silver embroidery that Adeviye had purchased for her in Paris.

Latife, carrying a single white rose in her hand, wore little make-up out of deference to Mustafa Kemal's wishes. Her hair was covered with a violet scarf and she had matching gloves.

[...] Mustafa Kemal himself wore a dark blue, three-piece business suit with matching tie sparked by a red design. His blondish hair was partially concealed by a kalpak of grey astrakhan; in his breast pocket he wore a white handkerchief.[4]

Six people sat down at the table. Latife's witnesses were Chief Aide-de-Camp Salih and Abdülhalik Bey, governor of Izmir; Mustafa Kemal's were two generals: Fevzi Çakmak and Kâzım Karabekir. Although Asım Paşa refers to only two witnesses, the marriage papers list the signatures of four. Around forty guests watched this historic ceremony.

Mustafa Kemal said, 'If I had been younger, I'd be having a somewhat different ceremony. I'd have ridden up, scooped Latife Hanım on my saddle and eloped. But now I realise I'm no longer that young.' And he asked the *müftü*: 'Dear sir! Latife Hanım and I have decided to marry. Will you please do the honours?'

The *müftü's* long prayers bored Mustafa Kemal; he turned to his friends:

'I hope the time will come when the governor himself can solemnise marriages,' he said, hinting at his plans for the future regarding religious marriage ceremonies.

The marriage was solemnised at five o'clock in the afternoon on 29 January 1923. The marriage certificate also bears the signature of Ömer Fevzi ibni Hüseyin, the chief *kadı*. Lütfü Efendi, the *müftü*, had brought gifts of his own: a Koran box and a copper pitcher enamelled with prayers, all for the nuptial chamber. These gifts are still preserved by Latife's family.

In transforming a house party into a wedding, Mustafa Kemal might have considered the security aspect and thus advanced the date; it is also possible he worried that the Uşşakizade family might turn the wedding into a grandiose affair. Those were days of privation; he wanted a simple ceremony. Although he was marrying the daughter of the wealthiest family in Izmir, he had to take his own precautions.

The fact that she had got out of the kitchen to sit at the marriage ceremony table had upset the order of proceedings Latife might have had in mind and had shown her that she had to be prepared for any eventuality. Speaking of the ceremony a year later, she is quoted in the *Current Opinion* article mentioned above:

'And I now realise why my husband wished to have it done that way. He himself wanted to set the example to the rest of our countrymen. It is true that since our innovation many of my young countrymen have married in western fashion. Of course, it will take years to break down the prejudices of centuries, but we are progressing rapidly, and before many years the hand of the past will cease to rule us any longer.'

A modern wedding

The marriage ceremony was conducted on a Monday and not a Thursday, as was the custom at the time. Tradition dictated an agent represent the bride at the religious ceremony. Yet here was Latife, at the table, in person, being asked for her consent.

The solemnisation was made on the basis of a symbolic amount of ten dirhems of immediate settlement. This pledge covered money and goods a man would settle on his wife as a form of financial guarantee. The low sum was interpreted as a desire to create equality between man and wife.

The marriage certificate lists Latife's year of birth as 1899, so she was twenty-four years old at the time they married. Mustafa Kemal was forty-one; his address was recorded as house number 46 in Göztepe, Izmir.

A 1917 Civil Code Order that regulated marriages had been suspended during the occupation, but had not yet been superseded by a new regulation. This marriage was therefore solemnised in full compliance with the Civil Code Order.

The form of the marriage ceremony was also crucial to the Lausanne conference. One of the key topics in the first phase of the conference was the establishment of a secular civil code in Turkey. Western powers had been presented with a determination to move away from sharia. The manner of his own nuptials proved that Mustafa Kemal would keep this promise.

They had no rings to exchange

The wedding was unusual on one more count: they had not purchased wedding rings. İsmet would bring them from Lausanne instead. 'The ring was bought for him at Lausanne by the delegates, who were as excited about the business as any school-children.'[5]

According to Muammer Erboy's account, Mustafa Kemal's gift to his bride was a handwritten Koran in a gold case the size of a matchbox that he had carried on his neck in battle. He said as he handed it to her, 'May this protect you.'

The Uşşakizade family are reported to have presented Mustafa Kemal with a precious cigarette case and a tiepin at this rushed wedding.

The first to congratulate the bride was the governor of Izmir, Abdülhalik Renda.

He kissed her hand as he said, 'Congratulations, My Lady,' then added, 'You have conquered the conqueror of Izmir.'

The Anatolian Agency featured the item in great detail in the daily bulletin. Particularly emphasised was the fact that during the ceremony it was Latife who had been asked first if she consented to the marriage, before Mustafa Kemal.

On 30 January 1923 the following report appeared in *Vakit*:

AN AUSPICIOUS WEDDING IN IZMIR

According to news we have received with great delight from both Ankara and Izmir, the wedding ceremony of His Excellency Gazi Mustafa Kemal Paşa and the daughter of Uşşakizade Muammer Bey has been conducted. With this marriage, His Excellency the Paşa carries out his mother's dying wish. His late mother wanted nothing more than to see her son happily married. The dear departed lady, whose maternal love for the highly virtuous son she raised was extraordinary, and who was also very sensitive, had insisted on a family home even before she had met her future daughter-in-law, and had developed a great affection for the young lady once she met her in Izmir.

Latife Hanım has exceptional qualities. Having visited all parts of the Continent, her knowledge of Europe is considerable. She speaks French, English and German flawlessly. Her musical skills are exemplary. Her Turkish writing is excellent. Uşşakizade Halit Bey has taken special care to teach Latife Hanım, whom he describes as highly talented. Those who have made her acquaintance sing the praises of her intelligence, resolve and willpower, and add that she is an ardent patriot.

The entire nation will welcome the fact that His Excellency Mustafa Kemal Paşa has selected a life mate with these qualities, and wish the happy couple all the best from the depths of their hearts.

Our newspaper would like to extend our sincerest congratulations to both His Excellency Mustafa Kemal Paşa and Latife Hanım.

The film news agency International News had shot footage of the young couple.

The item screened with the subtitle 'The first intimate scenes' went on to state: 'Mustafa Kemal Paşa and Turkey's richest girl, a resolute defender of women's rights ... The first intimate scenes ... General Kemal and his wife agree. It is impossible for a nation to progress if its women are excluded from its life.'[6]

The footage depicts a Latife confidently striding before the cameras, gazing boldly at the world, and even displaying little bashfulness when the wind whips her cape, revealing her figure. For westerners, this was a startlingly intriguing synthesis of the oriental and the occidental.

The New York Times: 'A Dowry of One Million Liras'

The wedding was reported on page 3 of the *New York Times*, citing 29 January, Istanbul:

Mustafa Kemal Marries; Bride Is The Daughter Of A Wealthy Merchant Of Izmir

It is reported that Mustafa Kemal Paşa, Turkish nationalist leader, was married today to the daughter of a rich Turkish merchant of Izmir, Muammer Uşaki Bey. Mustafa Kemal's bride is said to have brought him a dowry of 1,000,000 Turkish Liras. Educated in London and Paris, Mrs Kemal is known to be an advocate of women's rights and eschews the traditional Turkish veil.

The item goes on to convert the dowry value to US$660,000, a significant sum for Turkey, which had just emerged from a long war. A similar item appeared in the *Washington Post*.

As the news item indicates, the fact that Mustafa Kemal had married a world-famous merchant's daughter was noteworthy. The historian Feroz Ahmad compares this with the past:

> Mustafa Kemal's marriage to Latife Hanım, the daughter of a prominent Izmir businessman, may even be seen as a matrimonial alliance between the Kemalist bureaucrative élite and the emergent bourgeoisie; in contrast the Unionist heroes such as Enver and Hafız Hakkı Paşas married into the Ottoman household, revealing their social and political inclinations.[7]

The American magazine *Time* in its eightieth anniversary commemorative issue began its list of '80 Days that Changed the World' with 29 January 1923, featuring a photograph of Latife and Mustafa Kemal on their wedding day. The headline summarises a good deal: 'Turkey Forced Westward'.

The entire world wondered whither Turkey after the National Struggle.

The western press followed the wedding in Izmir with great interest; photographs of the newlyweds were highly sought after. The bride's European education, her outspoken stance on women's rights, how close husband and wife stood when posing for photos – all this stood for an image of a Turkey that faced westward. The wedding that was timed close to the break in the deadlocked Lausanne conference must have signalled to the world outside: 'We're doing fine; look, our leader is able to wed; we're set on our path.'

This was clever timing indeed: the conference had broken up on 27 January. Ahmet Emin Yalman, a celebrated columnist of the time, wrote in his memoirs:

> The clearest signal that Ankara was able to meet all with equanimity was the timing of Mustafa Kemal Paşa's wedding. Newspapers dated 30 January reported the news of the marriage ceremony of the speaker of the Grand Assembly to the daughter of Uşşakizade Muammer Bey. The bride is also the niece of the celebrated *litterateur* Halit Ziya Bey.[8]

10

Honeymoon

As the guests were leaving one by one, Mustafa Kemal signalled Kâzım Karabekir and Fevzi to stay. Then, holding Latife by the shoulders, he kissed her forehead.

'Come on, then, show your skills and prepare a wedding feast for our guests! Fevzi Paşa wants to see the bride prove herself.'

Caught unawares, Fevzi was sputtering, 'Paşam, that's not fair!' as Mustafa Kemal smiled.

'A soldier's wife's place is in the kitchen on her wedding night!'

Latife laid the single white rose she had been holding on Mustafa Kemal's lap, removed her gloves and ran out of the room.

She did magnificently. She decorated a crystal bowl she had overturned with flowers and leaves, all illuminated by tiny bulbs. Caviar and pats of butter were placed on vine leaves. A starched tablecloth, starched napkins and the finest china in the house were on the table, bedecked with a wealth of mezes.

The guests at the mansion were representatives of the Izmir press, and the topic was the Lausanne peace conference. The last of the guests left towards midnight. Latife's parents, brothers and sisters all retired to their own rooms, leaving the newlyweds alone.

On 31 January, Mustafa Kemal held a meeting at the former customs building to introduce his wife to the people of Izmir. Salih is seen standing next to Latife in a photo. Surrounded by a crowd of women, she holds a notebook in her hand; she must be taking minutes.

Mustafa Kemal began his speech with 'Ladies and gentlemen!' Stating his wish to speak as a humble deputy, he told the audience he welcomed questions: 'All that you see on this earth is woman's work. A society that contents itself with satisfying the contemporary needs of only one sex will find more than half of itself disenfranchised.'

Amongstst the questions posed to Mustafa Kemal, three came from women in the audience. This was the first time Latife had appeared in public together with Mustafa Kemal. She was all ears as he spoke of his vision for women before this crowd. The speech emphasised that the highest duty of a woman was motherhood, that this was the reason they needed education equal to that of men, and that they would stand beside the men in society and man and woman would walk together. He also stressed that science and knowledge were essential not only to men but to women, too, and that the hijab ought not to be allowed to marginalise women.[1]

What Latife thought of this speech, whether she shared the view of motherhood being the most important duty of women and what she said to Mustafa Kemal later we do not know.

They go on honeymoon

The newlyweds planned a short honeymoon trip in the Aegean region and so set off towards Balıkesir.

> Their honeymoon was spent in districts ravaged by the war. They stayed at the villages, where Mustafa Kemal talked with the peasants, listening to their complaints and saying what was expected of him. Even when they visited the towns, no one asked any questions about the lady accompanying him. At a review of the troops, she rode by his side like an adjutant. It was only then his officers knew of his marriage.[2]

Mahu Aygen and her husband would host the Paşa and his wife in Edremit, as theirs was the house with the largest reception room. Some seventy or eighty guests were expected for dinner. Sea bass was plentiful in Akçay, so a meal of sea bass, mayonnaise, savoury pies and pudding was prepared. The table was decorated with olives. Edremit was a pious town, where women were cloaked and could not address men. Mahu Aygen says, 'The female teachers, a few doctors' and solicitors' wives, and the rest of us, we decided to wear our cloak but no face veil to greet our guests.' In the room next to the reception room, she had prepared a bedchamber by putting two beds side by side. Around five in the afternoon, a group of men set off outside the town. Soon after, the district governor rapped on Mahu Aygen's door, at his wits' end. Mustafa Kemal had called on the Turkish Hearth and, seeing it shut, had lost his temper. Then he had gone to the Town Hall, which also was shut. He had ordered it open, and went in and sat down in a huff. They all trembled, worrying: what if he found the house they had prepared equally inadequate?

Mahu Aygen, her husband, and a group of women greeted their guests at the door. Latife was in an infantry uniform and a military coat. Turning to the women, she apologised: 'I had no idea such a warm welcome awaited us; that is why I've come in this outfit.' She removed her coat and hung it on the stand. Mustafa Kemal turned to Mahu and said, 'We are so grateful: you've made it possible for us to enjoy a civilised night. Here I am, travelling with my wife, yet we've not seen a single female face all this trip!'

They were standing at the bottom of the staircase. Latife walked on ahead and went up to the first floor. The ladies had surrounded Mustafa Kemal, and the headmistress was talking to Latife. When the torchlight procession came along, Mustafa Kemal invited all the women to join him at the window for his address. 'Come on ladies, let the people always see us together like this. Let them get used to seeing us together; this is the way of the future.'

When he saw that the women were not sitting at the table, Mustafa Kemal objected. Mahu tried to explain: 'We're serving the food.' He would have none of it, and seated Latife on one side and Mahu on the other. He had told her that night, 'We're coming from Balya. There, Latife Hanım and I stood in prayer side by side.'³ If Mahu Hanım's recollection is correct, then the couple had broken with tradition once more: man and wife standing in prayer side by side in a mosque would have been unheard of.

The short honeymoon tour gave Latife the opportunity to see Anatolia at close range. Vamık Volkan and Norman Itkowitz, biographers of Atatürk, interpret this tour:

She had witnessed the Turks' humiliation in Izmir at the hands of the Greeks and then their subsequent victory and the burning of the city. Whatever romantic notions she might have had about Anatolia were quickly dispelled by the harsh reality. The countryside was a wasteland. The excitement of the crowds cheering her hero was one thing, but the pervasiveness of need and poverty was another.[4]

The short tour ended on 10 February, and the newlyweds stayed in Izmir for a week longer. As Latife made her farewell visits and packed the goods she would take to Çankaya, Mustafa Kemal occupied himself with the preparations for the opening of the Economy Congress, on which he placed a great deal of importance. This congress would shape the immediate future of national economy policies and had long been planned. Ankara had originally been considered as the venue, but ultimately a decision was made to hold it in Izmir. The venue was the Ottoman Bank warehouse, the largest enclosed space in the city, capable of seating 7,000. Some 5,000 delegates were expected to attend, so additional dormitories were laid on; sadly, harsh winter conditions restricted the numbers.

The Turkish Economy Congress opened on Saturday, 17 February. The 1,100 delegates who attended had been appointed by the county councils, town councils, chambers of commerce and agriculture, the stock market and representatives of the Defence of Rights Association. Uşşakizade Muammer Bey was amongst the Izmir contingent. Women were also represented. A photography ban stayed in effect throughout the fortnight of the congress; official photographs were distributed to the press, albeit with a slight delay.

Women and men sat together. A 300-seat section had initially been allocated to female observers on the gallery, but the number of women attending reached 500. There was one more breakthrough for women at the congress: six female labourers from Izmir attended as delegates. Speaking on their behalf at the close of the congress, Rukiye Hanım thanked the organisers and said, 'Women are actively participating in the affairs of the country for the first time. That we were blessed with this honour delivers our hearts and fills them with pride.'[5]

Meeting the Lausanne delegation in Eskişehir

The honeymoon that was interlaced with politics had come to an end. It was time for Latife and Mustafa Kemal to set off for Ankara. At Eskişehir – en route to Ankara – Mustafa Kemal was scheduled to meet the Turkish delegation that had taken the decision to break off the deadlocked peace congress.

Two representatives of the foreign press were amongst the welcoming committee at Eskişehir station on 21 February: Larry Lue of the *Chicago Daily Tribune* and Ward Price from the *Daily Mail*. Larry Lue reported:

> [...] their train had barely stopped before Mustafa Kemal stepped off the car and helped his wife to the platform.
>
> Dressed in a smart tan sport suit, Mrs Mustafa Kemal, first lady of Anatolia, was unveiled and blushing. Laughing and waving her hands at acquaintances, she added gaiety and life to the scene, which otherwise was sombre. Despite the nation-wide hero worship for Kemal, his wife rather than himself was the cynosure of all eyes.[6]

He thought Mustafa Kemal's courtship must have been as impulsive as his war making.

Ward Price, who had accompanied İsmet, described the bride in great detail as she appeared at Eskişehir station; this was the woman the entire world wanted to know about:

> On the train from Istanbul to Ankara, in a train with broken windows, no heating, and no electric light, the Turkish delegation stopped at the small station of Eskişehir, to be joined by the Nationalist leader, Mustafa Kemal, accompanied by the wife whom he had married a few weeks earlier in Izmir.
>
> The Gazi – a Turkish military title conferred on 'Conquerors of the Infidels' – was dressed in a tweed suit, breeches, and cycling stockings, which contrasted oddly with patent-leather shoes. It was startling to see his new nineteen-year-old wife [sic], Latife Hanım,

wearing riding breeches, with high boots and spurs. She had a bright silk handkerchief over her hair, and her face was unveiled. Turkish onlookers were obviously startled by this costume, which no other woman in Turkey at that time would have dared to adopt.[7]

Arrival in Ankara, the Nationalist Base

The first question on everyone's lips was, was Latife pretty? Mustafa Kemal was a very handsome man; did they make a good-looking couple? Although not a striking beauty, her wholesomeness revealed itself on closer inspection. She was, however, blessed with regular features and sparkling brown-black eyes.

Harold Courtenay Armstrong describes her in *Grey Wolf* as 'dark-haired, with black, laughing eyes, small and dainty, now vivacious, now with a dignity of her own, tiny-limbed, and soft voiced as she talked the musical Turkish'.[1]

Halide Edib had replied to İsmet's question, 'What do you think of Latife Hanım?' with, 'She is very charming.'[2]

To the American journalist Isaac Frederic Marcosson, 'Latife was the most attractive Turkish woman' he had yet encountered:

Like other men of iron, he has his one vulnerable point, and having met Madam Kemal I can understand why he succumbed.[3]

Whilst we were in the midst of the interview the butler entered and whispered something in Kemal's ear. Instantly he turned and said, 'Madam Kemal is coming down.'

A few moments later the most attractive Turkish woman I had yet met entered – I should say glided – into the room. She was of medium height, with a full oriental face and brilliant dark eyes. Her every movement was grace itself. Although she wore a sort of a non-Turkish costume – it was dark blue – she had retained the charming head-dress which is usually worn with the veil, and which, according to old Turkish custom, must completely hide the hair. The veil, however, was absent for Madam Kemal was one of the emancipated ones. Some of her brown tresses peeped out from beneath the beguiling cover. A subtle perfume emanated from her. She was a picture of feminine Paris literally adorning the Ankara scene.[4]

Foreign newspapers of the time frequently referred to her as Kemal's 'beautiful bride'.

As for Mustafa Kemal himself, he had repeated once or twice that he did not find her to be a stunning beauty. Yet we also know that whilst still a houseguest in the Uşşakizade mansion, he had complimented her: 'You, child, are pleasant, no pleasantry. I shall henceforth call you Latif.' The play on words in first names borrowed from Arabic, which does have gender, afforded a variety of meanings: *latif* means 'pretty', 'pleasant', and *latife* means 'a pleasantry'. *Latif* is also used as a name, the masculine of *Latife*.

Süreyya Ağaoğlu remembers how Mustafa Kemal likened Latife to a *houri*, and how he teased her: 'The angels of paradise have mother-of-pearl skin and black eyes, just like you.'

Latife was much more beautiful in person than photographs give her credit for. Her charisma instantly enchanted and impressed anyone who met and spoke with her.

Curiosity, then, flowed through the welcoming committee: was the bride a good match for Mustafa Kemal Paşa?

Ankara station had been festooned with flowers for the early morning arrival of the newlyweds. The first to disembark was Mustafa Kemal, followed by Latife. Applause rose to the ceiling. Mustafa Kemal had departed a single man and come back married.

The welcoming committee of leading dignitaries greeted the delegation from Eskişehir. Accompanying Fevzi and İsmet Paşas were Prime Minister Rauf Bey, Nuri Bey Conker, Fethi Bey Okyar, Ruşen Eşref and countless Ankara natives. Latife had been looking out at the crowds. Salih reassured her that he would whisper the names of people whose hands she would be shaking.

The carriage had come to a halt before Rauf Bey. First to disembark was Mustafa Kemal, who then turned and assisted

Latife down, holding her hand. The first person to congratulate Latife was Prime Minister Rauf, whom Latife knew from his time in Izmir. She was delighted to see him again. She was given too many bouquets for her arms to hold; Salih took them deftly and laid them aside. The crowds were pushing one another to catch a glimpse of this young and pretty woman who looked about with sparkling eyes.[5]

The land of privation

The ceremony did not take long, and soon they set off for Çankaya. This was not the first time Latife had left home, but it was her first time in Ankara. And what a land of privation it appeared to be! Little more than a couple of hills on the bleak Anatolian plateau, the city was blessed with neither natural beauty nor modern conveniences such as domestic electricity or a piped water supply.

Those who speak of Ankara nights in that time all refer to a dark town. Frequently unreliable acetylene lamps were all they had to light their houses and streets. Going from one place to another at night was quite a feat that required a pocket torch. When electricity was introduced, the *Hakimiyet-i Milliye* newspaper carried ads listing 'Rooms to let with electricity'.

The Times of London had found the darkness of Ankara highly amusing, pointing out that even the most ardent patriot grants the difficulties of living there, where street lighting is achieved by half a dozen trembling electrical lamps, where running water is unheard of in houses and where a horse or donkey might be tied to even the Foreign Ministry doors.[6]

A curious, red and purple light illuminated this dun expanse that turned into a bleak and barren quagmire in the winter. It was this light that offered a glimmer of hope to the inhabitants, old and new, despite all the poverty and scarcity.

Ankara was all but barren. One day Falih Rıfkı headlined a column in the *Hakimiyet-i Milliye* with 'Verdant Ankara' only to then face insults of 'Sycophant!' So he defended his column:

'Gentlemen, either Ankara greens up, and gets a water supply, or it ceases to be the seat of government!'

Sadly, Ankara's water resources were quite scant. Most households had to make do with wells, whilst others went to neighbourhood fountains or paid water bearers.

Donkeys were the main means of transport, with locals often looking for their lost beasts. It was not unheard of to be snowed in for days at a time in midwinter.

Thankfully Latife had arrived in daylight; it was 20 February and a bitterly cold day. The ground had frozen. Çankaya was a twenty-minute drive from the station. They passed the occasional vineyard house on their way. The steppe stretched out into infinity but for a few spindly silverberry and pear trees.

The unpaved road up the hill was deeply rutted, making the vehicles rattle all the way. The stone house finally came into view: a rocky eyrie a few metres shy of the peak. The cheerful red paint on the window shutters allayed Latife's worries somewhat. The house emanated an air of total calm in defiance of the bitter winds around.

Black Sea bodyguards surrounded the house, wearing their traditional black costumes and headdresses, cartridge belts across their chests. Mustafa Kemal's adjutant and the servants welcomed the newly-weds enthusiastically.

Mustafa Kemal teased his wife:

'Here you are, Your Excellency Latife Hanım: your palace! Look, your chamberlain awaits you at the door.'

Ali Metin, the orderly, was smiling at her. Seeing a familiar face from Izmir cheered Latife up. The house was scrupulously clean and tidy. She loved the fountain hall. She kept asking questions of Mustafa Kemal, who replied as he dictated the guest list for the evening meal to Nuri.

Leaving Latife in her new home, Mustafa Kemal departed for the Grand Assembly to head a cabinet meeting. *The Times* reported in 21 February 1923 that Mustafa Kemal had returned to the city to debrief İsmet on the Lausanne conference after taking his new wife up to Çankaya.

The residence

Mustafa Kemal had initially arrived in Ankara on 27 December 1919, and since then the town had provided the base for him to direct the National Struggle. Ankara's support assured the town a permanent place in Mustafa Kemal's heart. In his words, the occupation had stopped at the gate as he stood in the centre.[7]

Çankaya was Mustafa Kemal's third residence in Ankara. It had been purchased for a sum of 9,000 liras, including expenses, paid for by the city council. Mustafa Kemal moved to Çankaya after a three or four month period of repairs in June 1921. His then companion Fikriye had furnished the house to please his tastes. She had hung burgundy curtains with stars and crescents in the windows and placed gifts that had come from around the world on the table in the centre.

There was a small marble fountain on the ground floor, right by the entrance. To its right lay a drawing room, giving access to the dining room. A wooden staircase next to the entrance hall ascended to the first floor, where a gallery gave on to the spray fountain below.

The ground floor had been laid out as an office–cum–reception room. The hall Mustafa Kemal used as a study held a large desk, bookcase and a few plants The modern-looking red morocco leather suite had come from Vienna. On the walls hung memorabilia and decorated swords as well as photos of Mustafa Kemal in Benghazi, and portraits of his mother. Anatolian rugs and carpets covered the floors; he was keen on fine carpets and braziers. Westerners described the house as a Victorian oriental. The famous stag dinners took place in the dining room on the other side of the hall. A billiards table had also been placed on this floor.

On the first floor were two bedrooms, one large, one smaller, and a primitive bathroom.

The Çankaya residence at the time consisted of two sections. Two more buildings stood in the grounds. One housed the aides-de-camp and their offices, whilst the other provided lodgings for the staff. The garden had two terraces surrounded by large trees; below them ran a fountain keeping a pool of a considerable size filled with water. Electricity to light the house was generated by a fan-belt motor housed in a shack nearby. The other houses used petrol and carbide (that is, acetylene) lamps, which were quite popular, as they remained reasonably steady in high winds.

We do not know if Fikriye's possessions had been packed away before Latife's arrival.

Impoverished Ankara

Ankara was little more than a village with no trees, water or shelter. Samanpazarı, the hay market, had neither a shack nor anything for sale. The peasants would have drawn their ox carts to one side and lain by their animals. The interior streets were too narrow even for a single cart. Everyone was very poor. In fact, the place called Ankara was a town that reeked of void and the barren desert. The worst fire of its history had occurred in 1917, and a large section of the town where Armenian builders and jewellers lived had burned to the ground.

The Christian population of Ankara had diminished significantly during the war. Falih Rıfkı relates this transformation in Çankaya:

When we arrived in Ankara in 1923, there were no Christian neighbourhoods, with the exception of a few vineyard houses. After alighting from the train, we used to pass down a quagmire on both sides, between a bleak cemetery and mud-brick and half-timbered shacks that belonged to merchants, and turn down a fire-ravaged area where the dust never settled. [...][8]

Ankara was the symbol of all Turkey outside the city walls of Istanbul. Everything in the way of life and prosperity had been dismantled and disappeared with the Armenians and the Greeks. It was up to us to build this city and country from the foundation all the way up to the roof.[9]

The population of Ankara had dwindled to 20,000 according to some sources, and 30,000 according to others, as a result of the fire at the end of the Great War. The castle walls were still soot blackened. Ramshackle adobe houses in a sorry state of disrepair clung to the sides of the steep zigzags that were the streets.

100 liras: an MP's salary

'Houses and furniture were all something else again,' in Falih Rıfkı's words, 'and the shopping so primitive that it was impossible to lay a table with matching china and glassware. We had ordered a custom-built table to serve for dining as well as a desk. None of its four legs matched. Yakup [Kadri Karaosmanoğlu] and I would frequently gaze at this table, puzzled at how it succeeded in standing upright.'

Come night-time, there was little to do other than chat and drink for hours around a table. There wasn't anything remotely like a restaurant.

Malaria was so widespread that both İsmet and Rauf had found themselves amongst the bed-ridden in the height of those politically charged days.

The Grand Assembly animated Ankara somewhat, initiating the construction of a couple of hotels and hostels. Student beds were appropriated for the members of parliament who could not find lodgings, and ultimately mattresses were stretched out in the teachers' college. MPs' salaries were 100 liras, of which twenty were withheld for their cigarette allocation.

The new MPs began arriving alone, or in pairs, but finding somewhere to stay was a major issue. Each looked for a family-sized house or even a shack. The most popular were the vineyard houses. The only hostel in town, Taşhan in Ulus, had converted all its rooms into dormitories, and MPs queued up before grocers.[10]

There was no accommodation for foreign missions in Ankara either. The Russians had a permanent residence, but other diplomats were forced to stay temporarily, as needed. The French embassy had, at one point, moved to the Ottoman Bank warehouse and created a reception room by laying Gobelin tapestry on the bare floors.

The Americans were amongst the diplomats who had failed to secure accommodation: Consul Robert Imbrie and his wife lived in a freight car, which they had converted into a home.

Women were conspicuous in their absence. The writer Falih Rıfkı says, 'The appearance of a deputy at the Karaoğlan Market, along with his wife in an Istanbul-style cloak, had caused vicious talk in parliament. There were no women to be seen anywhere. Not just at meetings, but at homes, streets or hotels.'[11]

A legend had grown around a mysterious beauty purported to be living in the same neighbourhood as Falih Rıfkı and Yakup Kadri. Rumour had it that she might reveal an arm behind the netting, or even a lock of her hair, every once in a while. Eventually, a painter created a 'portrait' of this evasive siren.

It was to such a 'womanless' Ankara that Latife had come as a bride.

12

The Bride Who Came to the Garrison

Mustafa Kemal told Latife when he returned home, 'I've invited a few friends to supper. Join us if you like.' He added, 'I suspect you may find it tiresome, though. I'll try to wrap up early.' Although disappointed at being left on her own on their first night in Ankara, she set to work transcribing the notes she had taken on the way and making a 'to do' list. Laughter rose from downstairs. So the conversation was not limited to Lausanne then ... İsmet Bozdağ says Latife read Bergson's latest book on philosophy as she waited for the guests to depart. First to leave was Rauf, and then the others followed. Mustafa Kemal ascended the staircase, a song on his lips. Latife was awake.[1]

A deep spring clean began as soon as Mustafa Kemal left for his office in the station building on the following morning. Not a single object was left untouched, not a doormat or a single lamp. The rugs were washed and doorknobs polished. Since Fikriye's departure, domestic arrangements had been left to the orderlies, who could only do so much. By evening, the residence was virtually unrecognisable.

The Uşşakizades owned the largest camel caravan of the Aegean region. The eldest daughter of the house would get a seven camel-load trousseau: silver, antiques, gold candlesticks, china, hand embroidered cloths, carpets and sitting- and bedroom furniture.

It only took a few days for Latife's trousseau to transform Çankaya from a middling commander's home into a grand house. The residence was completely overhauled once more.

İsmet İnönü's granddaughter Gülsün Toker Bilgehan explains the transformation:

The vineyard house on the stark Çankaya hill was stage to a festive day. Vehicles carrying the goods that had arrived at the Ankara station were climbing the hill one after the other. Sofas, side tables and bedroom furniture were offloaded and carried within; carpets were unrolled in the drawing room and tableware was placed into cupboards. The modest vineyard house, later to be known as the 'Turret Villa' – now a museum – was getting ready to welcome its lady.

The two-storey vineyard house had served as headquarters up to that time. It was quite small in fact.

[...]

She placed the yellow suite in the bedroom; it was in French Louis XIV style, and was very fine. Everything was yellow, from the silk counterpane through to the duvet. She had picked matching dressing tables and wardrobes. She rearranged the drawing room to the right of the entrance with the blue upholstered Louis XIV style furniture. The blue drawing room would serve for formal receptions.[2]

Latife set aside a section of the already cramped first floor for herself as she unpacked her trousseau from Izmir. She rearranged Mustafa Kemal's study and even created a sitting room for him.

Changes to his study irritated Mustafa Kemal exceedingly, claim several accounts.

The bedroom becomes off-limits to the aides

The idea of being his aide-de-camp appealed to Latife after her arrival in Ankara. One day she gently chided her husband: 'You've been calling me your aide-de-camp, yet I've not even a sword!' A few days later he handed her a small box. 'Here you are. This is for you.' Inside the box was a tiny jewelled sword made of gold and diamonds to suit his female ADC. The husband had gallantly proven himself equal to the challenge.

The entire Ankara contingent was in the process of graduating to a settled lifestyle from the guerrilla life they had all been living. Wife to the great commander, a solitary female in a sea of men, Latife was on her own in the midst of this huge headquarters. Most of the people at the residence were soldiers. The aides-de-camp, the orderlies and even the guests were all male.

Anyone could simply knock and enter, and Mustafa Kemal respected ceremony even less. Their bedroom was treated no differently from any other room, providing uninterrupted access to the national leader. Latife had to risk a conflict with Salih, chief ADC and mainstay in the household, just to claw back a degree of privacy.

One morning early, she met Salih bringing encrypted messages from the Foreign Ministry.

Latife shook her head in response to his question, 'Has His Excellency the Paşa awakened?' But he insisted, 'He has ordered me to awaken him in case of an urgent message.'

She said *she* would convey the message, but Salih dug his heels in; what if the Paşa were to ask, 'Who is my aide-de-camp? You or Latif?'

Latife repeated, 'Please allow me to give it to him.' She went in and awakened Mustafa Kemal. It was time this relationship changed; the bedroom had to be Mustafa Kemal's private domain.

Salih was cross, accusing Latife of usurping his position.

Mustafa Kemal's relationship with his aides-de-camp had deep roots. They had fought the same fight, stood side by side at the front, taking their chances with death. Despite the ever-present chain of command, their friendships went way beyond those of men who fought together. An outsider trying to break in would have a tough time of it. Worse yet for a woman, and one married to Mustafa Kemal. The peace treaty had yet to be signed. The prospect of more war flaring up again was all too real, and it was not the right time for Latife to designate their bedroom a private area. The female aide-de-camp would have to battle even Salih himself, whom she readily called a second father, as she fought to generate some privacy for her husband, a tiny enclave she would not have to share with his brothers-in-arms.

Latife goes to parliament on 1 March

Latife's first week at Çankaya was a very busy time. She met countless new faces, getting along particularly well with Mustafa Kemal's close friend, and one of the Nationalist notables, Fethi Bey Okyar and his wife, Galibe. Here were people of a similar mentality and age, and they lived nearby.

On the last day of February, Mustafa Kemal was dictating his speech to Latife, the speech he would make the following day at the assembly. He was about to open the fourth session of the first period. She would occasionally suggest *le mot juste* as the two worked together, and in three hours they completed it.

The speech referred to the need for unity in education and instruction, a subject that was very dear to Latife's heart. She wanted to listen to his delivery, as they had worked together. He concurred: public galleries ought to be open to females, too.

He delighted his wife when he said, 'You'd be setting an example.'

Not one for procrastination, he continued:

'Let's start tomorrow. Mahmut ADC will escort you to parliament. You can sit together at the diplomatic loge.'

There was no alcohol at supper that night. They put some western music on the gramophone and relaxed over a good meal, smiling and chatting. Latife related a story she had heard from a lecturer in France, to the mirth of the company. The Gazi asked in French:

'Why does the parakeet not speak in his own words?'

Latife replied in her lecturer's male voice:

'Because he has no ideas of his own to speak of!'

Laughter rang through the house.

That evening concluded with a visit to Fethi and Galibe. Latife kept her news to herself, determined not to spoil the surprise.

The next morning, time could not pass fast enough. She picked the most appropriate outfit in her wardrobe to set an example to Turkey's women and send out a clear message to the world. The only females who had visited parliament up to that time had been foreign journalists.

The gleaming Benz was ready. Mahmut ADC was waiting for her, his astrakhan kalpak tilted over his left eyebrow and a sheet of white paper in his hand.

The air was redolent of the spring to come as they arrived at the Grand Assembly building in Ulus.

When Mustafa Kemal had announced that parliament would convene in Ankara, there was only one building that was anywhere near suitable: the half-built Union and Progress Party offices. Even the roof had been left unfinished. The inhabitants of Ankara brought tiles they had been hoarding to repair their own roofs and then fetched old desks from schools. Acetylene lamps completed the preparations.[3]

The parliament Latife arrived at was this modest one-and-a-half-storey building.

As she walked a step ahead of Mahmut ADC towards her box, the entire chamber fell quiet. White turbans, red fezzes and dark kalpaks all turned towards her as she settled into the box. Two ambassadors got to their feet: the Frenchman Mengin and the Russian Aralov. This was a historic moment for Turkey. Mustafa Kemal had waved a signal flag by bringing his wife to the assembly. Soon silence gave way to murmurs, and yet furtive glances never left her.

Bells rang in the corridors; members of parliament entered the chamber to find their seats. Some had to sit on the desks, tucking their feet under. The lectern was a rickety affair. It all looked more like a small town meeting hall than anything.

One of the deputy speakers took the roll call and opened the session. Mustafa Kemal entered from one of the side doors; tumultuous applause broke out as he made his way to the lectern. The chamber might have been falling apart, nonetheless it exuded an extraordinary vitality.[4]

Mustafa Kemal began his speech, seldom casting an eye on the notes they had taken the night before. One by one, he detailed the achievements of the previous year and the objectives for the year 1923.

Latife watched her husband from the box. Everyone was silent. Mustafa Kemal was in his frock coat; on his head was his customary fur kalpak. She was so happy to be the first Turkish woman to have attended a session of the assembly as a visitor.

'A truly revolutionary assembly'

Latife got to her feet along with Mahmut; the diplomats rose to their feet again in greeting. In Mustafa Kemal's office were Ruşen Eşref and Hamdullah Suphi, along with Şeyh Servet, who had issued the original invitation to Latife. The Gazi got to his feet and showed his wife to a seat next to him.

Latife understood:

'I was so enthralled, Paşam,' she said. 'This is a truly revolutionary assembly.'

She knew just what to say to each person present and spoke French to the diplomats she had been introduced to. The French ambassador told her that his wife would be delighted to call upon her; they were in the midst of settling in Ankara. They agreed on a date and time. The Russian ambassador similarly desired to hold a party in Latife's honour, and asked for her permission as well for her to name the day.

She was perfect. She looked at her husband as she answered graciously, and consulted him before agreeing to dates and times. The room filled and emptied countless times for two hours. Confident in public ceremony, Latife deftly attended to and enchanted each and every visitor. Mustafa Kemal, too, gazed at her out of the corner of his eye even when he was talking to others. His delight was plain to see.[5]

Latife's attendance would feature in the domestic and foreign press the following day, interpreted as a triumph for Turkish women. Mustafa Kemal introducing his wife to members of the assembly had created a great deal of interest.

The Times reported, 'Following Mustafa Kemal's speech, his wife Latife Hanım held a reception for numerous deputies in one of the rooms in the assembly building.'

Either she had held a reception at the assembly building or Mustafa Kemal's introducing his wife to leading deputies, who in turn paid her their respects, had been interpreted as such.

Hakimiyet-i Milliye reported on 2 March 1923:

The attendance of Latife Hanım, the honourable wife of the Great Gazi, at yesterday's Grand National Assembly debate session has been an indisputable step in a de facto confirmation of the highest achievement of Turkish womanhood. This is due to the fact that Latife Hanım has been the first Turkish woman to attend a debate at the Grand National Assembly.[6]

13

Latife Entertains the Foreign Press
at Çankaya

Çankaya welcomed foreign correspondents in February and March. One particular party of late February, emblazoned on the front pages of leading newspapers, caused a sensation: 'Mrs Kemal Charms an American Visitor; Beautiful Bride Pours Tea for Foreign Newspaper Man; She Is for Women's Rights' and 'Kemal and Wife Pledge Liberty of Turkish Women.' Latife's pouring a cup of tea was interpreted as 'shattering five centuries of tradition and bringing a modern European atmosphere into the life of the new Turkish Government'.

Her confident and sophisticated poise and grasp of women's issues and world problems had impressed every single journalist present. Her declaration of intent to work actively alongside her husband in the fields of education and politics, as she outlined her work as his wife, had reverberated in particular. Her offer of tea to male correspondents was deemed of equal importance to the victory of the Great Attack. The fusion of the oriental and the occidental they confronted in Çankaya fascinated the journalists.

Larry Lue's account of the atmosphere of the residence appeared in the *Chicago Daily Tribune* of 28 February 1923; the same report also ran in the *New York Times*:

We entered a big anteroom with a marble fountain, which was not running, in the middle of the tessellated tile floor, and were ushered into a big room, where Premier Rauf Bey introduced us to Mr and Mrs Kemal.

The room itself radiated the personality of Kemal. It was a mixture of the orient and the occident. In a corner was a heavy Chippendale writing desk and in the centre a long table, where a copyist was busy. On a delicately worked brass centre table books and magazines were piled and also a big box of famous American chocolates. Crossed swords and daggers and pictures hung on the walls, one of which last was a gift from the city of Beirut, showing Kemal uniting the Arabs and Indians.

Gold incense-burners and oriental vases and bric-a-brac were on the shelves and tables. Leaning against the wall was a marble table of ancient Greek design, showing Turkey victorious, breaking the shackles of oppression and rising triumphant. In this semi-oriental atmosphere were heavy leather upholstered chairs, but one divan was covered in an oriental fashion.

After the exchange of formalities Mrs Kemal directed the conversation to the sphere of woman. She has numerous American friends, and her father is a former member of the New York Cotton Exchange. Though she has never visited America, she was educated in England and France and is therefore familiar with women's activities in the United States. She laughed when a correspondent declared that American women usurped all the privileges of men without taking over the responsibilities, and that America was the only country in the world where a sentimental jury would excuse the brutality of husband killing. This was not the goal of Turkish women, she said.

'My husband and myself are in perfect accord on the question of woman's sphere, as we are on all political questions,' she said.

She then translated the conversation, which so far had been in English, to Kemal, who replied that a woman must be regarded as a partner and comrade of a man, even to the point of abolishing men's clubs and women's clubs in favour of clubs for both men and women, without segregation.

Kemal's wife, since their marriage, has accompanied him everywhere he has had to go – to the front, to inspect troops, to social and diplomatic functions, banquets and receptions – yet nowhere has the majority failed to endorse her action, because she has been doing exactly what the majority of women wish to do.

Destined to do great things for her country

Mrs Kemal is a beauty of the Circassian type, with dark eyes flashing through long eyelashes, her small mouth, when laughing, reveals a perfect set of teeth, suggestful of a toothpaste advertisement. She wore the usual black satin Turkish dress and was unveiled. She had bracelets on both wrists, but she had only two rings, one a four-carat diamond in a deep platinum setting, and the other a platinum wedding ring, which İsmet Paşa, who dropped in during the interview, brought from Lausanne.

Kemal was dressed in a sack suit and soft collar. Tea was served in the dining room, which was decorated with oriental tapestries, the sideboard containing oriental and occidental services, gold and silver goblets and vases in themselves being sufficient to fascinate a collector.

Both papers described Latife as a woman destined to do great things for her country, and *The New York Times* of 28 February 1923 reports:

Kemal and İsmet remained in the dining room whilst Mrs Kemal served tea to Rauf Bey and the foreigners. She chatted gaily and recounted humorously the story of her three months' imprisonment by the Greeks in Izmir and her liberation when Kemal arrived. She said she was accused of espionage and understood a sentence of death was contemplated. She neither admitted nor denied the charge.

Then she told about her marriage. She said she had always been against marriage and had devoted her life to study, which eventually she desired to bring into service for the nation. She and Kemal had discussed the educational and political needs of Turkey and were so in harmony that it had brought them closer together. Their marriage had surprised her friends. Kemal had wanted her to work independently, but she had desired to work with him actively in the educational and political work.

It is difficult to impart the idea of the charming personality of Mrs Kemal, as well as give the impression of the guests as they sipped tea and listened to her talk on the rejuvenation of Turkey;

but her enthusiasm was catching, and even in the presence of the powerful personality of her husband every one felt that she, too, was destined to do great things for her country.

The first time in 500 years

The same party appeared in the *Washington Post* on 9 March 1923 with the headline 'Mrs Kemal Pours Tea'.

Mrs Mustafa Kemal poured tea for foreign newspaper men the other day at her country home near Ankara, and the news is flashed around the world and is given front-page space in many newspapers. It really is of considerable importance. For 500 years nothing of this sort had happened in Turkey, and it is about as good a proof as one could have that the old Turkey has passed and that a new one has been born. The change is not yet complete. Not all the Turks have adopted Kemal's western ideas, of which his conception of woman's place is only one, but the old day is evidently drawing swiftly to a close. It is said that to the Turks Kemal is what George Washington is to us. His influence is enormous; his example is sure to be decisive. The Turkey of the past is dying, if not dead, and we shall find a very different Turkey ten years hence.

George Ward Price, the second guest

Amongst the correspondents visiting the residence in March was George Ward Price, the *Daily Mail* correspondent who had met Latife and Mustafa Kemal at Eskişehir station. His report must date back to the second half of March; he had arrived at the residence accompanied by the former ambassador to the Court of St James's, Rauf Bey, whom Price for some reason refers to as the Grand Vizier.

I was invited to take tea with Mustafa Kemal and his young bride. [...] We were shown into a lofty hall, in the midst of which a fountain played. Latife Hanım was wearing a black dress in the Turkish style, but she had large diamonds in her ears and on her fingers. Her figure was short and rather plump. Her face had a wilful expression, and she was obviously well aware of the importance of her position.

'If I tell you anything you may consider it just as authoritative as if you had it from the Gazi himself,' she said, rather condescendingly.[1]

In *Extra-Special Correspondent*, the recollections he later collected in a book, Price continues:

> She went on to inform me that her father, Uşaki Bey, was a merchant in a large way of business in Izmir. After that city had been destroyed by fire, Mustafa Kemal had taken up quarters in the country-house of her family. It was there that she had met him, and at the end of three weeks he married her.
>
> 'How well you speak English!' I said.
>
> So far the Gazi had not appeared, but his wife led the way into another room, where tea was served, and he soon joined us. He proceeded to deliver a long explanation of his plans for the emancipation of Turkish women. Wives and daughters of the peasantry had always mixed freely with their menfolk, said Mustafa Kemal. The harem and the veil were snobbish innovations copied from the Arabs.[2]

Turkey's finances and Lausanne also came up on the agenda during the interview. Mustafa Kemal told Price that they would fight to the last unless approached on a basis of equality. Price also notes that whilst they had conducted the previous interviews – in Izmir and in Istanbul – in French, this time they spoke in English, with Latife and Rauf Bey interpreting.

Berthe Georges-Gaulis: 'Your first defeat yet!'

The third visitor who published impressions of Çankaya and Latife was the French journalist Berthe Georges-Gaulis, who had followed the National Struggle closely. She had originally arrived in Turkey in 1896 accompanying her husband, who was the *Le Temps* correspondent at the time; she decided to stay on after his death and took up his job. Georges-Gaulis occasionally corresponded with Mustafa Kemal throughout the National Struggle years and had even been invited to stay at one of the houses in the Çankaya compound in 1922.

She returned to Ankara on 11 March 1923. A reception was held that night for some diplomats, members of the cabinet and some leading deputies, along with their wives. The French correspondent and Mustafa Kemal had long enjoyed an informal relationship. The account here is taken from her 1924 book entitled *La Nouvelle Turquie*, although the original must have first appeared in the newspaper.

> As soon as I entered the large study where in December 1921 we had held such frank debates, I found my dear friend. We smiled at each other, all differences forgotten. In any case, finding him so 'well settled into married life' had amused me hugely.
>
> That impalpable diffidence particular to all newlywed men wherever they may be in the world had settled upon him, too. So I had to tease him with my opening words, referring to the thoughts of empire and republic builders on marriage. 'What happened to all our principles?' I asked.
>
> He was laughing, too, saying, 'She'll explain it all.'
>
> I had to add immediately, 'This is your first defeat yet!'
>
> He conceded the point and said, 'You'll soon understand why.'
>
> Everything around us had changed. A woman's hand had placed fine oriental ornaments on the tables, laid fabulous carpets on the floor, moved the furniture and books around, and thus rendered the already spacious room even bigger. This hand had also bedecked the study with flowers. Soon she entered; her attractive appearance was in total harmony with the environment she had created.
>
> Alluring and determined, with the wonderfully unshakeable courage that only the very young have, Latife Hanım had no self-doubt, nor doubted anyone else. She moved forward in her exceedingly simple, yet chic frock from a celebrated Parisian *maison* that flattered her oriental beauty.

She spoke French like a Frenchwoman, in full command of the finest nuance of our tongue. She chided us for launching into grave matters so soon in her vivacious and joyful voice, frequently accented with her generous laughter. She appeared to be accustomed to command and her own power. Raising her beautiful head, she said to me, 'I am my husband's aide-de-camp.'

So feminine, and such a comrade, too

Underneath the quick wit, sparkling laughter and pride that comes from happiness lay the games of a sharp and flexible intelligence. She played her attributes with the skill of a virtuoso. Her capacity for hard work and deep observation skills were also very much in evidence ... I now understood what it was that had put paid to his decision not to marry until final peace had been achieved, and therefore his famous so-called principles.

They were both peering at my face, trying to work out my first impressions. He said, in his most determined and convincing voice:

'She's promised me she will tell you about our marriage. Soon she will take you up to her quarters.'

I was still focusing on this large space that still preserved some eastern characteristics despite the outwardly western appearance. I, the housewife, looked over this room that revealed the two aspects of her character, westernised, still eastern. She could read what was going through my mind in a disconcertingly accurate manner and immediately repeated it out loud.

I thought she had the qualities essential to capture and keep a man such as Mustafa Kemal. That is, all woman, yet all comrade, a work-, journey- and helpmeet, a lover, and an accomplished friend to boot. A friend who did not violently resist Mustafa Kemal's unstoppable energy; one who bent him to accept her own energy. Which of these two would prevail? One would ultimately have to yield to the other. This was the one thing all around them wondered, but that none could work out.

Latife was more than adequately equipped to protect herself. Yet, she was under the constant attraction of that extraordinarily bright intelligence that had hitherto rejected all manners of domination, and had constantly changed in both form and structure. Which one would win?

We in the west struggle to understand today the marriage between two orientals whose powers are virtually equal, and who share the same intellectual and religious formation. This union could only exist between two people with common roots. However liberal the religious views, the indelible traces of Islam would remain.

In his wife, he found the traits he had admired

Sharing the same ideas, emotions, traditions and customs, but also her western culture, how well she knew Europe, how she received her guests as though they lived in the west: all this Mustafa Kemal admired hugely, and here he was, the husband of a woman with precisely these qualities. The confidence she had developed through many years of defiance delighted him. Mustafa Kemal, who never suffered the slightest vulgarity or even discourtesy, listened to the vivacious replies of his sparkling wife with great pleasure. The fact that she was Muslim also gave her great freedom in speaking out, enabling her to enunciate criticisms that no foreigner would dare mention.

This situation also made it possible for Mustafa Kemal to put into practice his precious 'total equality between the sexes' theory. He enjoyed setting an example in this respect. Thus had he replied to those who would criticise him over not practising what he preached. Conversely, it was his defiance of customs, in his desire to introduce his wife to society, that drew criticism. But he was accustomed to overcoming; let them talk, he would have said.

The woman he had picked would have delivered what he expected of her. She was energetic and talented. She must have loved danger – otherwise what was she doing here? – and was highly likely to be very ambitious, too. Ambition is no mean attribute; it provides one with resilience.

She moved back and forth in this grand salon where the guests were entertained.

And yet she was bashful

Latife Hanım recounted her comments on the events as we spoke, her flawless Parisian French lowered. She took Aralov under her wing and succeeded in cheering him up despite the fiery stares of Madam Aralov. Just then, a stunningly dignified and simply dressed Turkish woman entered the salon. Her entrance brought the Paşa back to our time. The true face of Ankara had briefly shone in all its nakedness before sinking back into its usual inscrutability. Taking the opportunity created by the noisy conversation that had resumed after a brief respite, Latife Hanım and I ascended to her private quarters at the top, like an eyrie, and which she had decorated with wedding gifts. Before I even had the chance to look at my surroundings, she began telling me how she got here.

Despite everything, she was still bashful. Begging my indulgence, she recounted the tale of her return to Izmir at the beginning of the Turkish push: 'None of this has sunk in; it's all like a dream.' Her voice grew more determined.

Her incredible energy had saved her. She had made a pledge. Should Mustafa Kemal enter Izmir in triumph, she would offer their house to him as lodgings.

Just as Berthe Georges-Gaulis was listening to the tale of the wedding, the door opened.

'I hope I'm not disturbing you; may I come in?' asked the Paşa, 'Has she told you all?'

Latife's fantastic confidence faltered for a moment, but it was replaced by grace instead. She was flustered for the first time.

'Come on,' said the Paşa, 'let me tell you about our honeymoon trip.'[3]

14

Touring the Country Together

Latife and Mustafa Kemal packed for a thirteen-day trip round the country. The time had come for Latife and the country to get to know each other. On the itinerary were Adana, Mersin, Konya, Tarsus, Afyon and Kütahya.

It took two and a half days to get to Adana. The couple had a special carriage, and their entourage travelled in the sleeper carriages. As they drew into Adana station, they spotted a multitude of women on the roofs and at the windows. The women trilled their *zılgıt* in greeting as the men clapped in rhythm. The crowds were hugging and kissing Mustafa Kemal in his marshal's uniform; Latife took her share of the warm welcome, too. A young girl of fifteen or sixteen years of age who spoke for the group requesting the annexation of Hatay brought tears to everyone's eyes, Latife included.[1]

They inched through the crowds. Just then a group of women, all in black cloaks, approached Mustafa Kemal; they wanted to entertain his wife. Mustafa Kemal's face grew grim; making no secret of his displeasure, he said, 'My wife goes nowhere I cannot.'

The newspapers of the day had carried a remarkable statement by the *müftü* of Adana: that there was nothing against religion in Mustafa Kemal travelling with his wife, and that her outfits were perfectly acceptable and in compliance with sharia. Latife was in a long two-piece suit. On her head was a smart scarf that revealed her face.

'See! How our girls made you cry!'

Konya welcomed them equally jubilantly, applause flanking their path wherever they went. Mustafa Kemal had a meeting in the town hall as Latife had some tea with representatives of Konya's women in a separate hall. Four tables were laid for dinner at the county hall, and Latife was at the women's table, again in a separate hall. Mustafa Kemal gave a long speech at the Konya Red Crescent Women's Group, explaining his hopes for the future of women. Denouncing vehemently the excesses of big cities and provinces both, he criticised women who always wore party gowns, and others who slunk away, obscured in shapeless dark cloaks. He spoke of his own displeasure at the segregation of Turkish society into women and men. He concluded by expressing his thanks for the warm congratulations he and his wife received.[2]

The Konya Women Teachers' School staged a show. The play was based on the love story of a war veteran and his fiancée. The crippled young man wanted to return her ring, but the girl refused to break the engagement. Mustafa Kemal surreptitiously reached out to wipe the tears in his eyes with his handkerchief. Latife smiled as she said:

'See! How our girls made you cry!'[3]

When they supped at the Sufi lodge, the leader's elder daughter shared their table.

Delighted with his wife's accomplishments

The journalist İsmail Habib couldn't fail to notice just how proud Mustafa Kemal was of his wife. He writes of that particular day:

> Latife Hanım was quoting from European notables on the topic of women. 'Kant has said that a woman's finest adornment is her virtue. Descartes has said that ...' We had all noticed time and again how delighted he was each time an opportunity arose that enabled his wife to display her accomplishments. He'd use any pretext to ask her to recite a Byron poem, adding that although he didn't understand it, he enjoyed the harmony. As soon as she finished her pealing recital, he'd ask her to recite something from Hugo this time so that he might understand.
>
> One day, when his wife even interpreted between him and some Greek prisoners of war, his eyes turned to us, sparkling with pride, as if to say, 'What a gifted wife I have!'[4]

She wore a Russian headdress

There were many women in the crowd welcoming the couple to Tarsus, mostly dressed in their regional black-and-white check cloaks. The majority had come to see Latife. Mothers would later tell their daughters, as they spoke of that day, 'We all went to see her; we were burning with curiosity. Thankfully Latife Hanım had not covered her face. She wore a Russian headdress.'

Their bed was made with embroidered linen. Torches outside the house burned all night, and folk dances rang through.

As Latife and Mustafa Kemal walked down the streets in Tarsus, locals sprinkled flowers and rose water on their heads from the windows. Mustafa Kemal was in good spirits. He danced the *zeybek*, sang folk tunes and asked for poetry readings. As İsmail Habib recited Nazım Hikmet's 'The Prisoner of the Forty Thieves', Mustafa Kemal gazed into the distance.

They arrived at Kütahya on 24 March. Mustafa Kemal had begun his speech at the Kütahya Lycée by addressing the teachers, female and male, pointing out that the army of teachers who shaped the future generation was no less crucial than the army of soldiers who fought a war of liberation. 'Ladies and gentlemen: you, teachers, are the command staff and officers of the army of enlightenment.'[5]

Throughout the trip, the people received Latife with open arms. The couple were presented with a three-sided gold seal in an Adana lycée they visited: on one face was engraved the name *Mustafa Kemal*; on the second, *Latife Mustafa Kemal*; and on the third, *Adana*.

The woman who walks alongside her husband

Chroniclers note how Latife tensed up occasionally during the six-stop tour. The first marital row, as the books describe it, occurred in Adana. The argument is said to have stemmed from seating arrangements in the car. Latife took exception to being forced to sit in the back of the car that had come to collect them at the station, and asked, 'How could you insult me, Kemal?'[6]

Latife knew how much Mustafa Kemal appreciated her, so why he might have told her to sit in the back, we do not know. She would normally have expected to sit in the front.

She wanted to be the woman who walks alongside her husband, not behind him.

Reading İsmail Habib's account gives an indication of the gaiety that permeated the trip on the whole, Latife's insistence on equality notwithstanding. Many people have observed how frequently the Paşa consulted his wife about his speeches and how the two debated affectionately at some length. Instead of nodding at his every utterance, Latife defended her own ideas, in her own inimitable style.

15

The 'Impertinent' Bride Who Wears Spurs

Latife and Mustafa Kemal enjoyed a relaxed relationship, free from hierarchical concerns.

At a time when most women addressed their husbands as 'My Master', or even 'My Paşa', Latife's call of 'Kemal!' was most unusual. On the whole she did tend to address him as 'Paşam', referring to him as 'His Excellency the Paşa', but there are people who chose to remember only the occasions when she called him 'Kemal'.

Her sister Vecihe summarises, 'We all used to address him as "Paşam" – "my paşa". Latife Hanım also did likewise. True, she did occasionally call him "Kemal", but Atatürk preferred "Paşam". He, in turn, called her either "Latife" or "Latif".'

Every time Latife said 'Kemal', women blushed and men were angered. Some thought her simply spoiled; others, disrespectful. Memoirs make much of the irritation this form of address caused Mustafa Kemal; it is likely that third parties' resentment of Latife's relaxed manner ultimately grated upon *his* nerves.

Soviet documents note, 'She calls her husband "Paşa". Several quotes in this book concur: she called him 'Paşam' in company and 'Kemal' only in the most intimate gatherings. Another note refers to how 'she does not fall prostrate before her husband like ordinary Turkish wives'.[1]

Did she somehow disappoint certain circles who expected her to behave differently? Still, Mustafa Kemal would never have married her if he had wanted a submissive wife.

She was so stylish

Latife was a very stylish lady. After her wedding, she continued to wear outfits ordered from top European boutiques, just as she had done all her life. She wore no *çarşaf* or veil.

She tended to wear predominantly black, occasionally adorning
her ears with diamond or brilliant earrings. The solitaire that was her
father's present never left her finger.

Western journalists visiting Ankara reported on her outfits at some
length, taking pains to emphasise that she did not wear a veil.

The *New York Times* of 14 March 1923 ran a column headed 'Mrs
Kemal's Clothes Are Pledge of Reform', and commented on Latife's
outfit: 'Her riding breeches indicate her intention of sweeping away
the harem conventions.' The article continued to report that she was
dressed as a man, in riding breeches, high boots and spurs, and wore a
jaunty cap on her head. She may not have been the first woman to go
out unveiled, but as the spouse of a leader, everything she did assumed a
symbolic significance, and so her attitude, behaviour and style all came
to exemplify change.

Pointing to the increasing emergence of women in Turkey's social
life, the *New York Times* observed how the *yaşmak*, or 'veil', was
disappearing. The column declared, 'One of the most laudable aims of
the Nationalist régime in Turkey is to emancipate the Turkish women.'

On 17 March 1923, the *Illustrated London News* published a photo
of the husband and wife standing side by side, with the subtitle 'Kemal's
unveiled wife: The symbol of freedom for Turkish women'.

Not only did Latife go around unveiled, but also she stood as a role
model for the abolition of the veil that was still prevalent at the time.

Paul Gentizon, the Turkey correspondent for *Le Temps* between
1922 and 1928, had observed:

> [...] and more to the point, he had no fear of taking his unveiled
> young wife along to military inspections and restaurants alike. She
> dressed like an amazon, wearing riding boots. Mustafa Kemal had
> certainly declared himself against the veiling of women; he wants
> it to vanish, just like the fez.[2]

Mustafa Kemal's wife symbolised the new Turkey before the entire
world.

İsmet's wife, Mevhibe Hanım, had similarly divested herself of her cloak on their way to Lausanne, lest she misrepresent the new Turkey. The well-wishers who came to see İsmet off at Sirkeci station on 8 April 1923 saw an unveiled twenty-six-year-old Mevhibe beside him.[3]

İsmet had, rather inadvertently, given her quite a scare once when they were in Lausanne. A large cardboard box tied with ribbons, clearly from an exclusive boutique, was delivered to their room one day. Mevhibe untied the ribbon and opened the box. She was stunned to discover one exquisite outfit after another: a two-piece in the latest style, a gown and a fine coat ... All far too modern, far too European for her. Could her husband have purchased such apparel without consulting her first? She didn't know what to think; there were so many possibilities to consider! Finally she sat down before the packages and began to wait for her husband. She grabbed him by the hand as soon as he returned from the conference and led him into the room. Pointing at the outfits on the bed, she asked, 'Paşam, what is all this?'

İsmet Paşa smiled as he replied, 'Rest easy, My Lady; true, I knew of them, but trust me, I am totally innocent. These goods belong to an august lady. Latife Hanım ordered these outfits when she was still in Izmir, and she gave me full instructions on the shop name. I am to send these on to her.'[4]

'Oh, to have my picture taken in ballgown ...'

Latife may have wrapped a scarf round her head, but her outfits were all from Europe: jodhpurs, two-pieces and capes.

An anecdote İsmail Habib Sevük relates might give an insight into her true feelings. Sevük had personally witnessed her discomfort with this enforced style; he certainly sympathised. Her station in life demanded a very modest style of dress, one which she regretted each time she saw herself in published photographs.

On their return from Konya, İsmail Habib had gone up to Çankaya to read Mustafa Kemal a speech he'd just finished. Latife and Yusuf Bey Akçura were also in the drawing room. Just then the post arrived. On top of the pile was the magazine *İnci*, with a lovely photo of Müfide Ferid on the cover.

Yusuf and Ferid Bey, then the ambassador to Warsaw, were brothers-in-law, so Müfide Hanım was Yusuf's wife's sister. 'Look at my sister-in-law!' he seemed to say as they looked at the cover, and Latife wistfully sighed, 'Oh, to have *my* picture taken in a ballgown ...'

İsmail Habib sympathised:

She's right. All through the trip, dressed in a semi-masculine fashion, patent leather boots on her feet, jodhpurs on her legs, a black wrap that covers all her head down to her ears ... All that is visible of her face is the bit between her eyebrows and her chin. All the photos of her that were published in the press depicted her thus. No matter; they might not have flattered her, but they most certainly were the most significant milestones of our feminine revolution.[5]

Many women, forced by a series of wars – the latest in the Balkans – to take over from their husbands in shops and offices by the 1910s, started relaxing the rules of hijab: the çarşaf was far too cumbersome, and head coverings eventually transformed into a large scarf, wrapped round the head and tied under the hair at the nape.

Outfits that revealed the entire face were still restricted to private parties. Out on the street, discretion still proved to be the more advisable route. Uncovering the face entirely only became more acceptable after the peace.

So whilst the idea that 'liberating women from invisibility, from wandering round like bogeymen' was being promoted, political expedience demanded Latife herself 'cover up'.

We see a covered woman in her photographs. Yet none of these coverings is particularly Islamic. On the Tarsus trip, she did indeed try what was then called a Russian headdress. We do know that she and Mustafa Kemal frequently reviewed the political situation, and Latife asked on more than one occasion, 'Isn't is time to get rid of this cloak?'

The only photograph of Latife with an uncovered head taken

throughout her marriage was one where she, Mustafa Kemal and her family posed together. She stands right at the back, as though unwilling to be spotted. All the other women in the family are uncovered, their heads, necks and arms revealed by their outfits. Latife, on the other hand, is in a high-necked white two-piece. She does not, however, wear a scarf over her neat chignon.

We also know that Mustafa Kemal the politician was opposed to the covering of women. He most certainly did refer to this topic in his speeches at the time. Yet his personal attitude to women and their clothing could have been very different, according to Falih Rıfkı. He reminds us that however much Mustafa Kemal might have insisted on women's social emancipation, as a man, he remained firmly in the traditional camp:

> He is not particularly western when it comes to women. To the extent that he even disliked nail polish. He was exceedingly jealous. Almost a man of a harem ... That is what he is accustomed to, and that is his personal preference.[6]

The Paşa's wife in déshabillé

Critics took exception to the appearance of a woman as self-confident as any of the men surrounding Mustafa Kemal in photos. One of these photographs was used in a handbill distributed in early 1923, the text little more than a vulgar rant. The so-called Anatolian Ottoman Revolution Committee bulletin featured a photo of Latife seated with her legs crossed. Also depicted were Mustafa Kemal, Recep Peker and Rauf Orbay; the photo originally appeared in the French magazine *L'Illustration*. The bulletin claimed:

> [...] Just ponder that your wife and daughter will be forced into this state tomorrow; how cheap your honour and virtue will become, and listen to your conscience! Understand how your religion and virtue have become toys in the hands of a national leader of such calibre! Oh, fellow Muslim! No need for more words; if

you do not break today the hand that reaches out into the most sacred heart of our religion and race, say a farewell for ever to your religion, your Koran, honour and virtue![7]

Despite all the care she took to present a conservative image, photos of her at the station on the Mersin trip were distributed in Anatolia as negative propaganda.

Bullet Holes in Latife's Clothes

Latife and Mustafa Kemal returned from their tour on 25 March. Extraordinary events were waiting in the wings: Ali Şükrü, leader of the opposition known as the Second Group, vanished on the 28th, on the heels of a series of frank attacks on the cabinet, which had infuriated Mustafa Kemal.

All this took its toll on Latife, too.

Bitter debates raged in the chamber, and the arrows of recrimination were aimed at Mustafa Kemal as the leader of the assembly. The smell of murder was in the air. Hüseyin Avni Ulaş, a key member of the Second Group, concluded a speech expressing his hope that the murder had not been politically motivated:

'The mouth and pen of a deputy are nothing less than the nation's honour. Strike down the hand that dares violate this honour!'[1]

Premier Rauf responded to the condemnations: 'The independent forces of the judiciary, police and *jandarma* will all do their duty unhindered.'[2]

Ali Şükrü had been seen at the Kuyulu Café in Karaoğlan Market earlier on the night of his disappearance; later, he had been spotted leaving arm in arm with Mustafa Kaptan, an MP close to Lame Osman. Reports of screams in the night and the sighting of a carriage – that ostensibly collected some furniture from Osman's house – on the following morning all added to a sense of foreboding.

Lame Osman came from Giresun in the Black Sea region. He had joined the National Struggle to crush Pontic Greeks after Mustafa Kemal's arrival in Samsun in May 1919, and he formed a volunteer corps that had grown to 5,000 irregulars. He might have risen to the rank of lieutenant colonel, but he himself remained ignorant and illiterate, and his brutality was legendary. Mustafa Kemal's bodyguard, a band of

Black Sea braves, was under Osman's command.

The murder victim was another Black Sea man: Ali Şükrü Bey, thirty-nine, MP for Trabzon, his hometown. A graduate of the Naval College, he had joined the Fleet Society and resigned his commission when he became a commander. He led the Second Group in the assembly. Having studied in the United States, he was fluent in English, and he was a well-informed, enlightened man.

He had a reputation for being an obstinate and choleric opponent, and he launched the *Tan* to promote the views of the Second Group: he personally wrote the editorial. *The Times* had interpreted the launch of the paper as 'an 80-man party of opposition in Ankara.'[3]

The six-days-a-week *Tan* managed to publish only sixty-eight issues.

'Whatever makes you say I've come to a decision?'

The events that unfolded following the disappearance of Ali Şükrü led Mustafa Kemal to dissolve parliament and hold fresh elections.

> Latife and Mustafa Kemal were taking a walk in the gardens at Çankaya, when Latife asked:
> 'What were thinking, Kemal?'
> 'What was I thinking? How do you know I was thinking?'
> 'When you blow smoke rings, I know you're thinking ... So what decision have you come to then?'
> 'Oh, well! Say you know I'm thinking, by the smoke rings; whatever makes you say I've come to a decision?'
> 'You'd have lit another if you hadn't. When you stub it out in the ashtray, twisting with your thumb, I know you've solved the issue and have found a way.'
> 'Well, well! It seems I've no more secrets left! Just tell me what I was thinking, and then I'll be fully convinced I've married an oracle and not a woman!'[4]

Mustafa Kemal enjoyed saying, 'Latife can read my mind.' That was how he had prefaced his announcement at the Azeri embassy of his intention to marry at the beginning of the year. His wife was truly skilled; she could foresee his next move.

Mustafa Kemal steered the conversation to the Lausanne conference. He mentioned the chilled relationship between Premier Rauf and İsmet, who had been conducting the negotiations.

'Even if İsmet Paşa succeeds in signing a viable treaty in Lausanne, we'll have a tough time ratifying it in this prejudiced assembly. That's why I need to go for a dissolution and fresh elections.'

Latife concurred. 'I've been hearing very much the same at dinners in the past few days.'

She followed Ankara politics closely, using her 'sight' to anticipate the assembly's moves. She, too, was completely engrossed in politics.

Fresh elections

At Mustafa Kemal's insistence, a decision to hold fresh elections was taken on 1 April.

Ali Şükrü Bey's disappearance had shocked Ankara. A thorough search finally revealed his body on 2 April, under a mound of soil and a cloud of flies in the garden of Topal Osman's summer house known as the Priest's Vineyard, close to Çankaya. He had been a big, strong man, whilst Lame Osman was scrawny ... The deputy had clearly resisted, and it must have taken several men to overpower and strangle him with tent rope.

Arrest warrants were issued for Lame Osman and Mustafa Kaptan. The former had vanished, but the latter was taken into custody. Referring to the balance of power of the time, Rıza Nur states that Justice Minister Rıfat Bey belonged to the Second Group, and the judges and the *jandarma* all sympathised with this strong opposition in the assembly.[5]

The residence under risk of attack

Even Parliament Police and its chief inspector would divest themselves of their sidearms before entering the chamber, whilst this band of brigands walked in armed to the teeth, bombs and all. They felt no need to ask for permission before putting their heads round the door of the chamber.[6]

A new regular guard corps had been formed and would be commanded by İsmail Hakkı Tekçe. Yet no one had dared inform Lame Osman of the dissolution of his band, and their worst fears came true when the irregulars took Mustafa Kemal in their sights.

Rıza Nur – minister of health at the time – relates what happened when Lame Osman threatened Çankaya:

> Mustafa Kemal was sitting on the sofa in his big hall. He was leaning forward. His face had gone yellow like the earth. He was immobile. I saw İsmet was sitting, facing him. Aviator Fuat and Recep – who later became home secretary – were on their feet. They looked like two wax statues. We all stood immobile, and finally Mustafa Kemal asked, 'What shall we do?'
>
> I said, 'In my opinion, you ought to go down to Ankara without delay.'
>
> Mustafa Kemal replied, 'Osman is usually composed; I could handle him. But what about the chamber?'
>
> İsmet and I returned and spent the night at the General Staff building.[7]

The residence was in danger of attack any moment.

Latife on orange crates, kalpak on her head

The worst happened: Lame Osman's band surrounded Çankaya. Latife's sister Vecihe was a houseguest at the time, so her grandson Mehmet Sadık Öke knows the story well:[8]

> The leader of the National Struggle was under threat. There was a short debate. Mustafa Kemal's safety was of the highest importance. Were he to come to any harm, none of the others would have survived anyway. Negotiations began with the band

outside. Then came the customary 'Women and children out!' Those inside made a plan: Mustafa Kemal would have to leave in disguise, along with the women and children. But someone had to stay in the house. Latife volunteered, saying, 'I can string them along!' Mustafa Kemal Paşa objected violently at first, but her resolve was unshakeable. She had already placed one of his kalpaks on her head and donned a coat. She commanded one of the orderlies fetch some orange crates from the kitchen, and laid them side by side below the windows.

Mustafa Kemal donned the cloak Vecihe picked from the wardrobe, and then he left along with Vecihe and the servant women.

The house was ablaze with light, the interior visible from the garden. Latife walked up and down on the orange crates to disguise her height, pretending to be Mustafa Kemal supposedly still in the house, disregarding the threat to her own safety. Mustafa Kemal, meanwhile, had reached the station building and begun to plan the attack against Lame Osman.

Lame Osman and his men rained bullets down on the house and finally broke in. They were furious when they realised the deception. Latife herself was roughed up. Just then, the guards surrounded Lame Osman and his band.

Lame Osman's trusted man Haliloğlu Rasim had a son, Rasim Aydın, who many years later related his father's side of the story. The account that was published in *Yeni Aktüel* supports Vecihe's account. Rasim says Osman and his men broke into the house upon the order to attack; finding Latife instead of Mustafa Kemal Paşa, they knocked her about. Their claim was that Mustafa Kemal had been threatened by a plot cooked up by – amongst others – Latife; so they had surrounded the residence to 'rescue' Mustafa Kemal, not to kill him.[9]

Rıza Nur relates the story in his memoirs. 'Latife told me later that Osman actually shot at Mustafa Kemal's house. To the extent that bullets had pierced through her clothes in the wardrobe.'[10]

Latife had come to the brink of death. This was the first time, but it would not be the last.

Parliament takes a blow

Kılıç Ali states in his memoirs that the inquest into Ali Şükrü's death had gone all the way up to the Gazi. He adds, 'İbrahim Bey of Ankara, appeal court prosecutor, and the Circassian Neşet Bey, chief inspector of Ankara, had gone up to the residence to take Mustafa Kemal's statement.'[11]

Lame Osman and some of his men had been killed. But worse was yet to come. His body was later exhumed and hanged by the heels at the door of parliament: a grave blow at a time when the Turkish Grand National Assembly was under such close scrutiny by the entire world. Çankaya's peaceful atmosphere had been disrupted.

The peace treaty had yet to be signed. The murder of an opposition deputy, followed by the summary execution of the suspect in an armed exchange, without due process, and then the desecration of the grave: none of this was desirable.

Cemal Şener, who published his research into Lame Osman, states, 'Today, the right dislikes him, and those who style themselves of the Kemalist left also disown him.' He adds, 'The only group who come to his defence are Giresun people, from the right or the left ...'[12]

The mausoleum of the murderer Lame Osman now rises on a hill in Giresun, and the largest thoroughfare in the city honours his name: Osman Ağa Caddesi.

And in Trabzon there stands a statue to the murdered opposition politician Ali Şükrü.

Latife Wants to Stand for Parliament

At the top of the agenda was the peace treaty that would conclude the Lausanne conference. Parliament had passed a motion to dissolve, and new elections were in the offing. The time was ripe for the new régime to come to a decision on universal suffrage. Latife had been pressing Mustafa Kemal on women's political rights since their return from the Adana trip. She intended to stand for a seat in an eastern county. Salih ADC comments on her political aspirations in his memoirs:

> Latife had a bee in her bonnet about becoming a deputy, but women had no voting rights, so naturally she couldn't have been elected! However, she kept pestering the Gazi Paşa, asking that he arrange for her to become a deputy by extending suffrage to the women, and also by giving them the right to be elected as well as to vote.[1]

She knew from her schooling that British women had gained the right to vote as well as stand in a public election in 1918, and that women had entered the House of Commons in the same year. True, the French Revolution had done little to advance women's political status, but she also knew that fifty years of suffragism had borne fruit, so that by 1923, women had gained full political rights in dozens of countries as diverse as New Zealand, Armenia, Russia, Hungary, Burma and the United States of America. Countless Turkish women viewed régime change as the ideal environment in which to advance their own emancipation. Nezihe Muhiddin led a group who had already made political demands, and other prominent women seeking political rights included Matlube Ömer, Azize of Cyprus and Güzide Osman.

Latife's stance throughout her stay in Çankaya never wavered:

a resolute defender of women's rights, she never shied away from declaring her position to any foreign correspondent. Consequently, the western press repeatedly referred to the woman Mustafa Kemal married as a suffragette and champion of women's rights.

In the 1920s, women and children still had the same political status in Turkey; so that despite the lack of any specific restriction to that effect in the first constitution of 20 January 1921, the assembly had remained a staunchly all-male club.

The scheduled elections required a fresh new law. During the debates on the Election Bill of 1923, it soon became obvious that the argument was going in the direction of preserving the status quo of the nineteenth-century constitution, of constituencies based on 20,000 males.

A single voice rose in support of the women: Tunalı Hilmi Bey, MP for Bolu, whose objection 'Not only do you deny them the right to vote, or be elected, but you won't even count them!' caused a furore in the chamber. The session came to an unexpectedly early end when he shouted, 'Gentlemen, our sacred war left behind more mothers than men. Please do not stamp your feet; you're stamping them on the heads of my holy mothers and sisters!'[2] Nevertheless, the old system would ultimately prevail. The head of the household would vote until women progressed sufficiently to merit their own political rights!

Vakit, published by Ahmet Emin and Asım Us, ran a survey beginning on 18 April 1923. The topic was women's political rights, and a survey entitled 'Women's Suffrage' proved to be a massive hit.

The debate the paper initiated created a suitable environment for women's political demands.[3]

'She would nominate you as a candidate ...'

Encouraged by the initial interest, the survey added the question, 'Which woman should stand for parliament?' Latife's name featured amongst the responses.

Çankaya, too, had been following the survey closely. One evening, at a tête-à-tête supper, Mustafa Kemal asked his wife:

'Have you seen today's *Vakit*? A namesake of yours from Istanbul, a

Latife Bekir Hanım, is demanding equal rights for women. Were they to obtain the said rights, she would nominate you as a candidate for Istanbul.'

'I agree, Paşam,' she replied, and asked, 'Don't you?'

'With what?'

'With the idea that men and women must live as equals ...'

'This, I've told you on several occasions, is my wish.'

'Don't you think I'd make a good MP?'

'Whatever is it that brings this about? Yes, I do believe women should enter parliament, but I've no wish to see my own wife there ... I want peace at home, peace that only my dear wife can offer.'[4]

The entry of an aide bearing an encrypted message brought the conversation to an end.

The Women's People's Party

The women's political activity reached its peak on 30 May 1923. Thirteen women, led by Nezihe Muhiddin, announced their intention to fight for political rights. Other notable names in the group were Şükufe Nihal and Latife Bekir – the lady whom Mustafa Kemal had pointed out as Latife's namesake. They intended to hold a council in the first instance to determine their agenda.

They convened a fortnight later and announced their decision to form the Women's People's Party.[5]

An article jointly written by Arthur Moss and Florence Gilliam entitled 'The Turkish Myth' ran in *The Nation* of 13 June 1923. Somewhat prematurely crediting Turkey with universal suffrage, with no discrimination for race, colour, creed or sex, the article then focused on the presence of a powerful women's party in Turkey:

[...] and there is now an active Turkish Women's Party with at least as much influence as the National Woman's Party in America. (Kemal has recently been married to Latife Hanım, one of the leaders of this party.)

The similarity in first names as well as the First Lady's well-known advocacy of the same platform may well have led to the erroneous conclusion.

Salih ADC repeatedly refers to Latife 'making a problem of' political rights; she would not give up, even in the face of the Election Bill that so manifestly disregarded women.[6] There was a woman in Çankaya who demanded political rights for herself and for members of her sex.

Votes for Latife in the ballot box

The elections were held in June, excluding women after all. Yet, there were males who, fully aware that women could not be elected, had still cast their votes in favour of prominent women, Latife amongst them.

The first news came from Izmir. The ballot box had yielded one vote for Latife. She wired her thanks to the Izmir city council and the Defence of Rights Association on 28 June.

İleri of 5 July published the news of votes for Latife and Halide Edib, illustrating the article with their portraits. 'Izmir's voters, whilst selecting their deputies, have cast one vote each for Latife Hanım, the honourable wife of our Gazi Commander-in-Chief, and Halide Hanım.' Şarki Karahisar (a district of Giresun county today) had also cast two votes for Halide Edib.[7]

Latife and Mustafa Kemal were discussing the election results the following evening at supper. One of the aides entered, bearing the results from Konya county.

Mustafa Kemal laughed after casting his eyes over the results.

'Congratulations, Latif. You received thirty-nine votes in Konya. Despite not having the right to stand. So if you were to stand officially, you would have crushed the party list.'

'Really, Kemal?' she asked. 'Let me see ...'[8]

On the returning officer's list from Konya stood the name Latife Gazi Mustafa Kemal, and facing the name, a count of thirty-nine.

'Send a telegram to the people of Konya and thank them ... This gallant gesture will have facilitated our job for the future,' encouraged Mustafa Kemal. When she read out the message of gratitude she had composed, he said, 'Very good; let's wire this without delay ... Except, Latif, this is a historic document; make sure you sign it ...'

'So, Kemal,' she asked, 'are you still determined not to let me become a member of parliament?'

He would not budge. 'Women may have their place in parliament, but I cannot find another wife like Latif. Please indulge me: I have not changed my mind.'

'Oh, you're incorrigible!' Latife smiled, shaking her head. She passed her arm through his as they went up the staircase.

The results from Malatya and Diyarbakır were surprising, too, with votes for Latife, Halide Edib, Mevhibe Hanım, Nezihe Muhiddin, Kara Fatma, Müfide Ferid and Aliye Fehmi.[9]

The voter had proved to be more sensitive than the legislature.

Latife had been born and raised between the two Constitutional Monarchy eras of the Ottoman Empire. These were times when women were rapidly becoming politicised, rebelling against their lowly status. Women held international meetings and demonstrations that attracted thousands in the early twentieth century. European women led a powerful pacifist movement. Ottoman women, likewise, were awakening. Although the 1839 *Tanzimat* – 'Reform' – Edict had offered women little tangible improvement, the subsequent reform movement did embrace all subjects.

Equal inheritance rights had come into effect in 1847.

Girls' secondary schools opened for the first time in 1858, and a women's teaching college was founded in 1870. Equal inheritance rights were extended into land ownership in the same year.

Legislation opened the way for the education of girls in 1869. This was enshrined in the first constitution of 1876 as a fundamental right. Primary education became mandatory for both boys and girls.

Women obtained the right to work for wages in 1897 and to work as civil servants in 1913. Within a year, women were active in commerce and trades. Another higher education institution for women opened in 1914. Within seven years, this college became co-educational, and in another year, seven female students enrolled at the Medical College.[10]

Non-Muslim women, who enjoyed significant privileges at the

time, had been able to attend private schools since the nineteenth century.

The number of associations and societies with female members had reached nineteen by 1919.

Widely read women's magazines transformed their own dialogue into a debate for fundamental rights.

From the very beginning of the Second Constitutional Monarchy, women had been asking for change: to obtain social rights and status, to participate in public and political life, to work, to enjoy education and instruction and to be freed of polygamy and of quick, unilateral divorces.[11]

Leading women's activists were Makbule Leman, Fatma Aliye, Şair Nigâr, Emine Semiye, Yaşar Nezihe and Aziz Haydar.

The 1917 revolution had liberated Russian women, who then began to point the way for the rest of the world. Similarly, Latife drew strength from, and fully intended to support, the women's movement in her own country.

The women of Turkey were in a far better position in 1923 than their great-grandmothers of a hundred years earlier. Isaac Frederic Marcosson, the journalist, had visited Turkey in July, soon after the elections, and spoke with Latife.

Madam Kemal has definite ideas about the future of Turkish women. Just like Halide Hanım, she is strong for emancipation. Along this line she said:

'I believe in equal rights for Turkish women, which means the right to vote, and to sit in the Grand Assembly. I maintain, however, that before suffrage and public service must come education. It would be absurd to impose suffrage on ignorant peasants. We must have schools for women eventually, conducted by women. [...] It must be evolution instead of revolution.'[12]

The cabinet kept the Women's People's Party hanging for a response for months. The party finally took a decision at the end of 1923 to continue their activities under the Turkish Women's Union banner, postponing their demands for universal suffrage for the foreseeable future.

It would take another eleven years for women to enter parliament.

'I can barely contain my joy!'

July 1923 was an exciting time for the government; first there were the elections, and then Lausanne. Word from Lausanne was anticipated any day. The rift between Rauf's government and İsmet had caused a great deal of tension.

Rauf called Ali Fuat Paşa on the phone early on the 24th, and the two went up to Çankaya together. Ali Fuat relates the events of that morning:

> We reached the residence at 10:30. Soon after, the Gazi entered the room we were waiting in. He was in his fine burnous, which he used as a dressing gown. He apologised, stating he hadn't wanted to keep us waiting.

Rauf Bey began:

> 'You did well; our news will not wait. Here is the telegram, wherein İsmet Paşa informs us he has signed the peace treaty.'
>
> The Gazi was ecstatic, though he paled in his excitement. He couldn't wrench his eyes from the telegram.
>
> He explained his delight to his two old friends, and thanked them. And then he admitted:
>
> 'I can barely contain my joy! Let's have a cup of coffee and a cigarette to calm down.'[13]

Rauf was ready to tender his resignation immediately. Mustafa Kemal would have none of it, saying, 'Don't act in haste. Let's think awhile, until the Second Assembly convenes.'

There were celebrations in Çankaya. Elated with the good news, Latife and Mustafa Kemal departed for a short break in Izmir.

Life at the Residence

'Latife Hanım was a true helpmeet for her husband, one of his greatest assistants,' says her sister Vecihe in a summary of the one thousand days Latife spent at Çankaya.

She would be the first to get up every morning, and come downstairs to check the newspapers and agency bulletins. She would spread out the papers – that arrived with a couple of days' delay – and excitedly scan through them all. These papers published her photos as frequently as they did her husband's. *Time* magazine, which was launched in 1923, for example, had featured Mustafa Kemal on the cover of the 24 March 1924 issue.

They would then examine these international reports together, often chatting happily. She was his window on the world, indulging his weakness for newspaper reports throughout her stay in Çankaya.

Turkey's new leader fascinated the international press, and several items on Turkey appeared every day. Appointed general manager of press relations in the middle of 1923, Zekeriya Sertel began to publish a monthly news digest of reports published abroad. He recollects how Latife accompanied Mustafa Kemal on his tours around the country, notebook and pen in hand, recording as he read out his speeches. She also took dictation, and worked with him on his speeches and correspondence.

A journalist who visited Ankara noted how Latife chronicled Mustafa Kemal: 'I am acting as a sort of amanuensis for him. [...] and I have started to write his biography.'[1]

How many pages she managed to write, and what subsequently happened to her work, we do not know. It does not appear to have been listed amongst her effects. Mustafa Kemal frequently spoke to her about his younger years and wartime reminiscences. So she must have decided to write this wealth of information that she had first-hand access to.

Latife and Mustafa Kemal play games

Latife and Mustafa Kemal used to play little games of her invention in the house. She might move the objects around in the room and ask Mustafa Kemal to find them, for instance. One evening, she taped the small china plate hanging on the screen in the fountain hall underneath the seat of Mustafa Kemal's chair. When he failed to find the plate after a long time searching, she pulled it out from underneath him. This little game had amused them both for hours.

Mustafa Kemal used to say, 'Well, I give up! My wife has become an illusionist! I wouldn't be surprised if she were to pull out a rabbit out of my pocket, instead of a handkerchief one morning!'[2]

Riding was one of their favourite activities. Mevlüt Bey[3] remembers seeing Latife Hanım and her sisters, all three mounted, waiting for Mustafa Kemal one morning.

Photographs depict Latife and Mustafa Kemal sharing a walking stick. Here's one vignette from those days:

It was a snowy day in Çankaya ... Mustafa Kemal was at home. He was smoking in the fountain hall, first inhaling deeply, then blowing rings. Latife was reading that day's *Yenigün* in a corner. As he put his cigarette out, Latife asked, 'It's a lovely day. Shall we go for a walk?'

'Good idea; go get our walking stick,' replied Mustafa Kemal.

Latife returned presently, carrying the walking stick with the silver handle that they always took for a walk around the Çankaya hills. She might use it briefly and then pass it on to him. That is why it was 'their walking stick'.

It was bright and cold out. They walked up towards the hill, following the paths. Latife wrote Mustafa Kemal's name in the snow with the slender stick in her hand, her peals of laughter ringing out as the snow inscription slipped down the hill. She was singing softly, happy.

Play us some Tchaikovsky, wife!

As one of the first states to recognise the new Turkey, the Soviets had established an embassy in Ankara. Latife and Mustafa Kemal had paid a visit to Ambassador Simeon Ivanovich Aralov and his wife, Sofia

Ilinichna, at their summer residence, at a time when the Russian couple were preparing to return.

They had tea at the gazebo, along with the Iranian ambassador and a few members of the Soviet embassy staff. Mustafa Kemal was in a smart casual outfit. Two bear cubs, presented to the embassy as gifts, were frolicking in the garden, climbing the trees, picking leaves and coming to inspect the people, entertaining Latife and Mustafa Kemal with their antics.

An eagle with a broken wing was walking around in the garden. Mustafa Kemal commented on the bird of prey. 'The eagle was the symbol of the Russian tsar. Look at this eagle with the broken wing, wandering amongst us all; the Russians have expelled their tsar.' So the talk moved to the brotherhood of nations, and the glasses rose in cheers. Mustafa Kemal pleaded with Latife, 'Wifey! Play that dear romance of Tchaikovsky's for us, as a farewell ...'

Latife spent a good part of the day reading, as she had moved her books to Çankaya. Kâzım Karabekir remembers how her elegantly bound volumes, mostly rare and valuable books, covered all the walls on the first floor.[4]

Vecihe says, 'Latife would recite Byron or Hugo for him after a long day's work and meetings. The Paşa might not have understood all the words, but he was particularly fond of Byron. He was unstinting with his praise for the peculiar melody that moves the listener.'

Latife's penchant for literature made a deep impression on Isaac Marcosson when he interviewed her in Çankaya:

> We began to discuss books. Much to my surprise I found that Madam Kemal was a great admirer of Longfellow. She quoted the whole of the *Psalm of Life*. I was equally interested to find how well she knew Keats, Shelley and Byron. I referred to the fact that in the old days, Byron's books were forbidden in Turkey on account of his pro-Greek sentiments, whereupon she remarked vivaciously, 'All such procedures are now part of the buried Turkish past.'[5]

These words were a clear indication of her stance against censorship.

When asked about her husband's diversions, Latife explained that she played the piano for him when he wanted to unwind:

'He loves music and when he does find time to read he absorbs ancient history,' was the reply. Then pointing to three playful pups that gambolled on the floor at our feet she added, 'I have also provided him with these little dogs, to whom he has become much attached.'

Husband and wife sat together on nights they did not have company. She did her best to create a relaxing atmosphere for him, summarised the books she had been reading and entertained him with stories.

The brazier: 'Stick to your guns!'

They occasionally teased each other over some trifle. Mevlüt remembers how a brazier had led to a little conflict.

'Madam's asking for you,' he was told one day. He went indoors to find out what she needed. Fethi Okyar's wife, Galibe, was standing up, smoking, as the two ladies chatted. A fabulous brazier stood in the middle of the room; this richly decorated oriental object had been a present to Mustafa Kemal from India. Latife introduced Mevlüt and Galibe, and then asked:

'Mevlüt Bey, winter's out. I don't want to remove this brazier from the drawing room, and I thought of perhaps using it as a cachepot for a small palm tree ... I wanted to consult you, too. What do you think?'

It was a good-sized brazier, and a fine one. Mevlüt concurred, albeit with a qualification:

'Except you might like to have the fire bowl removed, have a barrel made to match the beauty and the size of the brazier, and varnish and perhaps even decorate it with mother-of-pearl on the outside.'

They were working with a tape measure, checking the depth and diameter, when Mustafa Kemal turned up, asking, 'What are you doing, Latife?'

When he heard the proposal, he objected, 'The fire bowl would be mislaid someplace, and that would mean the brazier would be no good; not a great idea.'

Latife thought the brazier would be too small for a planter with the fire bowl in.

She insisted, 'Please let us go ahead as we'd agreed. I promise to look after the burner.'

The Paşa left the room, saying, 'No!'

She couldn't believe that Mevlüt, the agriculture expert, had so little backbone. Would no one ever stand up to Mustafa Kemal?

'I'm surprised you wouldn't defend your ideas before the Paşa! How feeble is that?'

Mevlüt decided to order two barrels in different sizes, rather than support one side over the other. He told Latife, 'I leave it to you two to decide how to go ahead.' Clearly, working at Çankaya was bound to have its own challenges. He related the incident to Hayati ADC, whose counsel was 'Just nod and move on!' But the chief ADC had also been there. About a week later, Mustafa Kemal suddenly asked Mevlüt, 'Latife Hanım gave you some instructions about the brazier the other day. Have you done it yet?'

Mevlüt stared at the chief ADC, ill at ease. Mustafa Kemal Paşa snapped:

'Some agricultural engineer you are!'[6]

He had come round to his wife's point of view after all.

'You know best'

Mustafa Kemal's sister-in-law Vecihe says of life at the residence: 'It was a tidy, neat house. My sister took care of every little detail; she ran the household just like any normal housewife. Mustafa Kemal wasn't that interested in household management; he'd left it all to his wife. "You know best," he used to say.' Daily life was quite unassuming. During wartime, all his domestic arrangements had been seen to by the ADCs.

Vecihe continues: 'Even I have on occasion ironed his trousers and shirts. He used to change twice or three times a day. He was so fastidious, and he was always impeccably attired. My sister knew it, so she herself was quite particular.'

The official cook at Çankaya died soon after Latife's arrival, so she asked for her father's help. Her own nanny, Canan Kalfa, had already followed her to Çankaya. Muammer despatched his own court-trained cook, Mahmut Efendi. Nesim Efendi, a black servant, also court-trained, arrived at the same time. Yaşar the waiter joined the staff later.[7]

Vecihe remembers the kitchen at Çankaya:

Latife Hanım personally arranged the menus and informed cook. She and Mustafa Kemal would have already discussed it all; she'd make sure to please his tastes above all. There was a beaten dough pastry for example, filled with either white cheese or chicken. That was one of his favourites. He liked fish. Grey mullet, the type we call *topan kefal* in Izmir; he liked it grilled. He also liked Izmir's sea bream. Muammer Bey would send these fishes to Çankaya. And a little semolina pudding, but he liked it moist. He ate sparingly, in any case. He wanted a little bowl of roast chickpeas before him. He also loved a soft omelette, and pasta with Italian sauce. He frequently asked me for these dishes, and I used to run to the kitchen to see to it.[8]

Mahmut Usta would be most offended each time he saw Latife boil pasta or Vecihe cook an omelette, saying, 'Madam, why do you go to this trouble when I'm here!' But it was not just Latife who went into the kitchen. Mustafa Kemal would frequently go to the veteran cook's side, lift the lids and sample the food.[9]

Occasionally he lunched alone, and at other times ate with a few colleagues. He did, from time to time, lunch with the family, before taking a ten-minute rest in the bedroom.

When they dined tête-à-tête, they used the Sèvres china, a gift from Muammer.

The Uşşakizade family at Çankaya

Esat Nedim Tengizman, Mustafa Kemal's official photographer, took family portraits of the visiting Uşşakizades on 8 July 1923. One was an indoor scene, and the other was taken outside the house: Mustafa Kemal, Vecihe, Rukiye, Adeviye, Muammer and Latife. All the women in the photo are dressed in modern outfits, and none has covered her hair.

Her sister Vecihe kept Latife company for quite a while at Çankaya. Latife's rebellious brother İsmail is known to have worked at the Foreign Office, and he visited Çankaya from time to time. Mustafa Kemal is reported to have had a particular fondness for Latife's youngest brother, Münci.

Halit Ziya and Vedad

Halit Ziya, as the uncle of the bride, paid the newlyweds a visit at Çankaya. The trip might have been onerous given the conditions of the time, but he was nothing less than absolutely delighted to carry out his duty. The 'unexpectedly warm welcome' he received from Mustafa Kemal, as well as Latife's attention to detail in everything that was offered, had pleased him greatly.

After his return to Istanbul, Hamdullah Suphi, the head of the Turkish Hearth, invited some musicians to Ankara. Halit Ziya's son Vedad was a member of the trio.

The Turkish Hearth of the day was in a dilapidated old Greek building in a terrible state of repair. As it did not even have a piano, Latife generously offered to lend her own, 'despatching it in a car, over the rutted roads'. The concert was a great success. And Vedad was naturally invited to stay with his 'elder sister' at Çankaya.

Vedad told his father of his Ankara trip in great detail when he returned a few days later. He had been moved by the warm compliments he had received from both his sister and the national leader.

One night, at a party attended also by İsmet and Tevfik Rüştü Aras, then foreign secretary, Mustafa Kemal had listened to Vedad play the piano, then asked him to translate a few publications in French,

German and English. He then said, 'You must become a diplomat,' and even elicited assent from Tevfik Rüştü then and there. This was ideal for Vedad, for whom a diplomatic career was a dream job, as his heart was never in his bank job anyway.

Halit Ziya was a houseguest at Çankaya on his next visit to Ankara. They spoke of Vedad again; hearing that he was still working at the bank, Mustafa Kemal instructed the young man be wired without delay, recalling him to Ankara.

The writer nodded in gratitude. But when Mahmut left the table to despatch the wire, Latife followed. She then signalled her uncle with her eyes and called him aside: 'I instructed Mahmut not to despatch the wire. Mustafa Kemal has these ideas when he's drinking, and he forgets them the next day ...'

Halit Ziya took umbrage at her interference. He asks in his memoirs, 'Why had Latife prevented it? Why had she not found it appropriate?' but then adds, 'I wish those obstacles had continued, and my son still lived, albeit not in such a prestigious career as diplomacy ...'[10]

Despite her resistance, a clerical position at Çankaya was found for Vedad thanks to his command of foreign languages. As he settled in one of the annexes in the grounds, his father cautioned, 'Never forget: your position there is going to be quite delicate.'

Süreyya and Tezer

Entertainment opportunities in Ankara were quite limited: there was an old open-air cinema, and there was the Turkish Hearth. Going out usually meant Latife and Mustafa Kemal paying home visits to residents of Ankara.

They regularly visited the Ağaoğlu family once a week. Süreyya, one of the daughters, says, 'The Atatürk I got to know was a true family man. Ankara at the time was a large family, in any case. It was so sincere ... Everyone knew everyone else, and everyone treated everyone else with affection and respect, like members of a family.'[11]

When Süreyya finished law school, Latife and Mustafa Kemal invited the family to dinner at Çankaya in celebration: Sitare Hanım,

Ahmet Bey and the daughters Tezer and Süreyya. Mustafa Kemal seated Tezer on one side and Süreyya on the other. He was in his element that night, entertaining the company with tales of his life. The waiter held the serving dish out to Mustafa Kemal first, and he gave it to Süreyya. The young lady naturally took the dish. It was only Tezer who thought to return the dish to Mustafa Kemal. Ahmet glared in wrath at Süreyya.

Dinner was a happy affair. As they bade their guests goodbye, Latife turned to Süreyya:

'You're in for it when you get home; your father's furious!'

And indeed the young lady had a strip torn off when they got home.

The Proclamation of the Republic

There was a buzz around dinner tables at Çankaya of late; Mustafa Kemal was clearly on the threshold of a momentous decision. On the evening of 28 October 1923, Fuat Bey and Ruşen Eşref, MPs for Rize and Afyon, respectively, were waiting at the residence. They wanted to talk to Mustafa Kemal, whom they had failed to get hold of at parliament earlier. Latife, too, was waiting for her husband. She and Ruşen Eşref were discussing new French books when Mustafa Kemal arrived with an entourage: İsmet, Kâzım Özalp, Halit and Kemalettin Sami Paşas and Fethi. He insisted Ruşen Eşref and Fuat also join them at dinner. The evening's topic was critical indeed. They sat down to an abstemious meal; no alcohol was served that night. Presently, Mustafa Kemal announced, 'Tomorrow we shall proclaim the republic.'

He then asked Latife, 'İsmet Paşa will stay here tonight. Would you please have them ready his room?'

The two friends discussed the proclamation of the republic at length.

Latife: 'Will they take to a president?'

Mustafa Kemal had been discussing the topic of the republic with Latife, too. A conversation between Yusuf Kemal and Latife on presidency reveals she had been sounding out their close associates.

Of interest also is who actually arranged this meeting: it was Mustafa Kemal himself. A little before the proclamation, Mustafa Kemal had told Yusuf Kemal that Latife wanted to see him. So Yusuf Kemal paid Latife a visit, and she caught him off guard with an insistent 'Will the country accept this, do you think? Will they take to a president?'

Yusuf Kemal was confident: 'I see no obstacles. The only thing that changes is the title … In any case, hasn't he been the de facto president for some time now?'

Mustafa Kemal joined them after a while, and Latife related their conversation. Mustafa Kemal demurred at first: 'No, no, leave me alone; let me work as the premier. Let me battle on. Let's appoint Fevzi Paşa as the president …' Yusuf Kemal had little choice but to exclaim: 'Paşam, let's stop wasting time on dreams …'[1]

What she revealed to the *Saturday Evening Post* correspondent who interviewed Mustafa Kemal at length in Ankara in July was intriguing:

> 'He is not only a great patriot and soldier, but he is also an unselfish leader,' she said. 'He has built a system of government that can function without him. He wants absolutely nothing for himself. He would be willing to retire at any time if he were convinced that his ideal of the self-determined Turkey will prevail.'[2]

This interview was published a week before the proclamation of the republic.

A look at the chronology of October 1923 reveals that all went according to plan.

13th: Proclamation of Ankara as the capital.

16th: The Fethi Bey cabinet resigns.

23rd: Ali Fuat Paşa resigns as deputy speaker of the assembly.

The resulting cabinet crisis was obviously one of Mustafa Kemal's own design, as no one then dared to come forward for a ministerial post. In the end, he announced his decision at dinner in Çankaya and so solved the problem at the root.

On 29 October 1923, Mustafa Kemal awakened with a toothache. He also had a bad cold. He and İsmet had worked late the previous night. He crawled out of bed and got dressed, pinning on his Medal of Independence. Latife was also dressed and ready.

It was a momentous day: the day of the proclamation of the republic. Vecihe remembers that historic occasion: 'He and Latife Hanım went to parliament together. He made a very good speech – despite his illness – after being appointed as president. The entire household was so concerned about him as we all knew about his condition.'³

Other sources sadly overlook the fact that Latife accompanied her husband, as did her two sisters, on that historic day.

Three commanders sidelined

The proclamation of the republic sidelined three of Mustafa Kemal's National Struggle colleagues: Ali Fuat Cebesoy, Rauf Orbay and Kâzım Karabekir. Mustafa Kemal believed they objected to the republic, and he went to some length to explain his conviction in his celebrated speech:

> I saw no need to recall all my colleagues in Ankara, and to confer with them, prior to taking the decision to proclaim the republic, as I had no doubt they essentially and naturally shared my views. Yet there were some individuals who were not present in Ankara at the time and who, despite having no authority in the matter, took umbrage at us for having proclaimed the republic without consulting them or obtaining their assent.

It was only when they heard the gun salute that the leading commanders of the National Struggle realised the proclamation of the republic had gone ahead.

Enver Behnan Şapolyo, who worked for the *Öğüt* in Ankara and who witnessed the proclamation as parliamentary correspondent, narrates the events of the day:

> It was the morning of Monday, 29 October 1923. Bright sunshine. Floods of people were on their way to parliament, all the way from Samanpazarı and Karaoğlan. Men in kalpaks, turbans and fezzes, and some women, too; they'd all gathered in the Nation Park facing parliament.
>
> The people awaited the National Assembly's decision in a state of excitement. Several approached deputies they didn't know and sought some indication of news. The sun set. Darkness settled. Yet the crowds wouldn't disperse. We were all waiting impatiently.

A deputy came out of the narrow door. All the journalists there, we surrounded him. He said, 'There are auspicious and historic decisions being taken at this moment!' That was all the news that had leaked.

It was around six forty-five that the session opened. A dim light. To the right, an audience section, to the left, the journalists' gallery, and in the centre, the deputies sitting at school desks. Atatürk absent. The deputies were crammed into the seats. In the silence İsmet İnönü stood and offered to the floor the amendment to the first item of the constitution: 'The authority lies unconditionally and absolutely with the people. The form of government of the Turkish state is a republic.' It was eight thirty ... As of this moment, the name of the Turkish state was a republic.

Mustafa Kemal was elected the first president of the Turkish Republic with 158 votes. Of the assembly, 100 members had abstained.

Mustafa Kemal entered the chamber, mounted the lectern to cheers and applause and made his first presidential speech at around eight thirty in the evening. Latife congratulated her husband: 'I'm so happy; I hope this will be good for the people and the state.' She withdrew shortly afterwards. 'You've got to see to your colleagues now, with so many guests.' She dozed off on the chair. He looked into the study when he couldn't find her in the bedroom early in the morning, carried her in his arms to the bedroom and tucked her in. He had his bath and went back out to the parliament without sleeping.[4]

A big celebration dinner was held at Çankaya on the 30th: İsmet, Fevzi and Kâzım all came with their wives. The dinner was a merry affair. Rukiye and Vecihe ran back and forth all night to make it perfect, and Latife sparkled as she entertained.

20

The Groom Has a Heart Attack

Ankara was very tense in the days following the proclamation of the republic: Mustafa Kemal suffered a serious heart attack in the second week of November, followed closely by another.

Earlier in the year, in the summer of 1923, when Latife and Mustafa Kemal decided to enlarge the old residence in Çankaya, they had moved to the small, three-room house immediately adjacent during the build.

The autumn rains were relentless, and the rickety building leaked everywhere. Hasan Rıza, who visited Mustafa Kemal, remembers the bowls placed around the room.[1]

We do not know whether these conditions played a part, but Latife fell ill in the autumn and had to stay with her family to recuperate in Istanbul. News of his heart attack made her immediately hasten back so she could look after her husband, which she did tenderly.

To the other side and back

Mustafa Kemal returned to work twenty days after the heart attack. Ali Fuat Paşa, who visited him in the station office, detected signs of illness on his face.

> His usual pink complexion had sallowed. He exhibited signs of shortness of breath and the like. He also appeared weaker on the whole. This state of the Gazi I had left hale and hearty only a month ago pierced me to the quick.[2]

Mustafa Kemal kissed Ali Fuat on the cheeks and then showed him to a seat beside him on the couch.

'They've told me of your distress at my illness. Your sorrow is evident on your face. I am much better. Let's have a cup of coffee and a cigarette first ...'

He pressed the bell and continued:

'From now on, just a couple of cigarettes a day, and again, same with the coffee. I am to give these things up completely if at all possible. Not a drop of alcohol. I follow the diet list compiled by the doctors. You know just how strict Latife is when it comes to a diet regimen, in any case. Trifle with her at my own peril! I obey like a child.'

At first, Mustafa Kemal did look after his health and followed Latife's counsel. He truly believed himself to have come back from the brink of death. That was how he related the events of the day:

'It was around twenty days ago, when I had gone out for a walk in the garden. I wandered around and had a cup of coffee. And suddenly, I was overcome by a sense of utter exhaustion. Just as I was about to go back in and have a rest, I must have lost consciousness. I don't know what happened next. When I opened my eyes, I found myself lying in bed and quite weak. I could recognise those around me. But those at the door, I couldn't place at all. I didn't ask anyone anything; I wanted to find it all out myself. It seemed to me that I had gone to the other side first and then, by some miracle, had returned to this one. I was convinced I had stayed on the other side long enough to see the afterlife. Fuat, my brother: I survived a serious threat.'

Their close circles noted how frequently Latife intervened due to his illness. She limited friends' visits in the days following the attack, and in doing so earned their wrath. She also restricted his drinking, coffee and cigarettes.

Yet Mustafa Kemal defied these rules whenever he could. He'd convinced one of the servants to purchase a couple of cartons of cigarettes, and concealed them in his private office in the station. When Hasan

Rıza entered one day and saw a pack on the desk, Mustafa Kemal hurriedly put it away in the drawer and said, 'I brought some in to offer to visitors.'[3]

His coffee consumption had gone up as well, after only a few days of abstinence.

As the doctors concurred that he had to rest, Latife sought their counsel on a location. Neşet Ömer replied, 'Our unanimous view is that a seaside town would be good,' effectively recommending a trip to Izmir.

When they were left on their own, Mustafa Kemal said to his wife, 'Well, bravo, Latife! You've taken over quite convincingly. I had no idea you were so capable.' Preparations for the trip followed.[4]

Mrs Kemal could rule Turkey

A press release was issued to the effect that Mustafa Kemal had suffered from exhaustion. In contrast, there was speculation in the foreign press on potential scenarios should Mustafa Kemal become incapacitated.

Within days of his recovery, the *New York Times* of 23 December published a commentary entitled 'Widow of Kemal May Rule Turkey.' In it, Frederick Cunliffe-Owen noted the gossip around Ankara following from the national leader's illness, and even suggested that the caliphate might be moved to Mecca or Bombay:

> [...] Kemal Paşa, who, ailing for a couple of months, has been dangerously ill in Ankara during the past week, suffering from a grave affection of the heart. The whole existence of the republic and its government are wrapped up in him, and should he die, no one can say what would happen.
>
> Thus far no one has turned up commanding sufficient confidence amongst natives or foreigners to serve as his successor. Of course, there is İsmet Paşa, who was Kemal's chief plenipotentiary at Lausanne, and there has been Fethi Bey, the former Minister of Foreign Affairs and emissary to Paris and London, and there is Rauf Bey, the naval hero of the two Balkan wars. But it is doubtful whether any one of these would know how to control the varied

dissentient elements of the National Assembly, some of whom, delegates from the Kurdish mountain ranges, are still steeped in the deepest barbarism, completely blind to any consideration of international policy and with little or no conception of the necessity of keeping on friendly terms with the unbelievers.

There are, however, some who believe that when the moment comes, it will be Kemal's clever, progressive and wealthy wife, brought up entirely abroad and soul and spirit of the women's emancipation movement in Turkey, who will govern in her husband's stead.

The Queen of Sheba and the Japanese Empress Haruko had successfully ruled their lands for close to half a century, and it would be no novelty in the Orient were Latife Hanım to step into her husband's shoes in the event of his death or incapacity. No matter how much Mrs Kemal Paşa might become a dictatoress and President of the Turkish Republic, it is impossible to conceive her in the rôle of Caliph. For a woman to fill that office would be a violation of some of the most sacred canons of the Koran.

What caused Americans real concern was the caliphate. The monarchy had been abolished, but the supreme religious institution had survived. The west might have naturally expected the ruler of Turkey to also wear the caliph mantle. However capable they might have found Latife to rule the country, they clearly had reservations about her qualifications for religious office.

I do not know whether it would be an exaggeration to draw from this item the conclusion that Latife carried sufficient political gravitas in the international arena. That her name was mentioned alongside those of leading statesmen, and found to be in a stronger position by comparison, is certainly indicative of her status at the time.

21

Latife Shields Her Husband with Her Own Body

Latife and Mustafa Kemal set off for Izmir one snowy Monday evening. Their first brief holiday in the city of their meeting and wedding had begun on 27 July, after the Lausanne treaty was signed. This time it would be more of a convalescence trip for the ailing leader.

The party included Dr Neşet Ömer and Kemaleddin and İzzeddin Paşas, commanders of the Fourth and the First Army Corps, respectively. At the dinner table, Mustafa Kemal delighted in telling the story of how he and Latife had met and married. They all retired to their compartments towards midnight. One of the commanders left in Eskişehir, and the second in Afyon. By the time the train reached Dumlupınar, the weather had worsened considerably. As one of the bridges presented a hazard in that weather, the train stopped at Güneyköy. On the following morning, the train was divided into two sections before continuing.

They arrived at Basmane station in Izmir at four thirty on 2 January. They had specifically waived an official welcome ceremony, and so were met only by a company of troops. The plan was to go to a house in Buca rather than Latife's family home. Muammer and Adeviye might have been away, so the former home of Forbes, the British consul, had been prepared instead. This fine English mansion dated to 1908; it stood in the midst of a well-tended garden on a small hill. It was well furnished and had several reception rooms; the bedrooms had en-suite bathrooms. The entire house was heated with stoves. Yet, despite the trip having been on the agenda for six weeks, there had been no preparation for the guests. Mustafa Kemal didn't sleep a wink that night. Early the next morning he went into the room where Salih and Staff Officer Tevfik were billeted; both men were still in their beds.

Salih says:

His Excellency the Paşa was in his nightgown. He asked how we were, and then said, 'I haven't slept at all. There's no point in staying here. Please get up immediately and get ready; we must leave.'

By the time the cars arrived, they were all packed and ready. Salih, Neşet Ömer and Latife left first to check up on the White Mansion and prepare it, but thankfully the house was as neat as always. Latife had the stoves lit, instructed cook on lunch and allocated the *selamlık* section to the guests. Lunch was served immediately upon Mustafa Kemal's arrival; afterwards, everyone retired for a rest. They gathered for supper at the *harem* section. Salih would later remark, 'Our comfort at Göztepe was perfect, especially after the Forbes mansion.'

The governor of Izmir, Aziz Bey, was shamed into resigning for having failed to prepare the mansion adequately and was swiftly replaced by Murat Bey, the governor of Ankara.

Was it only the laxity of preparations that had piqued Mustafa Kemal?

Latife is wounded in the attack

Strangely missing from official records and memoirs is the assassination attempt in Izmir, where Latife and Mustafa Kemal had gone in such good cheer and came to the brink of death.

But it was widely reported in the international press – 'An assassination attempt on the Turkish president with a hand grenade' – on the 7 and 8 January. The first report, dated the 7th, appeared on page 3 of the *Toronto Daily Star* with the headline, 'The Bomb That Missed Mustafa Kemal Wounded His Wife.' The same newspaper would report nineteen months later that Latife had actually distracted the assailant and thus saved her husband's life (*Toronto Daily Star*, 18 August 1925).

As for the front page of the *New York Times* on 8 January:

According to a telegram from its Mytilene correspondent, published in the *Eleutheron Bema*, an attempt has been made to assassinate Mustafa Kemal Paşa in Izmir.

[...] the Turkish President escaped injury, but his wife, Latife Hanım, is said to have been wounded by the explosion.

The most detailed report of all appeared in the *Chicago Daily Tribune* on 8 January 1924: 'New Report Says Bomb Hit Kemal,' announced the headline, based on a statement made by a Paris radio service. The paper claimed that the assailant appeared at Mustafa Kemal's home and demanded to see him. Mrs Kemal received the men at first, and then called her husband. It was when the president appeared that the man threw a bomb. The report went on to assert that both Mustafa Kemal and Latife had been wounded.

An article entitled 'Turkish President Divorces Wife Who Brought Big Dowry' in the *Washington Post* – published on 14 August 1925, just after the divorce – claims, 'It was revealed that a Cretan was in prison charged with the attempted assassination of the president.'

Although this attempt on the president's life was kept from the Turkish press, Latife's nephew Mehmet Sadık Öke also confirms it happened at the Forbes mansion. He says his aunt distracted the assailant by leaping between him and Mustafa Kemal, and that she sustained an injury to her hand.

Latife wrote a cautiously worded letter to her friend Galibe:

7 January 1340 [AD 1924]

Izmir, Göztepe

My special companion, dear, precious Galibe,

You have been constantly on my mind since our arrival here in Izmir. However, some very unpleasant events prevented me from writing to you earlier. The Forbes mansion had not been prepared as we had envisaged. The building is a fine one, on the outside and in, but it had not been furnished at all. Never mind offering some comfort: it would as likely have made us even more ill than before! We spent one night entirely sleepless and moved to Göztepe early the next morning. I had been occupied with the arrangements until today. I organised new reception rooms. The entire house is being arranged for comfort. [...] We are at ease. The weather is good. It's all green, the sea and the fine views; I hope we'll get to enjoy it all.

The Paşa was quite cross on the day of our arrival, but is now calm and pleased. I am very tired and in real need of a rest. Vecihe and Rukiye are scheduled to arrive in a few days; I will hand over household duties and treat myself to a serious cure.

How are you? Is Osman better now? If you only knew just how much I think of you all! Several times a day, every day. We do get news of dear Galibe and Ankara, in any case. I wonder if you think about us at all. Or do you lose yourself in the depths of a book and forget about us completely? Somehow, I think not ...

Kemal gave a dinner party tonight. We all dressed for it, and now everyone is in the drawing room. I'm listening to music, as I scribble these few lines.

I have today placed the order for the shoes you wanted. I'm sending you pictures of others. Let me know which style you prefer, and I'll have those made for you; I couldn't decide.

The letter concludes with 'my precious sister' and is signed 'Latife Gazi Mustafa Kemal'. It appears the couple continued with their holiday once the tensions of recent events were over, and life had gone back to normal sufficiently for Latife to attend to the shoes Galibe had ordered.

'Is he a padişah or a caliph? Here, read this!'

Mustafa Kemal looked after his health and refrained from drinking; Latife had put him on a diet. They went on rides together, read and studied; this was a welcome break indeed.

She made him eat breakfast; he wasn't allowed to leave the table with his usual single cup of coffee. He soon developed a taste for piroshki pastries.[2]

As they were having a cup of tea one afternoon, an encrypted telegram came from İsmet: the caliph had complained that members of the cabinet visiting Istanbul had neglected to call on him. He was also seeking budget funding for the office of the caliphate.

Irked by this request Mustafa Kemal grumbled, 'Is he a *padişah* or a caliph?' Latife was curious. He handed out the transcription:

'Here, read this!' He shared official correspondence with his wife from the beginning.

She read the message and suggested:

'Hardly surprising really. A friend returning from Istanbul just the other day told me how court property is being secretly sold in Beyoğlu. You've abolished the monarchy and proclaimed the republic, but allowed the members of that dynasty to still live in their old palaces as caliphs. Now, don't tell me to keep my nose out of state business. Look at France: more than a hundred years since they've abolished the monarchy, and to this day, not a single member of the exiled dynasty is admitted. Do you not agree that the caliphate is a threat to the republic?'

'Bravo, Latif ... You've worked it all out. You're so right. Fetch a pen and some paper; let's write a letter to the cabinet.'³

He dictated a scathing denunciation of the institution of the caliphate. Latife remembered the item that had appeared in the *New York Times* only a month earlier, the speculation on whether she herself would take the reins of government should Mustafa Kemal somehow become incapacitated. So how would the west react to the abolition of the caliphate?

Mustafa Kemal drives a tram

The famous anecdote about the horse tram dates back to this holiday. Latife tells how one night a sleepless Mustafa Kemal announced his desire to ride a horse tram. She pointed out, 'But the entire city is asleep!' Surely it was impossible to procure a tram at that hour; she begged him to rest.

'You tell me it's late; I know it's late: that's precisely why I wish to make use of this opportunity to ride a tram.'

I roused the ADCs. They made a few calls, and a tram was readied towards three o'clock. He took the ADCs as well, and we all made to the site where the tram was and mounted.

The driver was an old man. He kept whipping the horses. Mustafa Kemal asked him, 'Do you always drive with a whip?'

'Yes, Paşam. How can you drive without a whip?'

'Why ever not?'

'We've not seen it done that way.'

'Move over; I'll show you.'

Mustafa Kemal swapped seats with the driver, took the reins in his hand, cracked the whip in the air and began to drive the tram, calling out to the horses, 'Giddy up!' He kept shaking the reins.

He asked the driver:

'So, can I drive them, then?'

'So much better than me, Paşam!'

'I am a driver, too, just like you. I've driven hundreds of thousands of men, driven them to their deaths. But I never used a whip. I drove without one.'

I joined in:

'Let me become the conductor, Paşam.'

He turned towards me, raised his hand, circled his palm in the air, and pretending to put it in his pocket, he said:

'Give us the ticket, but don't pocket the money!'

I was burning with curiosity. There must have been a reason behind all this. I was dying to know, but didn't dare ask. A few days later, he looked at me meaningfully:

'I know; you're still curious about that night and want to know what all the lunacy was in aid of.'

'Far be it from me to call it lunacy!'

'I know it looked demented, but believe me, I had no choice. One of my men, one who accompanied us that night, has been whip-driving in a manner of speaking, I found out to my great dismay. Yet he had served me and the country so well up to then. Another, who'd been chasing personal benefit, was the target of the "don't pocket the money" jibe. Sacrificing him would have been awful; if word got out, that someone in my entourage had behaved so badly, that is. Yet he needed a lesson. I couldn't have confronted him with it either. I would still have to dismiss him in that instance, and again, the reason would have become public knowledge. I wanted him to understand that I knew, and let this be a lesson!'[4]

Muammer Erboy confirms the story of that strange night, one that is now a family legend:

> Horse trams ran along the Mithat Paşa Road, the road that passed by the Göztepe mansion. Mustafa Kemal took the driver's place and drove like Jehu. Aunt Latife and he sat together. Who knows, he may even have passed the reins to her.

The name of the corrupt close associate remained a secret.

Visiting Mevhibe

İsmet Paşa and his wife, Mevhibe, arrived in Izmir, the city of İsmet's birth and childhood, in the autumn of 1922.

The couple had settled in a large Göztepe house that used to belong to an Armenian, a three-storey seafront villa in a good state of repair. The drawing room had fine French furniture in a dark mahogany, and beyond it lay the dining room facing the sea; both rooms had fireplaces.

A particularly cold winter had set in, all the more remarkable in balmy Izmir. No number of enamel stoves sufficed to heat the house, so braziers were also lit.

Mevhibe was delivered of a baby whilst Latife and Mustafa Kemal were in town.

> A phaeton drew to a halt before the Göztepe house gate.
> A tiny lady descended; her head was covered, although her face was unveiled. She wore an overcoat. Her large, dark eyes sparkled in her small face. She told the servant who opened the gate:
> 'Please inform them that the wife of the Gazi Paşa is here.'

Mevhibe's mother, Saadet Hanım, ran downstairs, and the distinguished guest was taken into the resting new mother's room.

They were about the same age, but these two women with widely different dispositions were meeting for the first time. Mevhibe surreptitiously inspected Latife, this young woman of whom she'd heard so much in the past. She liked what she saw. The visitor was very different; her sophistication, good breeding and dominant personality were immediately evident.

Mevhibe found her to be a suitable partner for her president.

Saadet Hanım entered, carrying the newborn in a lacy, blue carrycot. The little boy was a sweet thing, with blonde hair and blue eyes. As İsmet Paşa had yet to make it to Izmir, the baby had not yet been named. A novice to the practice, Latife took the baby – who would be named Ömer a few days later – in her arms.

'God has willed it, madam; I've never seen such a bonny child.' Mevhibe secretly prayed Latife, too, would have a baby. She suddenly saw a broody woman inside this progressive person who commanded such a strong social position.[5]

Indeed, many years later Latife would write to Mevhibe, 'As I hugged him to my heart, I noticed the maternal instinct welling up inside me *for the first time*'[6] [sic].

Commanders, journalists and professors in Izmir

Mustafa Kemal met with notables in many fields throughout this holiday: leaders of the press, the university and the armed forces. Mete Tunçay states that he would have sounded out these forces for their support prior to taking a party decision to abolish the caliphate.

Kâzım Karabekir and Ali Fuat, the two generals, were scheduled to arrive in Izmir presently to attend military manoeuvres. Mustafa Kemal and İsmet sought the agreement of the army inspectors and commanders whom they had gathered; they thought it expedient to obtain full support in all matters related to policies domestic and foreign.[7]

Ahmet Emin, the proprietor and editor-in-chief of the *Vatan*, relates the meeting with the press:

Latife Hanım arrived at eight thirty. The Gazi introduced his wife to us all. We then sat down to supper. The table had been tastefully and neatly laid. The Presidential Orchestra was playing suitable music, conducted by İhsan Bey. Everything indicated that the Gazi placed great importance on peaceful cooperation with the press in conducting matters of state. At the table were the Gazi, Latife Hanım, seven journalists, and Deputy Şükrü Saraçoğlu, Mahmud Esad, and Lieutenant Colonel Tevfik Bey, the president's private secretary.[8]

Mustafa Kemal had asked the journalists to build a steel fortress around the republic.

Latife: 'Education must be freed of religion'

The couple spent a total of fifty-two days in Izmir, a true second honeymoon.

They visited the Turkish Hearth and Altay Sports Club on 7 February, on the same day that the Turkish Women's Union was founded in Istanbul. News must have reached Izmir, but whether they discussed this development, we do not know.

The couple visited Kuşadası and the ruins at Selçuk and Ephesus on 9 February, and went to Söke. This was the day Premier İsmet Paşa and the generals Fevzi, Kâzım and Ali Fuat all arrived, to be greeted personally by Mustafa Kemal at the station. The Darülfünun – Istanbul University – delegation, who had originally gone to Ankara to discuss funding, had accepted İsmet's invitation to accompany them to Izmir. The White Mansion hosted a party given in honour of the generals that night.

The skilful hostess who was his wife captivated Mustafa Kemal once more. His happiness was visible, a smile radiating from the depths of his eyes. He broke his diet for the first time since the coronary attack and joined his friends for a couple of glasses of rakı. Eriş Ülger cites Salih Bozok, who mentioned Mustafa Kemal turning towards his wife on the eve of the manoeuvres:

Do you remember the time eighteen months ago, Latife? On a night just like this, we had watched the burning of Izmir helplessly. Those days are now in the past. You've heard the conversation at the table tonight. Each and every one a hero ... And I thank you, Latife. I've never seen you in the role of such a delightful housewife until tonight. You were the best hostess imaginable. You've prepared everything beautifully. Have no doubt; all my friends were utterly delighted.[9]

The Darülfünun delegation attended lunch at the White Mansion on 14 February. The discussion centred on the question of a national curriculum versus religious instruction. Mustafa Kemal thought education institutions should become secular. He asked how the Turkish nation would take to a secularisation drive. Latife's close interest in education is well known; she fully concurred with the need to secularise education. Marcosson had earlier reported:

> 'On one subject I have strong views: education and religion in Turkey must be separate and distinct. This is my ideal of the mental uplift of the women of my race.'[10]

The lecturers stayed until three in the morning; upon their return to Istanbul, they would despatch a collective telegram from the Darülfünun, pledging wholehearted support of democratic principles.[11]

Mustafa Kemal directed the military manoeuvres that began at the Izmir Officers' Club on 15 February. Eriş Ülger states that husband and wife watched the start together. On the following night, they attended a play entitled *The Precipice* at the Bahribaba Theatre.

'I'd shield you with my own life!'

On the scheduled day of departure, Mustafa Kemal made an unexpected proposal, as related by İsmet Bozdağ:

> 'We're returning to Ankara. But you can stay on for a few more days if you like.'

'Why would I not accompany you?'

'We've had so many guests, you must be exhausted. I thought you might like to stay in Izmir and rest for a little longer.'

'You know I relax best next to you. Is there another reason why you're suggesting I stay?'

'Well, yes, there is; but none I would disclose. You're such a worrier.'

'Are you going to kill me with curiosity, Kemal? I'll worry if you won't tell me.'

Mustafa Kemal continued softly:

'The police have been tipped of an imminent attack on my life. But no one knows where or when. I wanted to spare you.'

'Do you really think I'd stand beside you in glory, but run away in the face of death? Together in happiness and in death. I'd proudly shield you from a bullet with my own life!'

Mustafa Kemal held her by the shoulders:

'All right, child. We depart tonight. But tell no one we are going, not even those you trust most.'

Her devotion and courage had won him over.[12]

Mustafa Kemal informed the generals at his table that night of the assassination attempt. Speaking to Fevzi, Ali Fuat and Cevdet, he said:

Cabinet received warning of a death trap for me. Necessary precautions have been taken, but they advise discretion all the same. I have therefore decided to keep the train's departure time a secret. As a secondary measure, I'm planning on taking your [addressing Ali Fuat at this point] car to the station. Latife and I will sit in the car, with your aide in the front, next to the driver. No one else. What do you think?

Ali Fuat Paşa was unshakeable: 'I'm confident no harm will come to you; this is nothing more than a foreign plot.'[13]

Two and a half years later, another assassination attempt would be discovered on 14 June 1926. This next attempt would rock Turkey to the core, and bizarrely, Ali Fuat would find himself implicated.

Rumours of a death trap had dampened the happiness of this second honeymoon. They set off for Ankara in a gloomy frame of mind that night.

Mustafa Kemal had tightened security so as to prevent any obstacles to his proposed course of action. He was about to announce the religious policies of the new régime: Islam would be distanced from politics.

The announcement was made in the assembly on 1 March. The Ministry of Sharia and Pious Foundations was abolished on 3 March. The Unity of Education Act was passed; all scientific and education institutions became subject to the Ministry of Education. There was no room for a caliph in this new world. Caliph Abdülmecid Efendi was deported early in the morning on 4 March.

Although the Grand National Assembly passed the act that abolished the caliphate on 4 March, Islam remained in the constitution as the official religion of the state until 1928.

Mete Tunçay states, 'The abolition of the Ministry of Sharia and Pious Foundations, coming on the heels of the abolition of the caliphate, was the first crucial legal step on the way to secularisation.'[14]

Latife Prepares the State Protocol

Countless visitors descended upon the residence day in, day out; the aides showed them in, often with little regard to any systematic procedure. This was exhausting, especially as some of his friends even expected to see Mustafa Kemal early in the morning whenever they chose. Latife decided to regulate visits and official receptions at the residence.

She summoned Mahmut ADC and explained what she had in mind; he noted down her plans for the system.

Mustafa Kemal returned early that evening and found the two still working, pen in hand, sheets of paper all round.

Mahmut ADC explained, 'Her Excellency is dictating the residence protocol.'

'What protocol is this, Latif?' Mustafa Kemal asked.

'Anyone who wishes to see you is admitted directly into the drawing room. It would be better to show the visitor to a seat in the aides-de-camp room and inform you. The visitors you wish to see could then be admitted in the order you specify.'

But informality had long been the rule, and he could see the potential for upset:

'Latif,' he objected, 'the aides know whom to admit, and whom to turn away. And the people they admit into the drawing room are my closest friends.'

She held her ground: 'Kemal, what if all your closest friends were to gather one morning and come here; would you then meet with them one by one?'

Mustafa Kemal is rumoured to have put his foot down, convinced she had to drop this idea. 'Leave my friends alone; institute whatever protocol you wish on yours.'

Latife also wanted prior notice of evening parties. She ordered uniforms for the personnel and sourced white gloves for the serving staff, who, being veterans barely out of uniform, were thus made even clumsier.[1]

Lord Kinross comments on Latife's efforts to regulate dinner parties:

> She tried to order his dinner-parties, demanding to know in advance just how many guests were expected, and objecting to those she disliked: she insisted that wives should be invited with their husbands as in respectable westernised households. For a while she even introduced evening-dress, causing many to decline the invitation who, in this backwoods 'capital', did not possess it. One evening the guests, arriving in dinner-jackets, were disconcerted to find a palm court orchestra playing in the hall, and amused to see Kemal coming downstairs to greet them, likewise dressed, with a shrug of the shoulders and a mock-martyred smile on his face. Kemal disliked all social pretensions, and this was not the way he cared to entertain his friends, unless on a formal occasion. He was a natural host, polite in his manner and assiduous in his attention to guests, but he liked to do things in his own way.[2]

The young woman was determined to create a presidential residence out of the bachelor garrison. She was the perfect hostess, whose attention to detail included the starching of the linen. Today, several full-time personnel are employed to carry out the official protocol functions that she managed on her own at the time.

Muammer Erboy states, 'She had drafted the first official protocol of the Turkish Republic. Food service at the table, event management, and countless others: it was she who had devised all relevant procedures.'

Her work for children

First ladies around the world traditionally did charity work, and Latife did act as head of the Society for the Protection of Children for a while. Whether this was suggested originally by Mustafa Kemal or her own idea, we do not know. It is highly possible that she stepped in when the society was left without its chief official temporarily as Fuat Umay, who headed the charity, was scheduled to depart for the United States on a fundraising trip.

The society had been founded at the end of the Great War; its Ankara branch dated back to 1921, set up possibly to offer solace to those fighting at the front. Its beginnings were modest: a single room in the *Hakimiye-i Milliye* newspaper printers, and a starting fund of twenty liras, collected from ten donors. The society had later moved to the old school building on Hacıbayram Road. Treatment of sick children was the society's main activity.

The society was particularly active between 1923 and 1925, distributing food and pasteurised milk aid, as well as despatching midwives to villages. Food assistance to children began in 1923, reaching 517,000 children. A 'Milk Drop' was set up in Izmir and Ankara; the former in 1923, and the latter a year later. These institutions purchased a cow and distributed free, pasteurised milk. One million, three hundred and thirty seven thousand children had received milk in 1924. Thirty thousand children had also received other forms of support in 1925.[3]

Latife's speech

The speech Latife delivered at the Society for the Protection of Children on 10 October 1923 was published on the front page of *İleri*, accompanied by a photograph:

> We have been invited to undertake a noble and sacred duty: occupation with the tiny children of our holy nation, the nation that has sacrificed so much in the path of independence. I am convinced that we all will carry out this noble duty unhesitatingly, our hearts tender. No hesitation, indeed, in the cause of contributing to the creation of tomorrow's iron-fisted youth, these babes of the nation saved from death or penury by our own efforts and work. Helping the babes of the nation is a considerable and great service to the future of the country. I, for my part, am determined to work to the

best of my capacity, as a citizen convinced of the noble and sacred nature of these services. I am also convinced that I will be able to elicit the maximum backing from my honourable friends gathered here, whose actions have already proven their patriotic credentials.

My honourable friends: the duty we carry out is as pure as it is important and exalted. We can all be certain that the assistance we provide is not going to be limited to our work alone. Let us work with sincerity and determination. We shall succeed with God's will. Allow us now to move to our duty, after this heartfelt and humble introduction.[4]

The *Cumhuriyet* of 8 February 1925 reported that Latife donated 1,000 liras to the Milk Drop Institution's branches in Izmir and at the Istanbul University, an amount equivalent to US$660 at the time. This was a significant sum for impoverished Turkey. The report headlined 'An Important Donation from Latife Hanım' continues:

> The Honourable President of the Turkish Society for the Protection of Children, Her Excellency Madam Latife Gazi Mustafa Kemal has very generously donated the sum of one thousand liras to the Milk Drop Institution opposite the Istanbul University, the institution under the management of the society. The funds were entrusted to the deputy for Istanbul, Dr Hakkı Şinasi Paşa.

Latife expressed her delight at accepting the presidency of the Society for the Protection of Children, the report went on, and emphasised how her tireless dedication to the advancement and progress of the society justified the title of 'protectress of orphans and children'.

The society started to run an orphanage in 1923. This happened after the move to an old Keçiören building in grounds of 39,000 square metres. Latife's efforts and financial contributions evidently contributed to these developments.

Latife as a child, with either Ömer or İsmail.

Muammer Bey in a portrait taken as Mayor.

Latife Hanım and Mustafa Kemal in Uşak.

Latife and Mustafa Kemal in Tarsus.

Izmir after the great fire.

Two days after the wedding, Latife takes notes at the meeting in the Izmir Customs building. Salih ADC and her sister Vecihe are seated next to her.

Latife and Mustafa Kemal tour Afyon in a phaeton decorated by local girls.

Mustafa Kemal as he planned to proclaim the republic.

Latife at her piano in Çankaya.

Latife and Mustafa Kemal together with Galibe and Fethi Okyar.

Latife wearing the diamond and pearl necklace that doubled up as a tiara, a
gift from her maternal uncle Ragıp Paşa.

23

Women of the Time

This was a time when a woman's husband's title was deemed adequate to identify her. Even trying to elicit their first names was an issue: they were mostly known as 'this minister's wife' or 'that city's MP's daughter'. The man's position defined those of his entire family, with women and children sharing the same secondary status.

Seclusion still dominated the social life of the nation. Social life, especially in Ankara, excluded women entirely, with women and men bowing to custom and leading segregated lives. Yet throughout the war years, in the absence of men, women had gone out of the home and undertaken countless jobs. Some had gone to the front in the years of occupation, many women actively participating in the struggle behind the lines. Although a certain degree of emancipation had already been achieved, Ankara remained a 'womanless' provincial town, its arrival on the world stage as a capital notwithstanding.

A significant proportion of the assembly was quite conservative and fully in favour of the continuation of women's seclusion. A radical change was essential before women could breathe freely. The assembly required many families to move to Ankara, with the women putting up with the majority of hardships during this relocation. Those who could find a vineyard house settled in Keçiören or Çankaya.

Living in Istanbul had become a mark of shame, whilst living in Ankara was considered to be an honour. Yet finding a suitable house in Ankara was no easy matter.

Finding female chroniclers proved to be a highly challenging task, and most memoirs were written as though women hardly existed.

The women who had arrived in Ankara prior to 1923 had known Fikriye as Mustafa Kemal's consort; it was with her they had established a relationship. The way she ran the household and entertained visitors had pleased everyone. Even Halide Edib used to call upon Fikriye each time she returned to Ankara. A piano had been found for Fikriye to practise on. She used to go riding around Çankaya and attend Red Crescent meetings. When she first arrived, she was covered in a cloak, but later she discarded it, preferring two-piece suits instead.[1]

But Fikriye, who had gained acceptance as the lady of Çankaya, disappeared discreetly, replaced by Latife a few months later. Mustafa Kemal's close friend Süreyya Yiğit says, 'All of Ankara society was buzzing when the Gazi returned accompanied by Latife Hanım. Ladies of Ankara were convinced of her superior attributes, judging by the swiftness of the marriage, a mere fortnight after the demise of Zübeyde Hanım.'[2]

It was Memduha, wife of Cevat Abbas, who introduced Latife to the ladies of Ankara.

The ladies of Ankara ...

The majority of the leading names in the National Struggle had married educated women from prominent families. Many were of a higher social class than their husbands, and they had all overcome countless tribulations throughout the occupation.

Sitare was a well-educated lady who hailed from Baku; she was married to Ağaoğlu Ahmet Bey and was a founding member of the Protection Society that looked after female orphans and destitute migrants.

Reşide of Bursa, wife of Celal Bey, had graduated from a Rüşdiye junior school; she had famously denied access to the police – who had come to arrest her husband – during the occupation.

Hümeyra, wife of Kılıç Ali, had been raised in a Sufi lodge in Istanbul and educated in a French school; her father was a lecturer in economics at the Imperial School of Political Science.

İffet, the wife of Rıza Nur, was the granddaughter of Rıza Paşa, the minister of war. She had been raised in Europe.

Memduha, the wife of Cevat Abbas, came from a family that went back 400 years, and she had been privately educated. Her outspokenness was legendary: she had famously stopped Mustafa Kemal's private train to air her fury at the infrequency of her husband's home visits.

Latife got on very well with Galibe, the wife of Fethi Okyar. A highly cultured woman, Galibe had attended school in Germany when her father was the consul in Munich; she spoke English, German and Farsi and was very widely read. Mother to a son and a daughter, she was a godsend for Latife. Their photograph had been published abroad and made the cover of *Süs* magazine closer to home. Another group portrait dates back to the same period, this time with the ladies sitting in front of their husbands, a photo that has been reproduced in several books. Galibe appears less severely covered than Latife in all these pictures. Evidently Mustafa Kemal's wife came under stifling scrutiny from the ultraconservative circles.

Some of the women in the Çankaya set were more modern in their dress than others. Reşide Bayar preferred to cover her hair. Füheda, the wife of Justice Minister Mahmut Esat Bey Bozkurt, continued to wear her lattice veil long after her husband had signed the Civil Code.[3]

Mevhibe had first divested herself of her *çarşaf* on their way to Lausanne, on the insistence of her husband, İsmet Paşa. Galibe was always modern and chic, and the wives of Cevat Abbas, Kılıç Ali and Süreyya Yiğit all posed for photographs in those early years with their heads uncovered. The Ağaoğlu family women were all emancipated, in both mindset and their dress: Süreyya was the first female entrant in law school, and Tezer, who would later be elected an MP, was reading philosophy.

'At homes' in Çankaya

Segregation had to end if Ankara was to be transformed at all. Latife and Mustafa Kemal made careful plans before starting 'reception days' to attract ladies to Çankaya. Vecihe says these 'at homes' were held between 3:00 and 6:30 pm on Saturdays. Mustafa Kemal later altered their nature, requesting the husbands accompany their wives, as he himself wanted to attend.

These at homes became Ankara's top social event. The blue drawing room, which Latife used as the reception room, used to overflow with guests: Ankara natives as well as the wives of ministers, parliamentarians and journalists. Ladies flocked in, not only from around Çankaya but also from Keçiören and Dikmen. They sat quietly on the chairs in the blue room until Latife opened the dining room doors and invited them into tea with a 'Do come in, ladies.'

The table was laid as an exquisitely elegant open buffet. Embroidered tablecloths that came from Latife's trousseau ... Crystal dishes holding cakes ... Tea was taken standing up. Latife Hanım served everyone personally.

Latife was the perfect hostess and a gracious one at that. She dressed beautifully. Most of her clothes came from Europe, and some were made to order in Istanbul. During these 'at homes', the guests could hardly prise their eyes away from her outfits, her jewels – her father's presents – and especially the solitaire she constantly spun around her finger as she spoke. Latife had to do most of the speaking at these parties, her guests being on the whole too timid to do much but listen.[4]

Leman Karaosmaoğlu, a close friend of Latife's, remembers:

Cakes were lined up on embroidered tablecloths from Latife Hanım's trousseau. It was her ladyship's at home. The ladies of the time were quite reticent. No one dared reach out to anything, waiting on foot instead, according to old Turkish custom. Until Latife Hanım personally offered them something to eat or drink, they took nothing. She would insist, saying, 'Please, Madam, these biscuits are delicious, do take a plate.' Eventually she did succeed in breaking through some of the shyness of the Ankara ladies.

Embroidered net covers were placed over the trays to keep the flies off in the summer. The cook prepared all the food. The table was always richly laden. Everything Latife Hanım said would be repeated at home and would travel round the entire city, altering along the way.[5]

What did the ladies discuss? In those politically charged days, the next stage in the transformation of Turkey was the main topic. Gülsün Toker Bilgehan, İnönü's granddaughter, remembers her mother relating their tone:

> The atmosphere in the capital was magical: male or female, everyone's patriotism was in a heightened state. Everyone put up with all the privations and shortages uncomplainingly. The women were ready to take their place in society, just as Mustafa Kemal wanted. They had received their leader's message loud and clear. They wanted to prove themselves. Should they ever falter, Latife Hanım was there to teach them, renew their hopes and make sure they all faced the future confidently.
>
> The Gazi Paşa's consort had a major influence on the wives; they all feared and venerated her at the same time. Mustafa Kemal's devotion to his wife was well known; he treated her with great courtesy in public and valued her ideas. Precious Istanbul ladies were transformed into lionesses when they sat in Latife Hanım's room; the talk of the reforms Mustafa Kemal would implement animated them as one, and they all displayed their resolve.[6]

These so-called 'precious Istanbul ladies' had all survived a war, put up with oppression and contributed to the National Struggle.

Segregation

Süreyya Ağaoğlu and her friend Melahat began their internship at the Ministry of Justice, the first female lawyers in the country, but lunch was proving to be an issue. One day – with Süreyya's father's prior permission – the two ladies went to the Istanbul Restaurant, whose clientele largely consisted of parliamentarians. There had never been a single female patron to date at what was, in effect, the only restaurant around.

Ahmet Ağaoğlu received a call from astonished MPs. He had a chat with his daughter that evening. 'Premier Rauf Bey informed me that you and a lady friend of yours were eating at the restaurant, and that caused a huge commotion around town. And there was another lady who went to the library and who took her share of the gossip. I suggest you two come over here for lunch in the future.'

(Rauf would learn much later that the lady whose library trips had caused such consternation was his own sister!)

When he heard Süreyya's account of the incident, Mustafa Kemal commented, 'You're both right, you and your father.' On the following day, as Süreyya was working, Minister Necati came over and informed her that the Paşa personally would take her to lunch. Mahmut, MP for Siirt, and Muzaffer ADC accompanied Mustafa Kemal in the light grey car that drew up by the ministry. Mustafa Kemal said, 'Latife is expecting you for lunch.' The car first made a stop by the Istanbul Restaurant. Every single MP eating his lunch rushed outside.

Mustafa Kemal chatted with them briefly and then raised his voice slightly as he said, 'I'm taking Süreyya over to us for lunch today, but she will eat at the restaurant tomorrow.'

Latife illuminated the younger woman later at Çankaya. 'Kemal was furious with this restaurant business. He said *he* certainly would do something about it!'

On the following day, two more ladies appeared for lunch at the Istanbul Restaurant: Hamdullah Suphi's wife and Nuriye, the wife of İhsan, the minister of the navy. The male patrons of the only restaurant in Ankara had little choice but to accept the presence of women as of that day.[7]

Segregation came to an end first in Çankaya, followed by the Istanbul Restaurant. The time had come for other places. Falih Rıfkı relates the first Turkish Hearth meeting held in Ankara:

> A mud-brick building, apparently a former Greek school. Hamdullah Suphi had converted it into the Turkish Hearth. Mustafa Kemal's first mixed-sex party was held there when he invited his friends along with their wives.
>
> It's still so vivid before my eyes. The ladies on one side of the room and the men on the other. A mere handful of intrepid ladies

standing up. The women didn't even move to get anything from the buffet. No one was introduced to anyone else as a family. The men stared at the women constantly. Mustafa Kemal encouraged us: 'Lads, go and compliment the ladies standing up. Offer them something. Let's show up those still sitting down. Soon they'll all get up.' [...]

The women's movement developed at a fast pace. Mustafa Kemal and İsmet Paşa always took pains to hold mixed parties.[8]

The table

Mustafa Kemal's dining table was a place of good company.

Vecihe says, 'He used to sit down to dinner towards seven thirty or eight. Dinner went on for a long time. The earliest he got up was eleven, sometimes staying as late as one or two. And you couldn't leave the table until Atatürk gave you permission.'

Originally, the dining table had been an all-male affair, but the arrival of women transformed it. Salih says Latife attended these dinners regularly at first. If the conversation dragged on or moved into details that did not interest her, she retired to her room and read. She is reported to have withdrawn herself from the dinner table in the latter part of the marriage, rarely attending and certainly leaving early if she did: she went up to her room directly if Mustafa Kemal was entertaining his friends.[9]

She tried to regulate these dinners. Mustafa Kemal would sit and drink with his close friends once a week, and he also drank if he wanted to when he met with his political associates. The rest of the week, they would eat tête-à-tête and not drink alcohol. Husband and wife took regular walks together first thing in the morning.

Sadly, her plans were doomed to fail. She once complained to Salih, 'It's you, in any case, who leads him astray.'[10]

She wanted Mustafa Kemal to drink less and spend more time with her. He, on the other hand, frequently gave into the triple temptation of dining table–drink–company, however genuinely he might have wanted to please her.

Latife had complained to her mother, too:

Even if I were to be generous enough to admit, 'They're entertaining my husband,' that is *my* job, *my* duty ... The worst of it is how, although they all pace themselves, they make him drink copious amounts.

I spied on the table so many nights. Kılıç Ali, Nuri Conker and Recep Zühtü all made it till the morning with a single glass each. My husband guzzled bottles. You should see how he awakens after an alcohol-free night; you'd think him a battle sword drawn against an enemy, he's so sharp. Then there are the mornings after the nights before: yes, he does get up, but drags his feet as though wearing shoes of lead. If they had the slightest concern for the nation, the state, never mind me, they'd not make Mustafa Kemal Paşa, whom they all fuss around, declaring, 'none of this could work without you', drink so much, waste so much of his time. I am his wife. Naturally, I will fight them. Sadly, I have no weapons. I am alone.[11]

She must have resented being set aside as hostess in her own home and considered those stag dinners an offence. She wanted her husband to be a civilised, westernised man who would eat his meal in proper fashion, with guests accompanied by their wives and waiters serving food and drink with formal courtesy.

In her husband's presence, Latife once warned Nuri Conker never to come to the presidential palace again without his wife, threatening he would be turned back otherwise. Nuri retorted, 'As you wish, Madam, but if you send me out the front door, I will re-enter through the back.' He later boasted to his family how his rejoinder had amused Mustafa Kemal.[12]

It's not hard to visualise quite what went on at a stag dinner. These tables intimidated women: İsmet is reported to have always attended on his own, his wife, Mevhibe, paying Latife a visit only during the day. With most women still excluded in mixed company, Mevhibe would not have enjoyed these all-male parties.

That was why Latife considered women's presence at these dinners something of a civilising influence on the conversation. A stag dinner rang danger bells for her: it was a night with the potential to lead to strain.

Men who preferred to chat and drink until three in the morning naturally found her an insufferable hostess. Lord Kinross speaks for them when he says:

> Latife was omnipresent, a short stocky figure sitting at the head of the table, even on a bachelor evening when he drank with his cronies. She would try to lead the conversation. For, as the favourite spoiled child of her father, she liked to be listened to – and Kemal did not take easily to the listener's role.[13]

This paragraph gives an insight into Lord Kinross's own male viewpoint: women were lowly creatures, risible in their desire to join in. Latife attending a meal at her own home is defined as 'sitting at the head of the table', her shape a 'short stocky figure'. Staggeringly, he judges her attempts to lead the conversation as her being 'spoiled'. This biography was published in 1964, forty-nine years ago. Vast changes have occurred in how men view women since then. I am convinced that such misogynistic language in referring to the wife of a president would test the daring of any male biographer today. In any case, the prejudice evident in these lines may well summarise the statements of all the people he had interviewed, male *and* female.

24

The Women's Movement and Latife

Latife was only eighteen years old when she publicly criticised the Young Turks' policies on women, citing examples from the recent past. Beni Hasan mentions Latife's affinity with the women's causes in an article he wrote for *The Mentor* in New York. It begins with the early years of Mustafa Kemal, moves to his objectives and then introduces Latife:

> It was about that time the voice of a girl was being heard in Izmir. She was uttering things which in a way were far more shocking than anything Kemal the cadet, or Kemal the captain had said. She was saying that the Young Turk movement was a false thing unless it released not only the male population from political serfdom but also the women from social slavery. She was eighteen years old.
>
> It is likely that they would have clapped her into a prison, or, at least, an asylum for the demented, had not her father been Izmir's richest and most influential merchant – Muammer Uşşaki Bey. The girl's name was Latife. Possibly Mustafa Kemal had heard of her, but it was not until after the British landed at Gallipoli and embarked upon their disastrous campaign that she knew of his existence.[1]

What the article reveals above all is that, in the first quarter of the twentieth century, Latife was fully aware of the status of women well before she began studying in Europe. The number of similarly enlightened women was considerable at the time. Latife, like them, must have been nourished by the women's movements rising in both the Ottoman Empire and the world at large. What set her apart was her marriage to Mustafa Kemal and her subsequent influential position at Çankaya.

Her views on women's rights were crystal clear. She considered discarding the veil an issue of liberty, defended the right of political representation, insisted Mustafa Kemal support her ambition to become an MP, supported a Civil Code project that would abolish unilateral divorce and polygamy, and argued for the separation of religion and education as essential to the advancement of women. And in all this, she never once forgot she was the wife of a leader: she always averred that she fully supported Mustafa Kemal in the struggle to liberate women.

I consider it a great loss to the women's movement that Latife's pioneering role at the time has been forgotten, and worse, deliberately obliterated.

Tribute for her services to Turkish women

One of the leading names of those early days of the republic, Süreyya Ağaoğlu, the first female lawyer in Turkey, must have felt similarly uncomfortable, for she paid tribute to Latife Hanım as well as to Mustafa Kemal at the Turkish Bar Association on the occasion of the fiftieth anniversary of the republic. Süreyya was nineteen when Latife lived in Çankaya, old enough to appreciate quite how valuable Latife's input was.

She concluded her memoirs, entitled *A Whole Lifetime*, by saying:

> Before my eyes as vivid as today passed those days when we flung open the doors of the law school to the women, those friends and lecturers. How quickly the years had passed, Lord! I felt obliged during my speech to express my gratitude to Atatürk, and to Latife Hanım, his wife and friend standing beside him, and to those days. And I shall always be obliged to remember Atatürk and Latife Hanım, his helpmeet at the start, for their services to Turkey, and to the women of Turkey.[2]

What thrilled me most as I did my research was accessing the archives of foreign publications. As I flicked through, I noticed how frequently Latife's views on women made it into print. That Mustafa Kemal focused much more on the women's movement during his marriage to Latife is manifest in his speeches.

Substantial progress was made during their marriage in bringing an end to the seclusion of women and laying the groundwork for equal rights.

The world expected the harem tradition to come to an end. Major steps forward had been taken in the final years of the Ottoman Empire. The entire world wanted to know what the new Turkey would do. Latife and Mustafa Kemal's wedding ceremony had broken with harem tradition, and the Izmir Economy Congress that convened immediately afterwards had taken its place in history as the first public event in Turkey with female participation.

Mustafa Kemal had invited the Azeri ambassador Abilov and his wife, Tamara, to the congress, and laid on a special train so they might travel in comfort. Abilov was one of the first foreign diplomats of the Ankara of the day. The congratulations Tamara sent Latife on the occasion of her wedding to Mustafa Kemal were distinctly political in content. Her message stressed the need for oriental women's status to be raised, so that they might take their just place in society. Latife's response was dated 8 February 1923:

To Her Excellency Tamara, wife to H. E. the Azeri Ambassador,
I thank you deeply for the sentiments and congratulations you have graced us with on the occasion of our wedding. The greatest happiness for me will be witnessing the rescue and deliverance of our and other suffering nations. I fully concur with your wishes for the elevation of oriental womanhood, as this is one of the top priorities amongst the conditions on which this rescue and deliverance depend. And my conviction of our ultimate success is complete.
Latife Mustafa Kemal[3]

The whole world's media placed Latife in the heart of women's rights from the day she got married. They had good reason; she was known to have challenged even Ankara's foreign diplomats on the topic of women's rights.

Her question on the state of feminism in Italy during a chat with the ambassador at a reception had caused some tension.

'Feminism, madam, has made little progress in Italy,' the ambassador replied with a smile. 'The women of my country have their own way of interpreting feminism; to them, it means making homes and presenting their husbands with fine, healthy children.'

'But how outdated!' exclaimed the first lady.

On 5 January 1926, in 'Story of Why Kemal Divorced Wife', the *New York Times* cited *Le Carnet de la semaine*, which claimed this to be the precise incident that led President Mustafa Kemal of Turkey to divorce his young and beautiful wife, Latife, the previous summer. The Parisian weekly then went on to assert that when she offended the Italian ambassador Mme Latife had already displeased her husband by her ambitions to share and direct his power towards modernisation.

On 14 March 1923, the *New York Times* ran an item with the headline 'Mme Kemal's Clothes Are Pledge of Reform', referring to two women as foremost exponents of women's rights in Turkey: Halide Edib and Latife.

It was evident that from the moment of her arrival she wished it to be emphasised that Mustafa Kemal Paşa, in his campaign for the emancipation of Turkish women, could count upon the full and active support of his wife.

It is not likely that Turkish women will discard their black skirts and shawls and their impenetrable veils for the unconventional attire of Mme Kemal, but it is certain that her advent will modify or greatly curtail the restrictions and obsolete customs prescribed for the women of Turkey by Mohammad. Mme Kemal insisted that the rules of conduct and dress prescribed by the founder of a faith centuries ago are not practicable today, and she intends to inject some western customs into Turkish feminine life.

'Evolution instead of revolution'

Latife made two public declarations on the subject of the veil: the first was during the interview with Isaac Marcosson in the days preceding the signing of the Lausanne treaty. She declared her stand against the veil, but rejected the idea of a speedy change, stating that it would take time and adding, 'It must be evolution instead of revolution.' Six months later she explained in another interview that liberation from the veil was an aspect of the struggle for freedom:

> It was nothing new for the women of Turkey to discard the heavy veil, especially in Izmir, Istanbul and in cities of European Turkey. My husband is fully determined that Turkish women must never again hide their faces, and the women of Turkey are with him. Some of the men might object to the women showing their faces, but it matters little what these men like or dislike. We have espoused the cause of freedom, and no nation can claim freedom whilst enslaving its women.[4]

Lord Kinross states that Mustafa Kemal discussed with her especially his plans for the emancipation of women.[5] Vecihe also relates how Latife worked with her husband on reforms relevant to women. Her reply to the question 'Did Atatürk consult with Latife Hanım on women's reforms?' was unhesitating:

'Absolutely. They worked hard together. At a time when men and women never sat together, *they* did. The revealing of a woman's face, for example ... the discarding of the *çarşaf*, for another ... "What do you say, Latife; shall we do it this way? What if you were to do it that way?" That's how they created the "Russian headscarf". They always planned their next move together.'

She relates an incident that occurred in January 1925, during the couple's second trip to Tarsus. Latife went out of the room on a prearranged signal given by Mustafa Kemal, as they were sitting in the house where they would stay the night. When she returned, her head was uncovered and she wore a plain, modern frock; this outfit impressed their hosts.

Mustafa Kemal asked, 'How do you find this new outfit?'

They replied, 'It's very fine, Paşam!'

He told them, 'This is how the women of Turkey will dress from now on.'[6]

Whenever he was on tour, he displayed sensitivity to the locals' reactions to the changes in clothing he wished to effect.

Johannes Glasneck writes of the speeches Latife made on the 1923 springtime tour of the country:

> Latife also mounted the dais to speak, under the stunned stares of the audience. This tour taken together had a massive impact on their contemporaries. Mustafa Kemal considered a family structure within which the man and the woman shared the rights and the duties essential to guarantee social advancement.[7]

She rehearses speeches in the Çankaya gardens

Vecihe reminds us that Mustafa Kemal asked Latife to speak at women's meetings and societies. Latife therefore had to rehearse in the garden of the Çankaya residence.

Hüsrev Gerede interprets her hard work as the attempt of a commander's ambitious wife to take centre stage. 'It is well known that Latife Hanım had political pretensions of her own and attempted to make public speeches on the Gazi's country tours, still in her cloak and veil. As Atatürk later told me, she used to rehearse speaking in the gardens of the old Çankaya residence, rather like Demosthenes, to improve her voice and posture.' He then comments, 'A childish act, rather like wanting to be Atatürk's equal, to compete with him.'[8]

The number of people who viewed Latife's penchant for public speaking as somehow defying Mustafa Kemal was considerable. Hüsrev Gerede implies displeasure on the part of Mustafa Kemal.

But Gerede was wrong. In reality, Latife was merely doing what she thought was expected of her as an adjutant capable of addressing the public when called upon. The fact that she rehearsed her speeches is evidence of her perfectionist attitude. The gardens in Çankaya were part of her home, after all; she would either rehearse before the mirror or out in the open air. Yes, it evidently suited the purposes of some males to belittle her efforts, accusing her of ambition and pretension, but those men must therefore have ignored Mustafa Kemal's own efforts to bring women into the public arena. It was Mustafa Kemal who had welcomed and actively encouraged female students and teachers to speak in public on all the trips he and Latife had taken together. Afet İnan, who accompanied him after the divorce, took oration lessons during her Çankaya days, particularly encouraged by Mustafa Kemal, and *she* is known to have rehearsed before the mirror.

The Civil Code

The key indicator of change in matters relating to women's rights was the law, with polygamy and unilateral divorce still obstructing any real emancipation for women. On 14 March 1923, the *New York Times* commented, '[...] the modern Muslim woman insists that her husband shall have only one wife [...]'.

A Civil Code had been one of the first promises at the Lausanne peace conference; Turkey had two clear alternatives. One was a multitiered system to accommodate the minorities (and this was the least palatable), whilst the other was a secular system based on western legal norms for the entire populace. It was this second one that was preferable on every count.

The parliamentary Civil Code commission was formed in early 1923. The original starting point was *fıkıh*, Islamic jurisprudence, guided by principles accepted by modern nations. The first draft preserved in its entirety the tradition that gave males superiority in matters of polygamy and unilateral divorce.

The Civil Code Bill that came before the assembly at the end of 1923 brought two opposing factions head to head.

Let us briefly examine these debates.

Ahmet Ağaoğlu accused the conservatives of hypocrisy on 26 December 1923 and on the following days regarding the matter of the bill.

Women held a big meeting at the Istanbul Turkish Hearth in early 1924, publicly voicing their opposition to the sharia-based clauses of the Civil Code Bill then in debate in the assembly. They criticised its overt subordination of the female. Nezihe Muhiddin, who took the stage as the representative of the Women's Union of Turkey, summarised women's pathetic status in the matter of divorce:

> What wife, conscious that her status dangles by a tie even flimsier than a thread of cotton, subject to a dismissal by a single syllable at any moment of sudden fury, this tie supposedly repaired by a contemptible caress of the cheek or a despicable patch like a trick, would feel secure in her lifetime companionship and espouse, even warm up to her tiny corner, as one should a temple? A woman in such an ignominious state could hardly become a noble mother, dignified wife or a sincere housewife! It is our right to expect of the secular republic not to differentiate between its nation's sexes to safeguard the rights of both men and women equally in matters of marriage, divorce and inheritance.[9]

Many women believed change would take hundreds of years, but others were demanding their rights immediately.

Vasıf Çınar took the stage and made a speech supporting women:

> There are two tragedies in our family life: polygamy, and divorce. Polygamy may have been acceptable in the olden days, but our republic can no longer suffer it … Regrettably, the bill clearly refers to it. And the matter of divorce is another. Of course there are times when an intolerable marriage is better ended. But this should only take place after grave consideration. Yet in our country, any drunkard can, and does, wield divorce.[10]

The women present took a decision to form a commission and draw up a report, which was handed to Minister of Justice Mahmut Esat Bozkurt when he visited the Women's Union of Turkey. President Mustafa Kemal and supporters of change did their best to encourage women against the conservatives.

Enver Paşa's Family Decree

The idea of a western-style Civil Code had first come to the Ottoman agenda after the *Tanzimat* reforms, but no consensus had been reached.

The state addressed the matter of marriage and divorce for the first time in 1881. A marriage licence became essential to conducting the contract: Muslims would have to apply to the sharia courts, and non-Muslims would seek a licence from their own religious leaders. The imam or the clergyman solemnising the marriage was obligated to inform the register office within a fortnight. The clerks who issued licences reported the addresses of newlyweds to the register offices each month. Similarly, in the case of divorce, the imam of the neighbourhood or village, or the leader of the congregation in the case of non-Muslims, was obligated to inform the register office. In other words, an official registry procedure of marriages and divorces was already in place.[11]

With thousands of men having to go to the front in the Great War, women achieved the status of civil servant, rearguard in battle or merchant in business. Countless others had no choice but to take up jobs as labourers. This situation created the need for a legal overhaul, and in 1917 a Family Decree was issued on Ziya Gökalp's insistence and Enver Paşa's initiative. Some of the clauses included a lower age limit for marriage, marriage before two witnesses and a judge and posting of the banns. The current wife's consent became a prerequisite of polygamous marriage.

Even these limited changes in favour of women had attracted massive opposition from the conservatives.[12]

Following the occupation of the Ottoman Empire in 1919, this regulation was suspended, as the minorities had also objected to the law interfering with their customs. However, in the absence of any subsequent regulation, we have to assume the 1917 rules remained in effect.

The 1923 Civil Code Bill was essentially a repeat of the 1917 Family Decree that had been suspended. But expectations had changed in the interim, prompting the formation of a new Civil Code commission on 19 May 1924, entrusted with drafting a new bill based on western models.

On 8 September 1924, London's *Evening Standard* commented in an article entitled 'The Harem Collapses':

> The feminist movements that have arisen recently in Turkey have become an effective force thanks to the support the Paşa's wife has provided. With the new ideas Turkish suffragettes defended at a big meeting recently held in Istanbul, they have demonstrated just how far removed modern republicans are from the prototype described by Pierre Loti in his famous work.[13]

The Swiss Civil Code was eventually identified as the most appropriate model. The bill would be published in its entirety, albeit with a few minor alterations. Halil Cin states that translation work started on 11 September, and the commission disbanded soon afterwards.

The Civil Code went before the assembly on 20 December 1925 and was published in the *Official Gazette* on 17 February, to go into force on 4 October 1926. Latife must have contributed on a subject so dear to her heart, but I was unable to source any documentary evidence. It is not hard to envisage Latife, who had read law, playing an active role during the drafting process. Although Turkish sources remain reticent on this point, there are references to her efforts in shaping and inspiring the Civil Code in the foreign press, notably in 'Kemal Pasha's Divorce', which appeared in the *Washington Post* on 16 November 1925.

In an article enentitled 'Divorced' from the 24 August 1925 issue, *Time* magazine claims that a significant part of Latife's contribution to the struggle for women's rights focused on monogamy. 'Her position and her prestige she used to further the cause of women, but in a land, traditionally conservative, she was not able to get them enfranchised. But her advocation of monogamy has to a great extent been effective.'

Letter to the Soviets

Documentary evidence of Latife's ideas on women's issues exists in the form of a 1924 letter.[14] She had mentioned to Ambassador Surits her interest in the women's movement in the Soviet Union. Surits passed this on to Kameneva, a champion of women's rights, asking for her assistance. Sister to Trotsky, a leader in the Bolshevik revolution, and wife to Kamenev, Davidovna Kameneva was thirty-nine years old at the time. In 1908, she accompanied Kamenev to Paris, where she edited the Bolshevik magazine *Proletariy*. When they returned home after the revolution, she headed the theatre division of the People's Commissariat for Education. Kameneva promptly despatched a booklet to Latife, outlining the women's movement. The booklet has not survived, but the letter has: Kameneva states that absolute equality between the sexes had been achieved in the Soviet Union and therefore 'there existed no women's issue in her country on the whole'.

In her response, Latife thanks Kameneva for the article, which she says was very helpful, and explains the situation in Turkey.

Dear Madam,

I am delighted to have received your letter dated 16 May. Please accept my deepest gratitude.

I have read with interest the abstract you graciously sent me. I am grateful to Mr Surits for having made possible this correspondence of ours that has enabled me to learn so much about the status of our friendly neighbour Russia.

Our revolution is not limited to politics alone; it also encompasses the social.

It has undertaken as a priority the elevation of women's cultural standards and the subsequent liberation of women. It is this objective that forces us to follow with great interest any matter of relevance to the advancement of women in the world. You will now understand why the best representatives of Turkish women are curious about the mental and physical conditions of their sisters in other countries.

As I have already noted, the abstract you have sent me has been very useful in this respect.

I would like to add, in the hope that you find it of interest, that Turkish women have been achieving results that promise success for the future. That village women of Turkey have, in addition to the great role they played in the National Struggle, continued to participate, with all their might, in the advances kindled by the revolution is quite evident, and this is a crucial factor in ultimate success. Now they are reading law and medicine. They go to universities in Turkey and abroad, and enter not only the private sector but also countless other fields that used to be monopolised by men, and thus determine their own fate.

In marriage, too, they are no longer slaves to their husbands; they are equals, and accompany them with equal rights and duties.

The advances made in the field of family and private life give us hope for their participation in the near future in the political life of the country.

This is the reason women of Turkey would be delighted to follow in the footsteps of their Russian sisters, whom they respect greatly.

In conclusion, dear Madam, I thank you for the note and the book you sent me. The Russian talent for fine arts shines through in an undeniable fashion. I would be eternally grateful if you would continue to keep me apprised of the advancements made by women in your charming country.

Begging your leave to express my true gratitude and deep respects,

Latife Mustafa Kemal

Latife therefore must have viewed the Soviet revolution favourably, and she was determined to learn more. Her use of 'sisters' in referring to Russian women is quite revealing. But her vow to follow in the footsteps of Soviet women is even more intriguing. In view of the achievements of Soviet women of the period, this was a highly ambitious position.

She also writes of the institution of marriage in her letter, and of women freed from the status of being slaves to their husbands, participating equally in society.

Although we do not know if they continued to write to each other, the letters indicate they may well have done. The foreign press also picked up on the exchange between these two women, as noted in *The Times* in April 1925.

Contacts with the Turkish women's movement

The public face of the women's movement in Turkey was Nezihe Muhiddin, leader of the Women's Union of Turkey. Although we have no details on the amount of contact between Latife and the union, we do know they sought her support to establish an orphanage. WUT applied to Mustafa Kemal's wife on 8 May 1924 with a request to convert a former imperial palace. They had scoured 540 neighbourhoods in Istanbul to assist war orphans and identified 2,000 such children who needed somewhere to live. Latife replied; she informed the minister of education. WUT took this as evidence of her backing. The minister asked the WUT to apply with a project, and they duly complied.[15]

Earlier I referred to the item published on 13 June 1923 by the US magazine *The Nation*, to the effect that Mustafa Kemal had married one of the leaders of the Turkish Women's Party. The error is understandable, as Latife's affinity with the views of the WUT was well known.

A letter signed 'Latife Mustafa Kemal' found in the archives of Fatma Aliye Hanım is held at the Atatürk Library. This lady was known as the foremost *Tanzimat* woman of all, and the letter is further proof of Latife's stand on the women's movement.

The letter in which she refers to the women's movement as her sisters is dated 9 April, and the year must be 1924.

> My very dear lady,
>   I thank you with all my heart for your letter, and your noble sentiments. I have read out your lines to the Paşa, as per your request; he, too, was deeply moved.
>   Your wishes are very important to us as, Your Eminence, you are a truly valuable mother that the entire world of women should be proud of. I extend my affectionate greetings to my sisters, and kiss your hand by your gracious leave.[16]

Latife's interest in the women's movements reached beyond the Soviet Union, all the way to the United States of America. Dorothy Detzer, the United States national executive secretary of the Women's

International League for Peace and Freedom informed a *Cumhuriyet* correspondent, 'I would like to travel to Ankara after the conclusion of my meetings in Istanbul if at all possible. I would like to meet with Her Excellency Latife Mustafa Kemal Paşa. Countless Americans and Europeans, I assure you, are very interested in Turks. I, for my part, have been lecturing to promote Turks wherever I go. I am delighted to be visiting your beautiful country.'

The world press was almost unanimous in describing Latife as a feminist, suffragette and defender of women's rights.

Ignoring Latife Hanım

Official history has always staunchly ignored Latife Hanım. I would summarise the general attitude of studies into Atatürk's life as one that disregards women on the whole. What is worse is that Turkish biographers of Atatürk seem to either completely write Latife Hanım out of history or sprinkle in a few derogatory lines. I have not found a single biography that even mentions her contributions.

In contrast, many foreign biographers of Atatürk give her credit for her role and influence in the advancement of women's rights.

The German writer Dagobert von Mikusch describes her function in a fresh new light in his *Gazi Mustafa Kemal*, published in 1929:

> For two years Latife Hanım had played an important part, being the First Lady of Turkey, and a kind of consort, and taking considerable share in social reform, especially in the liberation of women.
>
> She was now the spouse, but still more the helpmeet of the great man. At the same time Mustafa Kemal wished to show by his own example that the age-long bonds the East had imposed on women had gone for ever, and that she now stood on a social and human equality with man.[17]

The Argentine diplomat Jorge Blanco Villalta says, 'Mustafa Kemal was delighted with Latife's participation in the implementation of the reforms, and in particular, those that impacted upon women; he was truly proud of her. With her participation, she had gone way beyond the status of a mere first lady.'[18]

Even the women's movement of Turkey paid her scant attention. Her relatively early exit from the public domain might have played a part, or she might simply have been considered inconsequential. The prejudice that her husband's sponsorship was the only aegis that empowered her may well have been another cause.

I do not subscribe to the view that only Mustafa Kemal's patronage enabled Latife to speak out. She simply did not have the disposition to seek out such backing, nor would she ever have subjugated herself to her man. I am convinced of her genuine desire for the deliverance of her sex, which led her to become a role model.

Whether her appointment to social projects was more symbolic than genuine at a time when female intellectuals were invited to participate in public affairs is a perfectly justifiable question. My own view is that she herself took the initiative in each instance.

She left Çankaya, her work undone. The consequences and full ramifications of the union between Latife Hanım, the feminist, and Mustafa Kemal are not easy to analyse nine decades later.

25

Fikriye: The Former Consort Comes Back

It was May 1924. Latife and Mustafa Kemal were sitting and chatting when an orderly entered, distinctly ill at ease. He stared at Mustafa Kemal, hesitating between speech and silence.

Mustafa Kemal stared back quizzically.

'Fikriye Hanım has arrived, Your Excellency ...'

The Gazi said, 'All right.' The orderly left.

Latife immediately got to her feet and said, 'Let's not keep her waiting, Paşam; she has served you well in the past. Let's go welcome her.'

Fikriye was gazing out of the window when they entered the reception room. Latife went over and held out her hand. Petrified, Fikriye was unable to move her own arm. Mustafa Kemal spoke out:

'Welcome, Fikriye!'

She pulled herself together. As she stretched her hand out to Latife, she turned to face Mustafa Kemal, her face lit up by a huge smile:

'Thank you, Paşam,' she replied.

She made as if to embrace him when he moved to shake her hand, but he pulled away. They then sat down and chatted and dined together. Mustafa Kemal chided Fikriye for having left the sanatorium too early, but then relented, saying, 'Well, no use crying over spilled milk. Let's now see to your needs,' and changed the subject. At supper, he told her he would rent her a place in Erenköy, furnish it well, and that she'd not want for anything, but Fikriye was uninterested.[1]

This was İsmet Bozdağ's partly fictionalised account of the meeting.

Fikriye regarded Çankaya as her own home. Her side of the story is not hard to understand if we cast our minds back to her departure from Ankara. The trip she had taken to Munich on health grounds had ended so disastrously for her, altering the course of her entire life.

She had read of Mustafa Kemal's wedding in a newspaper whilst still in Munich. Shocked to the core, she returned immediately, news of which was wired to Mustafa Kemal on 6 March 1923. Fikriye wanted to come to Ankara. Mustafa Kemal cautioned Adnan Bey Adıvar by wire:

> I despatched Fikriye Hanım to Germany for treatment. Why has she come to Istanbul without seeking my leave? On no account could I allow her to travel to Ankara. I gave her sufficient funds. She must stay there and give me an explanation. I entreat you to command and inform all concerned not to allow her to travel without my permission.[2]

One account has Fikriye staying with a relation in Istanbul, although Şemsi Belli states – based on information he had from Handan Gören, Fikriye's landlady and family friend – that Fikriye had been living in Gelibolu for eighteen months, with no permit to travel to Ankara.

> She cried day and night. Her grief metamorphosed our house into one of mourning. She was inconsolable, no matter how hard we all tried. All she wanted was to be close to Mustafa Kemal in Ankara. She had absolutely no desire to imperil his marriage. But neither did she want to live in exile, so far from him. She had even contacted İsmet Paşa at one point, asking if he could get her a job near the Gazi Paşa in Ankara, but had failed to find a sympathetic ear.[3]

Handan Gören thought Fikriye had written countless letters to Mustafa Kemal, and that these letters had disappeared in the hands of the aides, or Latife. Salih confirms that Fikriye wrote twice a week to Mustafa Kemal from the sanatorium, and adds, 'Following the Gazi Paşa's orders not to reply to these letters, I would collect them in one corner, without even opening them.'

Süreyya Yiğit, a close friend of Mustafa Kemal's, says those who knew Fikriye were certain she'd come to Ankara some day: 'Everyone speculated what that crazed girl was capable of, but none of this gossip ever penetrated the walls of the residence.'[4]

No one appears to have noted down the date of Fikriye's first visit to Çankaya.

Her mind was already made up as she was on her way: not one for the cloak of invisibility, she was going to have a confrontation.

Fikriye's unexpected appearance might well have astounded Latife, but she behaved impeccably, and that first night passed uneventfully.

Ali Metin tried unsuccessfully to convince Fikriye to settle in Istanbul. When, by the following afternoon, Fikriye had silently tipped her hand by making absolutely no move to depart, a less than amused Latife asked the orderly, 'When is this lady going to leave?' She was worried that Fikriye wanted her man back and might insist on staying; this was a time when a man could legally have more than one wife.

By all accounts, the two women did not sit at the supper table together. Although not invited to the table, Fikriye came along of her own accord. Latife left the table when Fikriye arrived.

Dilek Bebe, Latife's niece, comments:

How would your wife react if a lady you'd lived with in the past turned up at the door and wanted to stay in your house? I would have taken exception. Compounded by the fact that this was the presidential residence. This would naturally cause tension between the married couple. It's not a normal situation. All her courtesy having failed to yield a result, my aunt must have uttered before Fikriye's door, 'Is this lady still here?' Fikriye Hanım heard her and departed. I'm sure Mustafa Kemal Paşa felt guilty at Fikriye's death. And then, his inadvertent use of Fikriye's name: it could not have been deliberate, but it must have pierced my aunt to the quick. That was when, to the best of my knowledge, she sent word out to her parents in Izmir, saying she wanted to leave.[5]

Fikriye returns to Çankaya

Fikriye came back to Çankaya. Kılıç Ali states in his memoirs that this time she had two handguns.

Several accounts agree on how Fikriye's last day unfolded:

She arrived in Ankara in the morning and made for the residence as soon as she disembarked from the train. She identified herself to the police and guards at the gate, who took her in without delay. They then informed Muzaffer ADC. Fikriye should have waited in the middle pavilion, in the guest waiting room, but she entered the green room instead. Sergeant Bekir went to awaken Mustafa Kemal when he saw who it was, and told him that Fikriye was waiting. Mustafa Kemal summoned Rusuhi, the chief ADC, and instructed him to talk to Fikriye to find out what she wanted. Fikriye wasn't familiar with Rusuhi, so he introduced himself. He would arrange for her to meet with Mustafa Kemal as soon as he learned what she wanted, but would she kindly move into the other room?

Fikriye was annoyed and retorted, 'I'm moving nowhere. I am the lady of this house.' It was this unnatural and agitated state of hers that rang alarm bells in his mind. Politely he insisted that she move to the guest room, and they finally moved to the middle pavilion. Fikriye went into the toilet at one point. When she failed to return after quite a while, Rusuhi told Muzaffer to open the door and check, a command that the latter disobeyed, modesty forbidding it. So Rusuhi opened the door himself; seeing Fikriye fumble in her handbag, out of which peeked a Browning handgun, he informed her that she could not see Mustafa Kemal on that day.

A distraught Fikriye bade farewell to the aides and left the residence. She walked towards the phaeton she had left at the gate. Then she sent word that she wanted to see Rusuhi again, but he did not respond.

Let us lend an ear to Kılıç Ali:

As the phaeton pulled away from the residence and reached the nearby Fuat Bulca mansion, Fikriye Hanım withdrew the handgun, one she might have placed in her bag with the intention of attacking the Gazi or Latife Hanım, and shot at roughly where her heart was. Flinging herself out of the phaeton in a desperate attempt to save her life, she collapsed then and there![6]

He believes that Fikriye had planned to kill Mustafa Kemal and Latife, and then commit suicide:

> A second handgun was found tucked into her waistband. We had surmised, in view of these two guns, and the fact that she had prepared one in the toilet, that – God forbid! – had she succeeded in securing a meeting with the Gazi, she would have, in all likelihood, shot the Gazi and Latife Hanım, and then committed suicide. As for her attempt to summon Rusuhi Bey after she left the residence, perhaps she thought she would take vengeance by killing him, since he had prevented her from carrying out her plan.[7]

Şemsi Belli relates Fikriye's final moments, based on the account provided by Dr Ömer Vasfi Aybar, head of Ankara County Hospital:

> Fikriye Hanım was rushed to the hospital as şoon as she had attempted suicide. I had her taken into a private room at once and began the treatment. The poor driver was a babbling wreck with the horror of the incident. It was difficult to get any reliable information out of him. The left lung had sustained a puncture of a large diameter, and the Browning bullet had grazed the exterior lining of the heart as it passed through. Dr Refik Saydam – may he rest in eternal peace – arrived as soon as I had settled the casualty.

Dr Refik told him that a disconsolate Mustafa Kemal wanted no effort spared to save her life. Dr Ömer Vasfi believes that she would have survived had she not contracted pneumonia a few days later. His prognosis was favourable. 'Sadly, a high fever took hold a week later. We examined her. It was a serious case of pneumonia ... She died two days later.'[8]

Official records list the date of Fikriye's death as 30 May 1924. A number of conflicting stories accompany her death. Can Dündar includes one in his book entitled *Fikriye* that claims it was murder, not a suicide. Abbas Hayri Özdinçer, Fikriye's nephew, found Can Dündar after the broadcast of the *Fikriye* documentary and related the story he had heard since childhood:

What we heard was that my aunt had been found inside the carriage, shot in the back. My father, Enver, wasn't informed of my aunt's death that day. It was on the following day, that plain-clothes men fetched my father to Ankara, on a verbal command from Çankaya. Despite all his pleas, her body wasn't shown to him. All her possessions, including the handgun mentioned earlier, were impounded. The judge cautioned my father not to persist in asking to view the body or mentioning filing criminal charges:

'Such complaints could have undesirable consequences for you. I am very sorry for your loss, Enver Bey.'

According to Hayri Özdinçer, his father's later investigations into patients at the hospital turned up information that a woman had been admitted that night, and she was shouting, 'Wretches, murderers, they've shot me!'[9]

Handan Gören also mentions the few lines on Fikriye's death that appeared in the *Hakimiyet-i Milliye*, an Ankara paper, as she speaks to Şemsi Belli. She states that plain-clothes men raided their house after Fikriye's death and removed all her belongings, bags, letters written but not sent, photographs and valuable mementos. But at no point does she blame Mustafa Kemal. 'There's no way the Paşa could have known.'[10]

Fikriye's death caused grief and a deep silence amongst her close friends in Ankara.

Muammer and Adeviye arrive

Although she had caused little bother other than a minor degree of marital strain when she was alive, in death Fikriye hurt them both, and the weight of her death smothered the marriage.

Latife and Mustafa Kemal had a blazing row soon after Fikriye's death.

Ali Metin places it some three or four days after Mustafa Kemal had sent Fikriye off, but it must have taken place after her death.

It was three or four days after the departure of Fikriye Hanım; Mustafa Kemal and Latife Hanım were sitting in the drawing room. The residence emanated good cheer. I was playing a horn gramophone, such a rarity in those days. The bitch we'd found at the front a while back and erroneously named Trikoupis had had a litter. She was playing with her two puppies. Atatürk was contented, sipping his rakı slowly. Happily watching the adorable antics of the puppies, he turned to Latife Hanım and said, 'Look, Fikriye, how sweetly they gambol!' Latife Hanım had a fit.[11]

Latife is claimed to have lost her temper, and said, 'It's you who killed Fikriye. Now it's my turn, is it? Never forget, Kemal, I'm no Fikriye, and I can look after myself!'[12]

He was furious with her for blowing it out of all proportion, his anger evident as he yelled, 'Latife!' Latife fainted with the stress. When she came to, she saw Mustafa Kemal by her side. Inconsolable, she said, 'Go! I don't want to see you!' and went up to bed.

Latife was nowhere to be seen in their bedroom when Mustafa Kemal went upstairs: she had moved to the next room.

The row as related in İsmet Bozdağ's book *Atatürk and His Wife Latife Hanım* is most probably based on what those present in Çankaya witnessed at the time.

Ali Metin says, 'Atatürk regretted the upset he had caused, however inadvertently. Two days later, we received a telegram from Muammer Bey, Latife Hanım's father, stating that they were on their way to Ankara. We showed it to Atatürk. He thought for a while, then he concluded, "Latife must have wired them." And sure enough, we found out that she had despatched sentries with a handwritten telegram to the Çankaya post office.'

Salih Bozok says, 'This row caused them to separate their rooms.'[13] Latife ate in her room on the following day and refused to answer telephone calls. And when she did leave her room, she sulked. Mustafa Kemal went to his office at the Agriculture School. When he returned towards the morning, Latife had long retired to her room. Mustafa Kemal then decided to ignore her until she brought his morning coffee. Neither was he particularly happy that she'd involved her parents.

In an interview that appeared in *Cumhuriyet* on 2 June, Muammer mentions a plan to visit Ankara in early June. He might genuinely have made arrangements to see his daughter after Fikriye's death. It is also possible that Latife's wired invitation arrived just then.[14]

'I want a divorce!'

Adeviye and Muammer arrived at Çankaya and begged Mustafa Kemal to stay with them as they chatted with Latife.

'I want a divorce,' said Latife.

One could have heard a pin drop. Then Mustafa Kemal asked, 'Why?'

'There are so many reasons ... I'm trying to pick the first one. I loved you as a man of progressive ideas. And I married you out of love, and happily. You were tender towards me. You took me along wherever you went; you shared your views and treated me like a western man would have ... Then you started concealing your thoughts. You dissociated me from your work. You began to drink and chat until the morning with some friends who surround you. I was left here like a concubine in a harem, all on my own in this residence. First at your service like a loyal adjutant, then pushed into the harem like a concubine. Of course this offends my pride. You had no right to treat me with such disdain. Yet I held my tongue. The Fikriye incident was the last straw. You married me, but you love another.'

Mustafa Kemal waited for her to finish:

'Fikriye was around when I married you. By the act of marrying I made clear my choice. She is now dead. I am truly sorry for her death. In my grief, if I have somehow slipped and called you Fikriye instead of Latife, I would expect to be excused. I fully understand your sentiments. But one single word is no reason to turn this house into hell. As for keeping you away from my work, the matters of state are my job, not yours! You're not my adjutant; you are my wife. Matters of state will naturally be outside your domain. Are you complaining that you are no Kösem Sultan then?'

Being likened to the most infamous, scheming harem wife with political ambitions upset her.

'Not at all! I'm no Kösem Sultan, but want to be the wife of a president. And this is my right ...'[15]

It was then that Mustafa Kemal reminded her of the comments in the papers after she had attended the chamber, replying, 'So I have mixed you up in matters of state in a way not even seen in the West!'

The talk had mollified Latife somewhat.

Muammer pointed out to his daughter she was in the wrong. Adeviye, for her part, said that although her heart agreed with Latife, her mind had to concede Mustafa Kemal's point. Together, they succeeded in convincing her that every marriage has its ups and downs.

These conversations indicate there must have been more than just Fikriye that irritated Latife. She thought Mustafa Kemal had changed and voiced her objection to being demoted to a concubine in the harem.

She confided in her mother again the following day, disappointed that her mother had sided with her husband.

'He'll always be in the right, till doomsday, because he's a man! Because he is Mustafa Kemal Paşa!' She described her spouse: 'A husband that you can't keep hold of, nor walk on his path, a husband in the limelight of the entire world! That's what's crushing me.'

Then she voiced her discontent with his friends: 'If they would stop wasting what leisure he has with their naughty boy pastimes, there'd be a way out. That's how he's spent his time at school, in the army, at war. He's addicted to some of his friends. Just like my brothers, who used to run out to ride their bicycles as soon as they found a free moment, whenever my husband has a free moment, he runs to his friends. I thought I'd join in, and even tried ... They didn't welcome it at all. Mother, I wish you could understand my problem.'

She told her mother the problem went way beyond Mustafa Kemal addressing her by his dead lover's name. She asked, 'Every woman has to deal with others in her husband's life. But what can you do if it is his male friends that are so indispensable?'[16]

26

Kick-starting the Economy

The Turkish Republic was formed at the end of an eleven-year period of war. Everything had to be rebuilt. The world press wondered, 'So they've won a miraculous military victory over Europe, but what will they do with the economy?' *Izvestia*, the official mouthpiece of the Soviet Union, summed up its assessment of Turkey's economy at the end of 1923 in an article later republished as 'The New Turkey as a Business Proposal' in *The Literary Digest* on 15 December 1923: 'The population is depleted after eleven years of war; malaria and syphilis are endemic; Turkey, which is an agricultural country, has to import 36 million Liras' worth of wheat just to feed Istanbul; exports are down to virtually nothing; even the tobacco industry, the only developed sector in the country, is on its last legs; taxes are crippling, which is why people are escaping abroad; the budget deficit is expected to be colossal ...'

The paper's claim of 36 million was exaggerated. The actual wheat import figure of 1923 totalled 3 million pounds sterling.[1]

The Ankara correspondent of the *Poslednie Novosti* reported, 'The demobbed troops have spread around the country like bashi-bazouks; they've no work prospect, nor funds to pension them off; western Anatolia has been scoured into a desert; the once teeming corniche of Izmir is now a dark, deserted stretch after eight in the evening.'

The article continued, 'The Turks pat themselves on the back for not having printed too much money throughout the war. The only reason for that was the commandeering of grains and cattle. The population was forced to work unpaid. There are no cattle left in Anatolia now, and agriculture is devastated.'

Throughout the National Struggle, each household had indeed been asked to provide a set of underwear, socks and shoes, and 40 per cent of the stocks of calico, cotton, shoe sole leather, nails, packsaddles, etc.

held by both merchants and private individuals had been requisitioned, with the promise of payment at some future date.[2] *Izvestia* summed up the situation:

> Turkey possesses two treasures that the Ottoman Empire never did: independence and sovereignty. Yet these two assets will only come into their own once the economy is rebuilt.

Mustafa Kemal had already declared the objective of the Izmir Economy Congress to be economic independence.

Mete Tunçay states that in 1924 nearly half of all foreign capital in Turkey was German; over a quarter was French, and one sixth British. The United States held less than 2 per cent.[3]

Turkey was paying reparations to holders of foreign concessions in order to maintain its ties with the capitalist world.[4]

The long war had affected Latife's family, too.

Seventy-two Uşşakizade properties had burned down in the fire of Izmir. The majority of these had been adjacent to the Armenian quarter – where the fire had started – where today's Fuar is located. (Rumour has it that the land where the Republic Square now stands also belonged to the family.) Turkey's new leader and his father-in-law agreed on putting Muammer's burned property to the use of the country. In return, Muammer would receive shares in the first petroleum company to be established – once petrol was found. Sadly, no petrol was found, and consequently the state never paid its debt. Some properties were deemed suitable for the purposes of the new Turkey and were asked for; these the family offered freely. Muammer astutely placed a clause specifying 'trade fair grounds' into the land deed. Even today, any mayor who has designs on this area confronts this clause and has to alter his plans.

I already mentioned, based on reports published in the foreign press, how generous Muammer had been in providing his daughter with a dowry of 1 million liras on the occasion of her wedding. At the prevailing rate of exchange, this was an amount equivalent to US$660,000. The republic's 1924 budget was TL121m, whilst the presidential budget approved in November 1923 was TL10m. The magnitude of Latife's dowry is better put into perspective when compared with the budget that allocated 8 million liras for economic development.[5]

It appears that the Uşşakizades gave this money to the post-war, poverty-stricken Turkey as a present. How Latife's dowry was used, need it be addressed, we do not know. It may well have been used to rebuild Ankara.

The İş Bank project

Mustafa Kemal mentioned to Muammer that he had some funds of his own. His father-in-law proposed founding a company along the lines of the East India Company, following the example set by the queen of England. What he had in mind was something like today's Department of Foreign Trade. This company would market Turkish goods abroad. His proposal did not take off, but a bank was founded to support exporters instead.

A variety of sources agree that the seed capital came from Indian Muslims and that the money was sent to Mustafa Kemal during the National Struggle. He donated the initial capital on 26 August 1924 and also opened an account with TL207,400.[6]

Muammer was amongst the founders of the newly established bank that had an initial capital of 1 million liras. Sadly the authoritative export association he proposed failed to find support. He was convinced that the bank would have been secondary, though certainly crucial to finance exporters, but it would have been the export association that would generate the wealth in the first place.

Muammer Erboy states that Muammer Uşşakizade gradually liquidated his commercial concerns throughout the marriage in order to prevent any speculation or gossip arising from his relationship with Mustafa Kemal.

The account movements listed in the *History of İş Bank* reveal that Muammer sold his shares in the bank to Mustafa Kemal from 1925 onwards. Mustafa Kemal paid Muammer TL12,500, or half the value of 2,500 shares on 30 December 1925. Another TL12,500 was paid for 2,500 shares six months later. A note next to this entry states, 'final part payment'. There are no more entries of payments from Mustafa Kemal's account to the Uşşakizades after that date.[7]

Autumn Tour

Latife and Mustafa Kemal set off on 30 August 1924 for a tour of the country that was planned to take six weeks.

They reached Eskişehir by midnight and Afyon by sunrise. Two aircraft saluted the train from high above to cheerful waves of acknowledgement from the passengers. A large crowd that included a multitude of women welcomed them on the second anniversary of the Battle of Dumlupınar. Film cameras rolled continuously as still camera shutters clicked constantly.

They arrived at the parade ground in a motorcar flying the presidential banner, and they passed under the specially prepared triumphal arch. Tents in which to rest had been erected. Kütahya MPs had brought along two very fine vases as presents. After a brief rest, they went to the proposed site of the War Dead Memorial, completely concealed under a hillock of floral tributes. Clearly visible amongst the wreaths was one from the then mayor of Izmir, Latife's father, Muammer.

The president, together with his wife, laid the first stone and then sat down in the shade of the wooden lectern. He delivered a very moving, poetic speech on the battle of 30 August 1922. 'Triumph on the path of civilisation depends upon renewal. This is the only way to progress and advance in all matters social, economic and scientific.'

Latife buys shares in the Uşak Sugar Mill

Nuri Efendi Şeker, the founder of the Uşak Sugar Mill, was also present at the ceremony. He wanted to issue shares to attract public participation in his proposed venture. The year was 1924; this was the first attempt to build a local sugar mill in the country: the Ottoman Empire had never gone beyond importing.

Nuri took the opportunity to explain his project to Mustafa Kemal, who was interested but said he had no money on him. He asked İsmet, who was by his side, to purchase some, and İsmet obliged: five shares for ten liras. But it was Latife, whose family had originally come from Uşak, who showed the most interest: buying twenty-five shares for fifty liras. The initial capital of the company was 200 liras, from a total of fifty founding shareholders who had paid in three instalments.

This one incident is sufficient to demonstrate that Latife had complete control over her own money: she was able to purchase a considerable number of shares without the need to consult her husband, especially as he had asked to be excused.

After the ceremony in Dumlupınar, they proceeded to Bursa, to another joyous reception by crowds flanking the main thoroughfare. They spent eleven days at the mansion in Çekirge, a gift to Mustafa Kemal from the city on the occasion of his previous visit. Latife accompanied her husband everywhere in Bursa.

The rest of the tour was a little more relaxed.

The cruiser *Hamidiye* awaited them at Mudanya. They would take a tour the Marmara Sea: Mustafa Kemal, who had not visited Istanbul once since the victory, could gaze at the city from the Marmara and the Bosphorus.

'Come on,' he said. 'Let's sail the Marmara for a few hours. We'll breathe in the sea air, and relax a bit.'

Latife was delighted; this would be her first time on a battleship. Her curiosity about the shells or torpedo casings knew no bounds; she inspected everything in minute detail. They sailed round the Marmara in a few hours.[1]

Istanbul spotted the *Hamidiye* in the distance towards eleven o'clock on 12 September, and every single vessel tooted in salute. A twenty-one-gun salute greeted the cruiser as it approached the Selimiye Barracks.

The *Hamidiye* disappointed the thousands who had crowded both banks of the Bosphorus expecting that it would moor somewhere between Üsküdar and Beşiktaş: it sped up the strait without stopping or bothering to acknowledge the city. Journalists constantly on the phone to the police stations along the Bosphorus all received the same response. Mustafa Kemal did not even wave at the people of Istanbul as he passed.

Şevket Süreyya refers to the state of the press: 'In short, these journalists had only the eyewitness accounts of Bosphorus ferry passengers who had caught sight of the cruiser to base their reports on.'

The Gazi was on the deck of the *Hamidiye*. He was in a black suit, and he was hatless. His wife, Latife Hanım, stood next to him. He was pointing to parts of Istanbul as he spoke to her. The seamen in their whites were standing to attention at the bow of the *Hamidiye*. Her Excellency Latife Hanım was wearing a black jacket over a white shirt.

These reports all were appended with lines expressing the longing the residents of Istanbul had for the Gazi. Why would he not come? Had Istanbul offended him? Why?[2]

No one wanted to return to Mudanya, so Mustafa Kemal said, 'Let's sail on!'

Husband and wife sing together

Having crossed the Bosphorus without stopping at Istanbul, they reached the Black Sea. It was a fine day, and a huge table was laid on deck. As the sun set, the tumblers rose, and voices were raised in song. Mustafa Kemal started: '*Black Sea, Black Sea, 'tis we that come, not the enemeee ...*' Latife was one of the first to accompany him. Their high spirits transformed the cruiser into a cruise ship. They stopped at the seaside villages and towns, chatted with the locals, stocked up on provisions and went back on-board. It was like a Blue Cruise.

They continued in this happy fashion all the way to Trabzon, but on the way, delight gave way to grief: Erzurum had suffered a powerful earthquake on 13 September. They did not drink that night, and the couple retired early.

Mustafa Kemal had planned to go back to Samsun to proceed to Erzurum by motorcar. Detailed information had been sought from

Ankara, and overland travel preparations were made in the meanwhile. He despatched a telegram to Cevad Paşa, the Third Army Corps inspector, instructing him to mobilise military medical teams.

The earthquake affected Latife badly. She is reported to have said to her husband, 'I'm so frightened. As though the earthquake had taken place inside me, and not in Erzurum ... I have a strange feeling as if something awful is about to happen.'

She objected when he said, 'Don't come; I could send you back to Ankara,' pointing out, 'Even seeing us might console them somewhat.'

Mustafa Kemal calmed her by proposing, 'Let's take a walk on deck. Breathe deeply. You'll feel much better in no time at all.'[3]

They reached Trabzon on the morning of 15 September to a rapturous welcome. They made directly for the city hall, and they rested briefly in the afternoon at the well-appointed mansion prepared in their honour. Latife chatted with the women of Trabzon. *Cumhuriyet* ran a report of the meeting:

> Considerable numbers of women of our city have today paid a visit to Her Excellency Latife Hanım. This visit has delighted and impressed Her Excellency.[4]

The wire that had come from Erzurum on 16 September reported heavy loss of life. But they could not motor from Trabzon as originally intended: there simply weren't enough cars available. They decided to proceed by sea a little further. Each time the *Hamidiye* was about to put in to port, rowing boats set off by the dozens or more, rugs were unrolled on the ground and animals were sacrificed in their honour. These heartfelt welcomes greeted them in Rize, in Giresun and in Ordu.

Samsun always enjoyed a special place in Mustafa Kemal's heart; this was the site of the start of the National Struggle. Well aware of this fact, Samsun people had filled the streets and the roofs. A huge ceremony took place at the city hall, after which they proceeded to the ground-breaking ceremony for the Samsun–Çarşamba railway. Mustafa Kemal wielded a silver pick and shovel at the ceremony.

They received a long line of visitors and later went to see a play at the theatre, which the locals also attended. At night, Samsun people cheered outside their house.

The motorcars that had set off from Ankara to take the company to Erzurum had arrived by this time. They proceeded to Amasya, where a torchlight procession continued all night. Tokat also greeted them with a torchlight procession; they fell asleep to the cheers of 'Long live the republic!'

Crisis in Tokat

Mustafa Bey, MP for Tokat and a former staff officer of Mustafa Kemal's, accommodated the president and his wife on their second night in Tokat. A scandal broke out at the table that night. Mustafa Bey spoke of the incident with Şevket Süreyya many years later:

> The table had been laid in our dining room; the guests had sat and eaten. It was still relatively early. But Latife Hanım insisted it was time to get up, trying to explain her concern for Mustafa Kemal's health and rest. The Paşa stalled for a while. Soon after, however, the request was repeated, more persistently this time. But he was essentially a night owl. He intended to talk with Tokat people yet. In short, her insistence exasperated both him and the guests. The Gazi still tried to placate her, but she sprang to her feet in a fury and rushed upstairs. The Gazi was regretful, embarrassed, yet also visibly relieved. But that wasn't the end of it. In a short while, the furious stamping of high heels was heard from the wooden floors of the bedroom above. The Gazi was at a loss.
> 'One of my mistakes was to marry,' he said.[5]

Kılıç Ali thought Latife was jealous of the women embracing her husband, but Eriş Ülger, who cites the other aide, disagrees: according to Salih, she was incensed when Mustafa Kemal took the aides in the same car.

The people draw their carriage in Sivas

The wave of affection shown Mustafa Kemal enveloped Latife, too. The welcome in Sivas was unforgettable: the people gathered at Gazhane, untied the horses on the city council road, and hauled the coach carrying Mustafa Kemal and Latife.[6]

On 28 September, they called at Zara, between Sivas and Erzincan. Latife's questions about local traditions on birthing and childcare attracted the local midwives, one of whom was able to brief her in more detail.

They were in Erzincan on the 29th. The Army Corps commander Asım Gündüz and his wife were known to Latife from Izmir. A big feast was held in their honour that night, and they stayed at the Gündüz home. Asım Gündüz saw a very happy couple.

Mustafa Kemal and Latife arrived at Erzurum on the 30th. He visited every single settlement that had been devastated by the earthquake, and Latife matched Mustafa Kemal's donations penny for penny. Their donations were listed thus: Mustafa Kemal, 10,000 liras from his pocket; Latife Hanım, 10,000 liras; members of parliament, 3,000 each; aides, clerks and others, one or two hundred liras.[7]

Latife viewed herself as equally responsible as her husband and as an extension of the cause; she exercised her free will as she spent her money.

They spent 4 October in Sarıkamış and the 6th in Kars, where a play about the town's liberation was performed. The surprise of the night was the folk dance accompanied by the 'Welcome' song, which received deafening applause. Latife and Mustafa Kemal got to their feet a number of times to salute the young musicians and dancers. Later they returned to Sarıkamış.

Joy and grief marked this tour of the country: the rapturous welcomes everywhere they went were inextricably linked with the images of the earthquake that carved themselves into their minds. A sudden marital spat cast a pall over the latter part of the tour.

Cracks in the marriage

The long autumn tour of the country failed to dispel the gloom cast by Fikriye. Kılıç Ali relates in his memoirs how tense Latife was on the way to Sarıkamış, snapping at everyone around her.

They were at the official dinner held in Mustafa Kemal's honour at the home of Ali Sait Paşa, the Army Corps commander in Sarıkamış. The guest list included the governor of Erzurum, military commanders stationed at Sarıkamış and other military and civil notables. Latife and Naciye, the wife of the Army Corps commander, were also at the table. Mustafa Kemal and Latife had not been speaking to each other since they had had a spat the previous day.

Aperitifs were followed by the food as Mustafa Kemal constantly flattered Naciye Hanım's beauty and speech. A waiter handed the dish of pasta to Mustafa Kemal. Then Latife raised her voice:

'Watch your feet, Kemal. They're reaching all the way to me.'[8]

A deathly silence fell. Mustafa Kemal begged to be excused, and they left the table together.

Their private quarters lay next to the dining room. Straining to overhear the conversation in the room, a group of guests, Kılıç Ali amongst them, realised all hell was breaking loose. But the raised voice belonged to Latife.

One story that has not made it into any of the memoirs is that Latife asked for a divorce. Her dignity would not tolerate him courting another, however gallantly it might have been intended.

Mustafa Kemal moved to a different room to spend the night. The original plan was to return to Erzurum the following afternoon. He appeared tetchy; Latife, regretful. Mustafa Kemal showed Naciye Hanım to his side when they got to the motorcars; Rusuhi and Salih were in the front. Latife was left alone, and she had to continue in Chief Private Secretary Tevfik's vehicle.

Very early the following morning, Salih knocked on Kılıç Ali's door. He related how Mustafa Kemal had not slept a wink, called him up late and informed him of his decision to divorce Latife, whom he intended to send back to Ankara.

Mustafa Kemal had also entrusted him with a letter to be handed to İsmet in Ankara. The row that had reportedly been caused by Mustafa Kemal paying court to another woman was about to break up the marriage. Latife first went to Erzincan, accompanied by Salih. She got on well with Asım Gündüz and his wife, and she spent the night as their houseguest. Asım Gündüz says:

> What a tragic coincidence it was that all those years later, when I was stationed in Erzincan as the Army Corps commander, the Gazi and his wife had set off on their tour of the East and been my guest one night. They were so happy, so content, that the wire I received from Sarıkamış a short whilst later knocked me for six. It informed me that Latife Hanım was on her way, escorted by an aide, and I was to accommodate her.
>
> Latife Hanım was disconsolate. She and my wife spent a long time discussing their troubles, but my wife was unable to ask what had happened and Latife Hanım herself wasn't forthcoming.[9]

Latife left a letter with Asım Gündüz for Kılıç Ali, who was due to arrive at Erzincan on the following day. There was a second letter addressed to Mustafa Kemal inside the first.

At this time, neither Kılıç Ali nor Salih behaved in a manner that might have suggested they supported a break-up. They could see just how upset Kemal Paşa was; it was clear he wanted a reconciliation.

They worked out a code: Salih would ask Kılıç Ali, who continued on with Mustafa Kemal, how the patient fared. Kılıç Ali would convey Mustafa Kemal's mood. Needless to say, Kılıç Ali had already informed Mustafa Kemal of both the code and the fact that Latife awaited word from them. Soon he, too, joined in the game.

The reply to Latife's wire, sent as soon as she had arrived in Erzincan, came from Salih: 'The patient is still running a fever.' They communicated again in Suşehri. The reply was the same. Mustafa Kemal was kept apprised of the coded telegram traffic.

As they motored, he would pull Kılıç Ali's leg from time to time:

'How's the patient doing Kılıç Ali; is he still feverish?'

Asım Paşa handed Latife's envelope addressed to Kılıç Ali, which contained a letter to Mustafa Kemal. Kılıç Ali placed it in his pocket and went to Mustafa Kemal's bedroom in the commander's headquarters, where he was lying down, doubled up with kidney pain. Rauf Bey, MP for Rize, was wrapping a woollen scarf round his waist to keep him warm.

Mustafa Kemal joked when he saw Kılıç Ali:

'What news? How's the patient's fever?'

'Where's that letter?'

Kılıç Ali immediately informed him of the letter Latife had sent, adding, 'Allow me to present this.'

'Leave it!' snapped Mustafa Kemal first, but then asked: 'Where's that letter?'

Kılıç Ali withdrew it from his pocket, ripped the envelope open and began to read it aloud.

In his memoirs he notes, 'The letter was truly masterful.'

Latife begged her husband's forgiveness and concluded:

'I have buried all my failings in the Erzurum's disaster area. Forgive me now. Let us return to our happy home, to Çankaya, together, in good cheer.'

The letter delighted Mustafa Kemal. 'Tell her the patient is well, and that she is to wait for us in Kayseri.'[10]

Salih later told Kılıç Ali, that once the wire reached them:

Latife Hanım was buoyed up indescribably. She couldn't wait for Mustafa Kemal's arrival. She sped eighty kilometres to meet him. Atatürk was also in a happy mood that day. He alighted from the motorcar where we reached him, and showing Latife Hanım and me into his car, he showered us with compliments.

When he and Latife were reunited, Mustafa Kemal quipped:

'Look, Madam, what was the need to rush back to Ankara?'

Everyone was happy. They stopped at a country garden for a cup of coffee and rested awhile.

Mustafa Kemal had not forgotten about the earlier letter he had written to İsmet – the letter he had entrusted to Salih wherein he'd expressed his decision to divorce. He enquired about its fate, and upon hearing the reply – 'It's still with me' – he instructed his aide to rip it up. Salih did as he was told, but kept the pieces, again as he was told. He did, in fact, keep all correspondence related to Latife. The cancelled letter had read:

> My very dear İsmet,
>
> Latife Hanım is preceding me to Ankara. We did not think it appropriate to continue the tour together. Because this two-year experience has given rise to the conviction that we cannot continue to live together. I have informed her of my decision. She is very sad and melancholy.
>
> She may well request your, and possibly Fevzi Paşa's, mediation to reconcile us. My decision is final. However, I have no wish to offend her, or her family's honour or dignity. I will maintain my respect and true friendship with her and her family. We will determine the manner of the separation in Ankara in due course. It is necessary to ensure her consensual and calm departure to Izmir.
>
> Kissing you on the eyes,
>
> Gazi M. Kemal[11]

They spent one night in Sivas before returning to Ankara via Kırşehir. Atıf, the governor of Kırşehir, presented Latife with a pair of Kırşehir carpets.

Ankara had missed Mustafa Kemal and welcomed the couple with a massive ceremony. Latife invited Kılıç Ali to stay at the Çankaya residence in gratitude for his role in the reconciliation; the tense tour had ended happily.

'Get me Veled Çelebi!'

Latife invited Veled Çelebi, the leading Sufi sheikh of the period, to Çankaya upon their return from the autumn tour. Explaining how she sometimes failed to work out just how to behave with Mustafa Kemal, she asked for his counsel. Çelebi reportedly said:

> Look, every young girl has her dreams prior to marriage; this is the prerogative of every maiden. Sometimes reality outdoes even the

most fantastic dream. Sometimes things turn out quite differently. You, my child, have married no ordinary man. You have married a tiger, a lion. You cannot imprison him behind iron bars. Even if you were to contain him, he'd break free. That is the source of all your problems.[12]

Remembering Veled Çelebi's words, Latife later said to her mother, 'I like being in the same house with a tiger. But I'm not trying to rein the tiger in; it's all I can do to avoid his claws.'[13]

The correspondence between Latife and the Sufi sheikh is kept at the Turkish History Institute: a letter addressed to Veled Çelebi is listed amongst the papers.

28

Days of Opposition

Political tension was lying in wait for Latife and Mustafa Kemal, who had so recently overcome their Sarıkamış crisis. Some of the old guard were conspicuous in their absence amongst the welcoming committee on the couple's return to Ankara; Mustafa Kemal knew this did not bode well. Disquiet was not, in fact, a new phenomenon.

It went all the way back to the days of Lausanne. During his premiership Rauf had been dissatisfied with İsmet's attitude at the conference and had even presented his resignation on the day of İsmet's return to Ankara. Many years later, in his memoirs, he would expound on his reasons for disagreeing with the postponement of the Mosul issue. Three leading commanders of the National Struggle, Ali Fuat, Kâzım and Rauf realised they had been excluded when the first they heard of the proclamation of the republic was the gun salute. The abolition of the caliphate had caused yet more tension; their objections had been met with accusations of being supporters of the caliphate, an allegation that had caused deep offence.

So many political decisions were made in Çankaya, and Latife followed it all carefully. She admired Mustafa Kemal one hundred per cent, yet she had her own opinions. She debated, objected and fearlessly aired her ideas. She had read law and had been attending Mustafa Kemal's 'school of politics' for two years. She was not a first lady who would limit herself to housekeeping, content to merely observe political events. As Armstrong stresses: 'Latife was a politician.'[1]

Heated debates loomed in the chamber, with a number of proposals on the Mosul issue already having been presented. But what caused the greatest acrimony was population exchanges: a series of questions had previously been asked in the chamber on the conditions of immigrants coming in from Greece, and there were rumours that certain members of the People's Party had filled their own coffers with the property left behind by departing Greeks. Kâzım Karabekir, then inspector of the Ankara First Army, resigned, followed closely by Refet and Ali Fuat Paşas. The commanders had joined the opposition, which was estimated to hold some thirty to forty seats in the house.

Latife had been close friends with Rauf, the former prime minister; she specifically invited Ali Fuat to join them at dinner as one of Mustafa Kemal's oldest friends.

The president clearly wanted to bridge the growing gulf between him and his old colleagues. The invitation did not reach Ali Fuat, however. Someone had attempted to prevent a reconciliation.[2]

On 1 November, Mustafa Kemal officially opened the new session of the assembly with a relatively short and optimistic speech on the 'state of the nation', in which he did not refer to the political tensions of the past months.[3]

The resignation of the generals had convinced Mustafa Kemal that he was facing a generals' revolt. He had for over a year suspected a military plot, and lost no time in taking his own measures. He had to be certain of total loyalty of the higher echelons of the military. He had full confidence in Fevzi Çakmak, whom he had entrusted with the army. He asked Fevzi to resign his parliamentary seat. The same demand was conveyed to the commanders of the First, Second and Third Army Corps. Their letters of resignation were read to loud applause and cheers in the House. Mete Tunçay says, 'Mustafa Kemal suspected a "Generals' Plot" and so reinforced his control of the army by pulling the commanders loyal to him away from the assembly.'[4]

I have not been able to determine how frequently Latife visited parliament. We do know, however, that on the following day – that is, on the 5th – Mustafa Kemal himself was present during the debates in the president's box accompanied by his wife, Latife.[5]

The 5th of November was an important day: parliamentary questions on the Ministry of Exchange, Urban Planning and Development had become a motion of censure. A recurring malaria attack had kept Rauf away. Nineteen deputies voted against the government. Immediately after the vote, Rauf and ten of his colleagues resigned from the People's Party.

Some forty to fifty more resignations were expected before long.

'We'd be left in the minority if we dismissed the dissenters!'

A meeting of the central committee and the leaders was held in Çankaya immediately after the resignations, with the express aim of finding a solution to the schism. A proposal was made to dismiss the dissenters from the party. Mustafa Kemal stayed silent, noting down the names mentioned one by one. He suddenly stopped and counted them with the tip of his pen. Smiling, he said:

'Friends, I note that if we were to dismiss the dissenters on this list, we'd be left in the minority.'

They all stared at him: was he joking? Mustafa Kemal summoned two of the alleged dissidents for a chat. The Diyarbakır MPs declared their loyalty as Mustafa Kemal opened the letters piled up before him.

'Friends,' he said, 'it's all sorted,' and he proceeded to read aloud the letter in his hand. Ali Fuat Paşa had presented his resignation from the People's Party and announced the foundation of the *Terakkiperver Cumhuriyetçi Fırka*, the Progressive Republican Party.

Mustafa Kemal seemed satisfied with the 'legitimisation' of the opposition that had for months been brewing in secret.[6]

The generals who resigned had declared their political plans for the future, and the tension of 5 November had at least yielded an opposition party. The Progressive Republican Party (PRP) was founded on 17 November.

A second party had arrived in the hitherto single party republic. The speed of resignations from the People's Party accelerated. Every single resignation came from members who had served in the War of Independence and had been in positions of significant responsibility thereafter. The change in their political stance would soon create an environment that would directly impact upon Latife.

Historians define the PRP programme as more liberal than that of the People's Party. Mete Tunçay, for instance, interprets the manifesto and the programme as documents that defended a liberal democracy in matters political and economic.[7]

Yet the PRP made no plans for female suffrage, nor had they developed any policies regarding women. Any past gains women might have made still failed to be converted into a permanent text.

The Party of Union and Progress, former rulers of the Ottoman Empire, had an official women's branch,[8] but even the People's Party had no women's branch at the time. Women still had no vote or any representation at the political party level.

Turkey in the eyes of the journalist Zekeriya Sertel

The journalist Zekeriya Sertel had headed the Official Printers before clashing with the government and tendering his resignation. His comments in *Resimli Ay* cast some light on the events of the time:

> [...] a degree of dissent had been brewing amongst the deputies throughout 1924. Those gathered around the president embraced the national movement and took pleasure in presenting the republic and independence as their own work ... The People's Party was a party of the masses; it was not ideological. Although it promoted a secular and democratic government, its ranks still included highly devout and conservative members. This extraordinary state of affairs could not last permanently. The time to disband the People's Party had come... Heading the new party were Rauf Bey and generals Kâzım Karabekir and Ali Fuat. In essence, their thinking was little different from those of the higher echelons of the People's Party, except that People's Party members tended, on the whole, to be much more devout and monopolistic, whilst the new party displayed significantly more liberal thinking. All this political hullabaloo brought the İsmet Paşa cabinet down. He was exhausted and had been ailing. What he needed above all was treatment and rest. So he tendered his own resignation and gave way to the Fethi Bey cabinet.

Sertel hailed the foundation of the PRP as the advent of common sense: the end of the monopolist thought would be good for the country.

> The foundation of the new party is noteworthy in revealing that the magic of victory and independence that had stifled the mind was now on the wane, and that the people were once again able to think sensibly. Following the victory, our eyes were dazzled and our capacity to think vanished. All that we could see before us were the august examples of victory, nothing more. But that period of ecstasy and thrill is behind us now. Now is the time of common sense. Now we may exercise our capacity to criticise and to approve. It is this wherewithal to wield this capacity to criticise that has enabled us to analyse those who were previously idolised. The People's Party grew proud and selfish with the absolute fealty it enjoyed in the initial period of astonishment and excitement. It appropriated the entirety of victory and began to exclude those outside even more. It was this monopolistic mentality that created such a reaction around the country and gave rise to the winds of opposition. The new party is the direct result of these winds.

Sertel does not mince his words when he summarises the events from his opposing standpoint. This comment, published in early 1925, is an indication of just how free the press was at the time. Sadly, Sertel would find himself amongst the journalists exiled by the Law for the Maintenance of Public Order parliament passed just a few months later.

He also points out the reluctance of the people of Turkey to relinquish their mentality of 'a militarist nation':

> Leaders of this new party were equally well qualified to reach high positions in the ruling party. But they desired something other than a ministerial portfolio. They wanted to prevent the dictatorship that was beginning to settle upon the country ... The political history of 1924 concluded with the foundation of a new party. The year 1925 will foster and raise this infant, the infant whose growth into a healthy and happy child is our heartfelt wish.[9]

'Declare martial law!'

Mustafa Kemal's reaction to the foundation of the PRP was quite calm, whilst İsmet suggested declaring martial law.[10]

Although opposition to the government in the assembly was not a new phenomenon, it had hitherto been contained within a single group: 100 deputies had refused to attend at the proclamation of the republic,[11] and there had been noes in the vote to ratify the Lausanne treaty. But a formally organised opposition party was an entirely different prospect altogether.

Erik Jan Zürcher claims that Mustafa Kemal had known of the plans long before the founding of the opposition party, and that he had weakened their support by meeting with key deputies from the eastern counties:

> Mustafa Kemal's policy with regard to the PRP at first was a very cautious one. [...] He seemed to follow a conciliatory course after the split had taken place.[12]

Was Latife a member of the PRP?

What was Latife's attitude to the PRP? This question occupied me for a long time. I consulted Ayşe Cebesoy, the niece of Ali Fuat Cebesoy, during our interview. Her reply surprised me: 'She was a member of the PRP.' If Latife was indeed connected to the opposition party, a new train of thought can be proposed.

Mustafa Kemal might well have thought it expedient for Latife to join the opposition party in order to calm the political tensions in the country. He had, after all, resorted to her offices in the past to smooth ruffled feathers.

Also worth considering is how Mustafa Kemal guided his own sister Makbule towards the Free Party in 1930, and how he was instrumental in the Free Party adding a clause on female participation in politics. Is it possible therefore for Latife to have joined a political party at a time when women were excluded from political rights? Yaprak Zihnioğlu writes that the first applications from women to join the Republican

People's Party were made in 1926.[13] But the title of Mustafa Kemal's wife might have conferred upon Latife a special privilege.

The Şeyh Said revolt

The most important incident between the founding of the PRP and the end of January was the change in the cabinet. Fethi Okyar formed the new cabinet after İsmet's resignation. İsmet had wanted to declare martial law after the division in the party; his resignation served to calm these troubled waters.[14] Kâzım Karabekir was elected as the first president of the PRP.[15]

Latife and Mustafa Kemal departed for Konya on 1 January 1925. They went to Adana, Tarsus and Mersin on what would turn out to be their final country tour together. They returned to Ankara on 2 February amid an atmosphere of complete change: the revolt that would have a massive influence on Turkey's future, and quite possibly prove to be a turning point in Latife's own life, had started. The sound of gunfire was coming from the south-east.

Ten followers of Şeyh Said – sought on charges of brigandry – responded with fire to a call for surrender by the *jandarma* on 13 January in Genç (a district of today's Bingöl county). The rebels captured Elazığ and surrounded Diyarbakır.

> A call was made in parliament for martial law in the region. Kâzım Karabekir supported the government and said that in the face of any internal or external danger the Turkish nation would always be one, [...] after which the government proposal to declare martial law was adopted unanimously.[16]

Tough measures required tough legislation. The High Treason Act was extended to include any activity that exploited religion for political means. The PRP did not oppose the motion.[17] What shattered the harmony in parliament was the forcing out of the Fethi Bey cabinet. İsmet, who had found the measures taken in the south-east inadequate, took over once more.

He presented the Law for the Maintenance of Public Order as his first act. Kâzım Karabekir stated that he was in favour of every lawful measure the government deemed necessary, but that it was wrong to undermine the basic constitutional rights of the nation. This law essentially gave government a free hand to do whatever it wanted for two years.[18]

Despite heated debate in the chamber and the PRP's opposition, the bill passed on 4 March 1925.

> On 6 March six newspapers (*Tevhid-i Efkâr, İstiklal, Son Telgraf, Aydınlık, Orak Çekiç* and *Sebilürreşat*) were closed down, followed by Hüseyin Cahit's *Tanin* a month later.[19]

Thirty-three socialists and communists were arrested and arraigned. The Independence Tribunals were working overtime.

Lord Kinross says, 'This was to give the government wide dictatorial powers.'[20] A time of oppression had begun. Countless members of the PRP were arrested in the eastern counties, and the PRP was forced to declare it had no connection with reactionaries or secret activities.

Şeyh Said conceded defeat on 15 April and surrendered. The suppression action continued until the end of May. The question of whether the Şeyh Said revolt was one incited by religious reactionaries or a national insurrection under the guise of religion is still debated. The complexities of the Şeyh Said revolt challenge historians even today ... On 29 May 1925, Falih Rıfkı asked in *Hakimiyet-i Milliye*:

> Was the Şeyh Said revolt a political and national revolution, instead of a religious fundamentalist insurrection, as we believed at the time?[21]

Latife, honorary president of the Turkish Hearth

The Turkish Hearth, much higher in profile than the Society for the Protection of Children, invited Latife to join the central committee in the spring of 1925. The society had kept female political representation on their agenda well before the advent of the republic. Although they had to halt their activities throughout the Great War, they regrouped with renewed vigour after the proclamation of the republic. By the end of 1923, they had over forty branches. Popular with notables of the period, the Turkish Hearth hosted plays and concerts, and provided a platform for philosophical debates. High-ranking statesmen wrote for their publication entitled *Türk Yurdu* (*The Turkish Homeland*). This essentially cultural institution promoted republican ideology, supported reforms in planning and even offered a platform for debate for these reforms. Its position in the drive for modernisation was therefore crucial.

Nationalism and Turkishness policies dominated the 1925 general meeting of the Turkish Hearth, which came on the heels of the Şeyh Said revolt. Latife represented the Kars Turkish Hearth at the general meeting.

On 2 May 1925, *Cumhuriyet* ran a front-page item on her address to the Turkish Hearth with the headline 'An Important Speech by Latife Hanım'. The same item appeared in the *Vatan* on the same date. The Anatolian Agency appears to have issued a summary of the text as a press release; points that were greeted with applause in the text were marked.

In this acclaimed speech, Latife pointed to 'the presence of religious and ideological schisms determined to divide the country, and the Turkish Hearth's constant struggle with, and effective results against, these schisms'. The way the text was presented to the press is an indication of just how much weight the government placed on the speech.

On 17 May, immediately after the general meeting, the central committee appointed Latife as honorary president of the Turkish Hearth. Two and a half years of tireless work at Çankaya was finally beginning to pay off: she had been asked to represent a highly influential institution in Turkish ideological life. Her battle to end political exclusion was beginning to bear fruit. Hamdullah Suphi, the minister of education, had been re-elected as president; Muhiddin Baha was elected as secretary general; and Celal Bayar, the general manager of İş Bank, was elected as treasurer.

Latife receives a medal of honour

Latife appears to have been particularly active and prominent in May 1925. The Turkish press praised her endlessly, with *Cumhuriyet* reporting on the 25th, 'The French ambassador in an audience with Latife Hanım ... M. Albert Sarrault, the French ambassador, was today received by Latife Hanım.'

Founded in 1925, the Turkish Aeroplane Society aimed to develop Turkish aviation; its first president was Cevat Abbas. The society presented its first females-only medal to Latife around the same time, prompted by her image as the exemplar of the selfless and noble nature of the women of Turkey.[22]

She thanked the TAS in a public message published on the 27th, expressing her wish 'for the success of the society, whose objectives and activities' she supported wholeheartedly.

The final days of PRP

Black clouds had been circling over the PRP; the presence of two political parties was far too much of a challenge for the assembly. An interesting note in the memoirs of Ali Fuat Cebesoy – who was of the opposition – shows how politically influential Latife was. She went to the People's Party Istanbul Congress, quite possibly at the request of her husband, whose boycott of the former Ottoman capital had yet to relax.

In relating the debates at the congress, Ali Fuat notes:

> Paymaster General Refik İsmail Bey spoke at length, accusing the Progressive Republican Party of reactionism and said, moreover, that in participating in the revolt, the party was guilty of treason, and he heedlessly claimed the party would soon be closed down. Her Excellency Latife Hanım – the Gazi's spouse – also present, replied to Refik İsmail Bey by saying, 'The preservation of a steely block of civilisation created by Turkish citizens is the only guarantee of the salvation of the Turkish homeland.'[23]

The congress had convened at Robert College on 25 May, in the week prior to the closing down of the Progressive Republican Party.

Ali Fuat's account reveals that Latife opposed the accusations levelled against the PRP and delivered a message of unity at the People's Party

Istanbul Congress. Were these words an expression of a last-ditch attempt by Mustafa Kemal to heal the breach in those final days of the PRP? It seems unlikely for Latife to have spoken out of her own accord in Istanbul.

The Progressive Republican Party was banned on 3 June 1925. The law would chase its members a year later, after the assassination attempt in Izmir; some would escape abroad, some would be tried and acquitted, and many would be hanged. Kâzım Karabekir and Ali Fuat Cebesoy barely escaped execution, whilst Rauf Orbay and Adnan and Halide Edib Adıvar had to seek asylum abroad.

The Eastern Independence Tribunal arrested leading Istanbul journalists at the same time, on charges of indirectly inciting rebellion. One such journalist, Ahmet Emin Yalman, would later write:

> The Istanbul press enraged the Gazi and his coterie. This gave the opponents of the press free rein to make waves. The issues that arose out of Izmir cost the country, and the press, very dear, leaving only a single genuine newspaper between 1925 and 1936.[24]

On 28 June, Şeyh Said and forty-six others were hanged outside Ulucami, the big mosque in Diyarbakır.[25]

He teased the military commander on his way to the gallows, saying, 'Come, General, say goodbye to your enemy.'[26]

What was Latife's political position?

The foreign press paid close attention to Latife's political influence. She explained her views on Turkey unhesitatingly, and in the early days of their marriage even stated to Ward Price of the *Daily Mail*, 'If I tell you anything, you may consider it just as authoritative as if you had it from the Gazi himself.'[27]

İsmet Bozdağ, in contrast, claims that Latife interfered in matters of state on the pretext of acting as an adjutant or secretary, and later chafed at finding herself sidelined.[28]

Latife, whose full involvement Mustafa Kemal had expressly sought in their first year together, had begun to see herself as a wife excluded in the second year. She had told her parents as much in front of Mustafa Kemal. Yet the prominence she appears to have regained in May 1925 indicates that the position had changed once more.

Memoirs on the subject of Atatürk on the whole condemn Latife's interest in politics as a flaw of character, of not knowing her place. Politics was a man's work, after all.

The Argentine diplomat Villalta makes a remarkable interpretation in his *Atatürk*:

Latife had realised that her husband's policies were not the most appropriate for Turkey; she didn't hold back in expressing her view before strangers, and even in public. She had begun to appear as an opponent of Kemal. He lost his temper; realising his mistake, he made his mind up swiftly.[29]

Armstrong also supports the view that Latife opposed him politically:

She had the most advanced and pronounced views on the position of woman in the state: equal rights and equal opportunities for the two sexes. As Mustafa Kemal became more dictatorial she disagreed with him and his unconstitutional acts. She sympathised with his opponents. She took up her own line in politics and developed ambitions in opposition to his. She criticised him in public as well as in private. She interfered with his work and his duties.

As long as she kept to her women's meetings Mustafa Kemal did not mind ...[30]

Both of these comments might suffer from a degree of hyperbole; Latife's political support of Mustafa Kemal at Çankaya is beyond dispute. It might have been her personality, constantly questioning and evaluating, that somehow fuelled speculation about her possible opposition. She neither issued an unequivocal challenge nor submitted absolutely. The country's frequent political upheavals must have played some part in their marital tensions.

Was It a Love Match?

Latife is an indispensable chapter in any Mustafa Kemal biography; anyone who studies him mentions his wife. The Volkan and Itkowitz title *The Immortal Atatürk*, a psychological biography essentially focusing on the internal world of Mustafa Kemal, offers an intriguing insight:

> The marriage had been made for reasons beyond Latife's sexual appeal and his enjoyment of her adoration. Mustafa Kemal seems at no point to have seen Latife as an individual but to have viewed her as a token of his success. She surely took great pleasure in marriage to her idealised hero, but had little or no desire to know him as a human being.[1]

There is no consensus on how much of a love match this marriage was, the union that lasted two and a half years and provided enough material to inspire countless films.

Şevket Süreyya believed reasons other than romance played their part:

> When Mustafa Kemal settled in Ankara as a head of state, he was forty-three years old, but quite inexperienced in matters of women and love.
>
> A woman does not automatically mean love. That said, he did marry for a while ... but this was no love match. Yes, he appeared to have formed a family. But there was no mutual love. This marriage began with a fait accompli and ended with another. All for lack of something.
>
> There was no mutual love.[2]

In contrast to Şevket Süreyya, Halide Edib was one of many who believed that Mustafa Kemal had fallen in love at first sight. She not only benefited from a woman's perspective, but was, in fact, a first-hand witness: 'She was dazzled by him, and he was frankly in love.'[3]

All the sources I have found agree that they beamed with happiness in their first few months.

Armstrong also writes that Mustafa Kemal was head over heels in love:

> Now he had met something new, a girl of breeding, free, self-possessed, educated in the West, absorbed in western ideas, capable of meeting him intellectually, of holding his interest beyond the passing of sex, capable of being a partner and a helper. And withal, soft and scented, rousing desire, exquisite and maddening. He was swept off his feet. He was on fire. For the first time he was in love.[4]

The deep passion Mustafa Kemal had for Latife is evident between the lines of these memoirs. He might not have been lovesick in the way Şevket Süreyya means, but he had met a girl he *would* want to love.

Latife's air of self-confidence, open-mindedness and sincerity had attracted him from the first. Deciding to marry a woman who demanded an equal relationship gave him the special pleasure of defying the prevailing attitudes of the time: his wife would be a role model for women of the future.

Lord Kinross interprets Latife's position:

> Not a wife to remain in the background, she made her personality felt. From the start of the marriage, Kemal had drawn from her companionship a stimulus such as no other woman had given him; moreover, practical help and advice in his work, so she still acted to some extent as his 'secretary'. She was intelligent and well educated; she was self-confident, with ideas of her own; they could hold serious discussions together. Here, as he saw it, was a relationship between man and wife on equal terms, such as prevailed in the West.[5]

Did money play a role in the marriage?

Şemsi Belli, who held long interviews with Makbule Atadan, Mustafa Kemal's sister, implies Latife married Mustafa Kemal for his money. He claims Makbule told him that Atatürk had said, 'Latife loved me for my money and my position, whilst Fikriye loved me for my own sake.'[6]

Mustafa Kemal's charisma as leader of the National Struggle must have played a part in Latife's love. But the idea that Latife married Mustafa Kemal for his money is hardly plausible, as she herself was the wealthy party. I find such an allegation on the part of Makbule difficult to believe.

The American journalist Louis Bryant, who had leftist tendencies, claims quite the opposite, arguing that Mustafa Kemal married Latife for her money:

> Latife is not the bravest, most beautiful, most intelligent, and most charming of Turkish women. She is the richest. She was the daughter of the richest man in Turkey, an Izmir merchant, and he was expected to supply the one thing Kemal needed: money.[7]

Latife loved Mustafa Kemal to a fault. She loved him before they met, and her love continued to grow after they did. We do know that she lived with his photograph by her side to her dying day and looked out at his statue, one she found particularly fine.

But her love was not unconditional. She would suffer no attack on her pride, defying him categorically, regardless of how many bridges she might burn in the process.

Battle of the wills

How would two such strong characters live together?

Berthe Georges-Gaulis asked herself this same question on the very first days of the marriage:

Which of these two would prevail? Inevitably one had to succumb to the other. No one around them dared to voice this question, the question on all their minds. Latife was more than adequately equipped to protect herself. Yet she had fallen under the perpetual spell of that magnificent mind, the mind that constantly metamorphosed itself, and had hitherto fought off any attempt at domination. Who would win?[8]

Von Mikusch says,

> Both of them having strong natures and being hard, proud and unyielding they were too like one another in disposition to live together in harmony. There must have been a secret battle between them to decide which of them was to rule.[9]

Vamık Volkan and Norman Itkowitz agree:

> Paradoxically, he married Latife because, on the surface, she appeared to be very different from his mother; her brashness reminded him of himself, always thrusting forward and testing boundaries. Soon, however, he would experience Latife's engulfing qualities.[10]

Armstrong says, 'Both she and Mustafa Kemal were equally imperious and domineering; both were strong-willed, hard and unyielding. She was as quick-witted and caustic-tongued as he was. She would not stand criticism any more than he would. There was no child to hold them together.'[11]

She wanted a family

Latife wanted Mustafa Kemal to become a part of the family they had formed. Şevket Süreyya comments, 'Latife Hanım sought a family man, a head of the household. Mustafa Kemal, on the other hand, had his lifelong habits, which he was loath to discard.'[12]

Latife was married to the man who governed Turkey, and she did not like him sitting at a table until daybreak. Süreyya Ağaoğlu says, 'Latife Hanım always kept his health foremost in her mind,' and adds:

She wanted him to get into bed by midnight, for instance. That's why his coterie disliked her. Latife Hanım didn't want him to drink. We, as a family, admired and loved Latife Hanım so much. I would also like to point out as a woman, if only Atatürk had stayed married, if only he had stayed with Latife Hanım ... He might well have lived longer ... And he might also have led by example on so many other counts.[13]

His wife's attempts to rein in his drinking tables irritated him, according to Lord Kinross:

Where Latife erred most in her psychology was in seeking too obviously to moderate his drinking habits. She tried to cut down the drink at the table. She would come into the room and exclaim before his friends, 'What's this, Kemal, drinking again?'[14]

In fact, a significant swathe of the people who charted Turkey's fate at the time had placed their hopes on Latife's success in this respect. Marshal Fevzi Çakmak explains, 'A crucial duty is expected of Latife Hanım, who is highly intelligent and well-bred. If she were to transfer the commander's drink table to the private domain of the family they have formed together, she will have carried out the greatest possible service to the country.'[15]

The number of people who expected Latife to exercise the kind of tact in directing Mustafa Kemal – who took no care of his health at all – to a more temperate lifestyle was not negligible. She did what she could, although a subtler and more skilful approach might have yielded better results in the long run. Instead, being the direct person she was, she was much more upfront, carrying the keys in her pocket as Mustafa Kemal chafed at the curbs on his freedom.

If only they'd had a child ...

Both Latife and Mustafa Kemal loved children. Hüsrev Gerede claims Mustafa Kemal was sterile,[16] which Rıza Nur suggests had been caused by a childhood disease. Precisely when Latife got to learn of this fact, or whether they ever discussed candidly it between themselves, we do not know. What we do have is a portrait of a woman who, for the two and a half years she lived in Ankara, paid visits to new mothers and named babies. It was Latife who named Kılıç Ali and Hümeyra's son Altemur. Her broodiness is evident in the letter she wrote to Mevhibe İnönü years later: she had first met Mevhibe as a newly delivered mother.

Was she overly jealous?

Mustafa Kemal's sexual life intrigues so many writers; most describe him as a womaniser. Latife was expected to turn a blind eye to his little escapades and to indulge him without fuss. After all, hadn't the rulers of the country run harems for hundreds of years?

Mustafa Kemal was a monogamous man struggling for equality with his wife in Çankaya at a time when polygyny persisted. Moreover, Latife expected nothing less than full equality. Marriage with a wife who was so set on equality compelled Mustafa Kemal to forswear many of his old habits. He tolerated Latife's challenges, but frequently found himself stifled. He is reported to have gone out for some fresh air when tensions came to a breaking point.

Ercüment Ekrem Talû, who was appointed head clerk to the president after the proclamation of the republic, says Latife wanted to read Mustafa Kemal's official correspondence as well as his private letters.

Esin Çelikkan, Ercüment Ekrem's daughter, comments on Latife's behaviour in her unpublished memoirs:

> Latife Hanım was jealous, petulant and capricious. She might have had good reason. It was not long since the time Fikriye Hanım had banged on Çankaya's door, insisting, 'I'm here to see my Paşa!' Then the flocks of ladies making eyes at her man. Latife Hanım wants to see the official correspondence as well, never mind private letters. My father refuses. 'I'm sorry, Madam.' He might have failed to hide his displeasure, so Latife Hanım tries to placate him. 'Relax,

Ercüment Bey, I was only teasing you.' Ercüment Ekrem takes a stand. 'All very well, but a joke and a pleasantry [a pun on Latife's name], they'll do!' Away with you.

Lord Kinross claims Latife grew jealous as Mustafa Kemal's initial ardour cooled:

> [...] for hers became at times a jealousy which she became unable, like any woman of the harem, to conceal or control. She was jealous of any woman to whom he might pay a compliment; jealous of his friends and their influence on him; jealous even of his dog and the attention he paid to it. One evening she made a scene when, in a gesture of congratulation, he patted the head of her young cousin, as he was playing the piano.[17]

Rereading all that was written on the subject of their rows reveals that three big quarrels occurred in the two and a half years. It was the last one that caused the divorce, and every single row is reported to have flared up over jealousy.

Süreyya Ağaoğlu says, 'Latife Hanım was, above all, in love with Mustafa Kemal. And like every woman, she was jealous. Women in love are. She was possessive; of this there is no doubt. Everyone says she should have been more charitable. I do not agree.'[18]

His candid friendship with Nuri Conker enabled Mustafa Kemal to divulge that he had remained faithful to Latife throughout the marriage.[19]

So Mustafa Kemal took pains to avoid offending Latife throughout their union. But Armstrong states that he lived recklessly, with utter abandon, after the divorce.[20]

Tales of stamping her feet

A well-known image of their marriage is of Latife stamping her feet. Aydan Eralp, the daughter-in-law of Ali Fethi Okyar and Galibe, denies these allegations outright:

A newspaper ran a serial on Latife Hanım. My mother-in-law kept the clippings without fail. The 'stamping feet' story made her so cross and distressed.

'Such calumny. For shame! She was an intellectual who adored and loved Atatürk, and she was blessed with common sense. She'd never do anything like that. How they insult her, yet she never once opens her mouth ...'[21]

The item in question, which ran in *Hürriyet* on 29 June 1973, is still preserved amongst Galibe Okyar's possessions. Galibe and Latife were very close until the March of 1925, when the Okyars left for France on Fethi Bey's ambassadorial appointment; the two women did keep in touch afterwards.

The displeasure some men felt about Latife 'stamping her feet' might well have been an expression of their discomfiture at nothing more than her presence. She stomped hard enough to shake the stairs, they claim. High heels and a determined gait on the wooden floors of those vineyard houses of the period might well lie at the heart of the legend.

She tried to lead him

The number of people who believe Latife tried to precede Mustafa Kemal throughout their marriage is considerable. Lord Kinross summarises these views by saying, 'Latife's fault lay in seeking to lead him.'[22]

Hüsrev Gerede wonders: 'Despite all her superior qualities, how Latife failed remains a mystery: failed to appreciate the need Turkey had for a supreme personality like Atatürk, and failed to make any compromises.' He continues:

Regrettably, Latife Hanım didn't know that you couldn't command a great commander, that a great statesman would never willingly share power. It was her ignorance that poisoned his home life and finally caused Latife Hanım's tears of regret, of losing the great historic blessing she once possessed.[23]

There is just one more thing to add to all that has been said to date. Mustafa Kemal, as he himself was frequently at pains to point out, was not a marrying man. He had already begun to wonder if he had not made a huge mistake. There had been talk amongst the residents of Ankara and even foreign diplomats that the marriage was on the verge of a massive crisis. Sadly, Latife was oblivious to it all.

Divorce

The row that would put them asunder for the rest of their lives broke out one midnight after supper had been cleared. It was either 20 or 21 July 1925, but precisely what happened remains a mystery. Mustafa Kemal was in the garden when Latife called out from the window. Whatever it was she said reportedly infuriated him into apoplexy. Puce with anger, sweat dripping from his brow, he strode into the study, picked up the telephone and ordered Salih ADC and Kılıç Ali to come over at once.

The aides entered the study together: Mustafa Kemal was stretched out on the sofa. Still incandescent, he was muttering: 'I need to run away; otherwise I swear I'll pour petrol over this place and set fire to it!'

Salih immediately loosened Mustafa Kemal's necktie and undid his collar button.

Lord Kinross claims, 'One night at Çankaya she again lost her temper. She turned on the friends with whom he had been drinking and tore their characters to pieces before him, one by one.'[1]

An Austrian Foreign Ministry document claims İsmet and Fevzi Paşas were present when this incident occurred.

Evidently Latife lost all control that night, voicing her anger before the guards and orderlies. But she never once spoke of it: she had given Mustafa Kemal her word. Whatever it was that caused their divorce remained behind Çankaya's closed doors.

Vecihe says, 'Atatürk and Latife Hanım subsequently swore to each other never to speak of their private life. I, too, was party to such an awful lot that I will never reveal.'[2]

According to Kılıç Ali, Mustafa Kemal first let off steam and then said to him, 'Wait here awhile; I need to clear my head. I'll go for a drive for a bit of fresh air.'

Taking Chief ADC Rusuhi Bey along, he got in the car and commanded, 'To Yozgat,' but actually spent the night at Marmara Mansion. His whereabouts were to be kept a secret. He also issued instructions for Latife to leave for Izmir at once.

Salih Bozok remembers Mustafa Kemal telephoning İsmet immediately after the row.

İsmet's pleas fall on deaf ears

There is a slightly different version of the events of the following day.

The doorbell of the Pink Mansion rang one afternoon. The butler opened the door. Recognising the president's voice, Mevhibe immediately came out to greet him. Taken aback by his glowering face, she muttered: 'Welcome, sir; how is Her Ladyship?'

A tense Mustafa Kemal snapped, 'She's fine,' as he stepped in to talk to İsmet. His mind was set on divorce. İsmet's voice trembled with grief when he told his wife. No amount of pleading had swayed Mustafa Kemal's mind.

The US Department of State report refers to Latife wiring Izmir to say she 'could no longer live in Ankara, and asked to be collected'.[3]

The news stunned everyone in Ankara. The capital was abuzz with gossip, and worse still, Mustafa Kemal was nowhere to be found.[4]

Rıza Soyak remembers that day:

> They must have had the most violent argument one night, and Atatürk left the residence, going down to his private secretary's office at the station. His decision to divorce, to end this life that made them both so unhappy, was clear for all to see, but he thought it expedient not to reveal his decision just then.
>
> He wrote a letter to Latife Hanım in the correspondence room; from what I've learned, this letter referred to how they were both very tense, a period of separation was essential for them both to calm down, and it recommended she join her mother, who was on her way to Ankara even as he wrote, and accompany her to Izmir for a bit of rest.[5]

Latife saved this letter to the end of her days.

> 22 July 1341 [1925 AD]
> Latife,
> You're tense, and you're tormented. I, too, am tense and tormented.
> I believe a period of separation to enable us to calm down is essential to healing this breach between us. I have written to your mother to accompany you to either Istanbul or Izmir throughout your illness so that you may recuperate. I am convinced that unless tranquillity is achieved through such a break, my own torment will not cease.
> Take whatever amount of money you require from the safe. You will have to spend some during your travel and cure. I am not entirely certain as to the amount; if it is insufficient, let me know. Leave the documents I need in the safe. Show Tevfik how to unlock and lock the safe. Instruct your nanny on the finer points of the household arrangements. I wish you peace and tranquillity.
> Gazi M. Kemal[6]

This succinct letter refers to a short-term separation, rather than a divorce, which is probably why Latife was convinced this departure would end with a reunion.

'Vedad, you can't stay here any longer!'

Before she set off for Izmir, Latife telephoned her nephew Vedad, who was staying in Çankaya. 'We're off, but you're here as my guest. You can't stay here any longer; either find lodgings in town or return to Istanbul.'

Vedad prevaricated, claiming he had to consult his father first. Halit Ziya was amongst the many who thought the marriage doomed. Father and son had held long discussions in the past, and Vedad had made it clear that in the event of a crisis, he would easily leave the foreign service and return to his old job at the bank.

Upon Latife's departure, Vedad wrote to his father: Halit Ziya's predictions had come true; Latife had been despatched to Izmir in the company of her mother, sister and brother. He was certain divorce would follow soon after. He was anxious and asked his father what he ought to do.

His father replied, 'You are there much more as the president's guest than as Latife's; it is he who is your patron; you ought to obey his command.'[7]

Last day in Çankaya

Mevhibe was one of the last people to see Latife before she left. Her face was white as a sheet as she pointed at the chaotic bedroom, mumbling, 'Oh, it's all such a mess!'

As she stared at Latife's possessions strewn around the room, the open drawers and the suitcases lined up against the wall, Mevhibe was convinced it was not the physical disorder that was meant. Latife knew the two and a half years she'd spent with Mustafa Kemal were worth an entire lifetime.[8]

In the morning, Latife got in the car that would take her to the train station, accompanied by Kılıç Ali and Muzaffer ADC, who would escort her to Izmir. Premier İsmet, Chief of the General Staff Fevzi and some members of parliament and the cabinet came to the station to see her off.

She had contented herself with packing some personal possessions. Kılıç Ali says she pleaded with him, 'You delivered me from a similar predicament in the past. I place my hopes on you once more.' This time, however, he did not think there was the slightest chance to repair the breach.[9]

'That black-hearted wretch ...'

Latife never thought this departure would be final when she left for Izmir. Mustafa Kemal must also have initially favoured a period of separation.

The letter she sent to Salih Bozok on 29 July from Göztepe supports this idea:

Salih Bey, you flare up and grumble, but you are blessed with great virtues. And you always speak the truth. What you cannot say to someone's face, you never voice behind his back. You are a father. [...] If you were in the place of that black-hearted wretch, you would never bedevil me so. [...] But no matter. His time, too, will come. [...]

My father is in Europe. [...] I am an orphan. I have no one. That is why I write to Salih Bey, man of his word, and second father to me. Please go talk to the Paşa. I have every confidence in my husband. He is compassionate. He has a noble soul. Please impress upon him my pleas to end the strain between us, that a fine future awaits us. In my letter to him, I asked him to send me the two of you, your wife and you. I have been without food or sleep for a week, a condemned woman. All for a childish outburst. Yet children are spared such severe punishment. I have every trust in your ability to resolve the situation peacefully.

Latife Gazi Mustafa Kemal[10]

I leave it to your imagination to work out who the 'black-hearted wretch' is.

Mustafa Kemal in a sweat

Whether Mustafa Kemal was already set on divorce when he told Latife about a separation or whether he made his mind up after her departure, we do not know.

The *talakname* – divorce document – that was sent to Izmir was drawn up subsequently. Latife received it two and a half weeks after her arrival. An announcement was sent to the newspapers via the Anatolian Agency on 12 August.

Mustafa Kemal spilled ink on the sheet when was writing the divorce document. A clean sheet was procured at once, but this time, with insufficient ink in the nib, the pen defied the words he was trying to write. He looked at those present and summarised his marriage in a single sentence: 'It started with a pen that wrote, and ended with one that didn't.'

Their relationship had begun in Izmir with a note written by Latife; Mustafa Kemal had expressed his delight by kissing the gold pen she'd used.

The task of presenting the divorce document in Izmir fell on Ali Rıza Bey, who was a close friend of Mustafa Kemal and married to Talia Hanım, Latife's cousin; it was Mustafa Kemal who had introduced them. And now he needed Ali Rıza's assistance in his own divorce. But there was a big problem: Latife did not want a divorce. She had to be persuaded, which might explain why Mustafa Kemal had taken such pains over the document. Ali Rıza was accompanied by Vasıf Çınar, the ambassador to Prague, and the two men finally convinced Latife to accept. Contrary to the popular belief, Latife was not divorced by an ordinary bulletin despatched to the Anatolian Agency; she made Mustafa Kemal sweat it out.

What Mehmet Sadık Öke heard from his grandmother VeciHe was this:

My grandmother says that the Paşa had sent a private letter to Latife Hanım along with the divorce document. The letter was very emotional, explaining how, despite being very much in love still, reasons known only to the two of them made the continuation of this marriage impossible. He wrote of his conviction that a woman who had deserted her home, taking her private possessions and jewellery, had no intention of returning, that this was way beyond a momentary bout of anger and that they would be happier apart despite still loving each other.

My aunt would have accepted the divorce. Resistance would have placed the Paşa in an impossible situation. He would then have to divorce my aunt Latife *in absentia*, causing a massive scandal. Latife Hanım would never do this to the Paşa. She saw the divorce as her duty to the state, a necessary evil to the survival of the Turkish Republic and the good of the Paşa, as well as his well-being.

Although Mustafa Kemal had originally written, 'I thought it expedient to release you,' he subsequently altered this text. The announcement text eventually read:

We have come to a decision to conclude our marriage of two and a half years with Uşşakizade Latife Hanım. I presented the aforementioned lady with a divorce document on 5 August 1341 [AD 1925]. I hereby plead and present the information to the government.

This final document referred to a consensual divorce and not to Mustafa Kemal divorcing Latife summarily. Evidently, the president was unwilling to be seen as a man who repudiated his wife with the customary proclamation: 'You're dismissed.'

His painstaking attention to fine detail did little to convince the world press or biographers. The fact that Mustafa Kemal divorced his wife with a government decree in the summer of 1925, when the Civil Code was imminent, was viewed as a scandal.

There were other issues that needed resolving: the return of Latife's goods and alimony. A draft document found amongst Mustafa Kemal's effects indicates he had intended to return the piano, the silverware and carpets. The engagement rings and diaries would be returned, but bedroom furniture and certain other objects would remain. The most important aspect of this note in my view concerns books. Mustafa Kemal states that he kept some, but would return others should Latife want them. His message proves the distinguished provenance of some of the valuable books still in Çankaya: Latife had brought them there.

She took approximately 20,000 liras from the safe when she left. Mustafa Kemal had scribbled, 'They should fear no evil from me,' but then crossed it out. Latife refused his offer of TL500 per month in alimony.

Her sister Vecihe would later comment how they had married like westerners and divorced like orientals.

When they married in January 1923, they had made their vows before a *müftü* and drawn up a marriage certificate. How did the dissolution of such a marriage by a government decree stand up in the eyes of the law and the prevailing conditions of the time?

Mustafa Kemal divorced Latife just when a new Civil Code was being prepared. Conservatives were reluctant to relinquish hundreds of years of supremacy over women, and so resisted such fundamental change to the Family Law. Mustafa Kemal's apparent departure in his private life from his radical modernisation in the public arena found little favour in the West.

Latife, who had worked so hard for a Civil Code, had been 'dismissed' quite unexpectedly.

In order for this divorce to find acceptance in public opinion, Latife had to be presented as a 'bad' woman. Bad enough to deserve this divorce. This might well lie at the core of the smear campaign that has persisted for so many years.

However much Lord Kinross might find the break-up reasonable, it is the manner of the divorce that he objects to:

> If there was an irony in the failure of the marriage – the failure of two headstrong oriental natures to come to terms with the give-and-take problems of a western relationship – there was an irony too in the manner of its end. In divorcing her, he reverted to the letter of Muslim law, which allowed a man to repudiate his wife without question.

He then points to the imminence of the Civil Code, 'A few months later his action would not have been possible.'[11]

'You ask how I could possibly divorce you? Very simply ...'

Mustafa Kemal must have occasionally wondered how he had commanded armies but failed to manage a woman. Many years later, during a relaxed chat on the Dolmabahçe Palace balcony, Atatürk suddenly mentioned his own marriage.

> The really strange thing was, Latife Hanım never believed I would leave her. Once, when the topic had somehow come up, she tried to point out a break-up would have been unthinkable. 'How come? How could the world famous Mustafa Kemal divorce his wife before the entire world?' She must have supposed the procedure

would have made it virtually impossible.

I replied, 'Very simply. I would not wish it in the first place. But if we had to, I'd ring the bell, summon Tevfik, my private secretary, dictate a couple of lines to go to the Anatolian Agency: "The Gazi has divorced his wife," and that would be that.' Latife Hanım was taken aback, 'So simple as that?' And I repeated, 'Yes, so simple as that.'

For someone as well versed as Latife in the stories of Henry VIII and his wives, or how Napoleon divorced Joséphine, *not* to have considered the possibility that Mustafa Kemal might one day divorce her is out of the question. But she did trust he would not divorce her just when he was trying to extricate the country from an unjust legal tradition that had prevailed for hundreds of years.

How badly Latife misjudged him: when Mustafa Kemal did indeed divorce her, it was by a government decree, a mere couple of lines, just as he had said.

Reverberations

A report despatched to the US Department of State

The breach between the presidential couple occupied the diplomatic circles in Ankara as detailed reports were despatched to their own countries. Shelton David Crosby, the US embassy chargé d'affaires, sent the following letter:[1]

> The Honourable
> Secretary of State
> Frank B. Kellogg
> Washington
> 10 August 1925

Dear Sir,

I hereby respectfully present to the attention of the Department unconfirmed, yet in our view, reliable rumours of a serious rift between President Mustafa Kemal and his wife Latife Hanım.

According to reports, following a bitter debate between the two, Latife Hanım wired her mother Mrs Uşşakizade in Izmir, asking to be collected, as she no longer could abide living in Ankara. Her mother arrived at Çankaya, stayed one night and returned to Izmir on the following day, taking her daughter along. Latife Hanım, who did not wish to see her husband prior to her departure, was reportedly seen off at the station by cabinet ministers in Ankara, led by İsmet Paşa, who tried unsuccessfully to convince her to stay. Her departure from Ankara has been explained as a change of climate necessitated by a fever she had contracted in order to prevent a scandal. She had gone to Izmir in the summer, but always accompanied by the president in the past. Mustafa Kemal is reported to have spent the morning of the day of her departure at his beloved farm, thus avoiding a confrontation with his wife. Mustafa Kemal's break-up with his wife is reported to have disturbed political circles in Ankara. There has been no news in the press about these developments, with the exception of Latife Hanım visiting her family in Izmir. Another cause of the rift is given as the failure of Latife Hanım to have borne the president an heir.

Shelton David Crosby
Chargé d'Affaires

A report by the Austrian chargé d'affaires

We have another document from the same time: the Austrian chargé d'affaires at the embassy in Turkey sent the following report on 20 August:[2]

Dear Herr Doktor Heinrich Mataja, Foreign Secretary:
Rumours had been rife for some time that the marriage that began in January 1923 between Gazi Mustafa Kemal Paşa and Uşşakizade Latife Hanım, daughter of a wealthy Izmir merchant, had not been without discord or strife; in fact, there had been highly discreet predictions that the marriage would soon come to an end. That the anticipated divorce, when it finally came, was announced only by an official bulletin, to which no Turkish newspaper dared to add a single syllable, is indicative of the severity of control exercised on the public agenda. This event, highly germane to the internal political developments in the country, has been accepted with no comment. Foreign journalists here have also felt the need to exercise maximum possible caution in following the events; to the extent that the *Neue Freie Presse* correspondent, offered a commission to write a serial on the subject, has not dared to accept lest he risk expulsion.

The background to the event is equally thought-provoking.
With your kind permission, I need to explain something of Mme Kemal to better understand the most recent argument between the

couple.

Latife Hanım has had the benefit of an exemplary education as the daughter of wealthy parents. She can speak and write all the major cultural languages of the world and knows Europe very well by first-hand experience; and beyond all this, she is extremely intelligent, smart and beautiful. Every single European who has had the opportunity to meet her praises the depth of her knowledge. Her personality, naturally, is complemented by certain tendencies that follow a parallel course with the majority of these virtues: a desire for supremacy, and the unjustly disdainful treatment of people she did not take to were indubitably dangerous characteristics in respect of her relations with her husband and his close circles. That being said, she was not entirely unjustified in her rejection of those she suspected of exercising a harmful influence on her husband. Around a month earlier, at the presidential residence in Çankaya, near Ankara, a supper party was given, attended by İsmet Paşa, Chief of the General Staff Fevzi Paşa, other dignitaries and a young piano virtuoso. After the supper, Mustafa Kemal invited his wife to play them some good music. She pleaded to be excused due to exhaustion, and Mustafa Kemal turned to the abovementioned pianist; at this time, Latife Hanım may have spoken out of turn. At the end of the piece, Mustafa Kemal congratulated the pianist provocatively by kissing him on the forehead. That was when Latife Hanım's patience ran out, and she berated the Gazi harshly before their guests. What then ensued is not only startling, but also apposite to showing the Gazi's character. He got up without a single word and slapped his wife noisily. The hand Latife Hanım raised in defence accidentally scratched the Paşa's cheek. Other incidents are also rumoured to have occurred. Latife Hanım left Çankaya that very night and returned to her parents' side in Izmir by the early train the following morning.

The Gazi issued instructions for immediate divorce proceedings, and the divorce was effected on 5 August.

The reflection of all these developments was the official bulletin dated 13 August, which I had referred to above, and a copy of which is enclosed for your perusal.

As in many similar instances, it is very difficult to come to a definite judgment on who the guilty party actually is. What is definite is that Latife Hanım may have overestimated her own power, to the extent that she has interfered in events for personal reasons. She had, for instance, engineered the appointment of her brother İsmail to the Turkish embassy in Paris without her husband's knowledge. The Gazi Paşa only became apprised of it when he saw the request for İsmail's dismissal – on grounds of a public argument with his wife in a bar that ended with him flinging a champagne bottle at her head. As one might expect, similar incidents, on the political level as well as administrative, had long been used injudiciously by court plotters – in a manner of speaking – hostile to Latife Hanım to sour her husband against her.

On the other hand, a claim that Latife Hanım's otherwise numerous beneficial influences on her husband failed to compensate for these regrettable incidents would be spurious indeed. There now stands no obstacle before these men of ill repute who surround the president and who were referred to in this report. The 'Saviour's' limitless popularity, gained both during the war of independence and thereafter, may now be vulnerable. The consequences of such damage would be momentous in respect of Turkey's internal political developments. It was this concern for the gravity of the situation that has prompted me to report on the unfortunate events displayed above.

Dear Secretary, please allow me to express my deepest loyalty,

Chargé d'affaires

Reactions to the divorce

The divorce divided their close circles; some pronouncing, 'She tormented her husband, and he divorced her,' and others lamenting, 'What a disaster!' İsmet Paşa and his wife, Mevhibe, were disconsolate at the break-up; he wore dark glasses for days afterwards.[3]

Fethi and Galibe Okyar, who were in Paris, were deeply troubled when they heard. The letter Galibe wrote Latife is still preserved by the Turkish History Institute.

Fahrettin Altay Paşa noted, 'The most deplorable event of the year was Atatürk's separation from Latife Hanım,' in referring to 1925 in his memoirs.[4]

Rauf Orbay, whose path had diverged from Mustafa Kemal's in those years, also describes the divorce as a great misfortune.

'She should have been more accommodating ...'

Latife's youngest sister, Rukiye, believed her eldest sister should have been much more accommodating. She once confided in her friend Leman Karaosmanoğlu:

> You know, Leman, my sister made a huge mistake. If I had been Atatürk's wife, I would have said, 'Love, my darling ... Love the entire universe ... Love, you deserve everything. You deserve it all.' And I never would have made a fuss.

Münci Uşşakizade commented, 'My sister is a wonderful woman. But she treated the Gazi as she would have an ordinary man. She didn't appreciate she had married a rare genius. That's why she was a handicap for him.'[5]

Sabiha Gökçen, one of Atatürk's adopted daughters, said, 'Had Latife Hanım been a little more patient, more clever, please note, I do not call her unintelligent, this marriage might have lasted an entire lifetime.'[6]

Her uncle Halit Ziya offers an insightful description of Latife's character:

> The entire family agreed upon Latife's intelligence, congeniality and easy-going nature; she was equipped with deep knowledge and culture, a unique girl, the pride of any family. She would have temporary outbursts, like storms in the springtime. I had, on one occasion, felt the need to illuminate and caution her.[7]

Many years later, Latife herself confided in Şehvar Çağlayan as she assessed her marriage. 'If I knew then what I know now, I would have managed things much more differently. We were surrounded by so much corruption, and I was too young to give battle.'[8]

Lord Kinross, Villalta and von Mikusch ...

Male biographers of Atatürk all believe Latife's petulance and dominating manner tried her husband's patience one too many times and so she deserved to be divorced.

Lord Kinross states:

> Latife, as befitted a western wife, would not be mastered. Nor had she the feminine tact with which to dissemble, to manage him without seeming to do so. She nagged at him and criticised him.

Adding that they had begun to offend each other, and with Latife's jealousy more than he could tolerate, he says Mustafa Kemal decided the end had come.[9]

The Argentine diplomat Jorge Blanco Villalta claims Latife went way beyond her position as the first lady of Turkey in the implementation of reforms and, in particular, in respect to women's emancipation, chafing at being restricted to her own circle with so much yet to achieve. He comments, 'so she wasn't as bright as she appeared,' and adds:

> Arguments had begun, and a distinct chill had set in. Latife had increasingly become more domineering. She demanded instant obeisance to her commands. She ordered her husband's life and habits around.[10]

Von Mikusch says:

> Latife was too able a woman to be satisfied with the narrow round of household duties, but she was not able enough to keep hold of her husband by her distinctively feminine endowments and make

up to him for what he lacked and needed. She seems also to have taken very badly with his autocratic mode of existence, wishing to impose restrictions on him, just as she had done at Izmir, when she deprived him of everything 'that was likely to injure his health'. This may have been the final cause of the breach between them. Just as suddenly as he had carried through the marriage ceremony, he wrote her a letter of divorcement – the ancient Mohammedan law still held – and Latife had to leave Çankaya.[11]

Joséphine and Latife

The Turkish press might have restricted itself to the briefest news report, but the world press dedicated hundreds of column inches to the divorce of Mustafa Kemal and his 'ultramodern wife'. The consensus was that the progressive Latife, the symbol of modernisation in the battle against reactionism, had been sacrificed due to her leading position in the women's movement of Turkey.

Surely these reports must have reached Turkey at the time, and yet none made it into books on Latife published in the country. This may be your first opportunity to read these comments that are valuable documents in their own right. In the year following the divorce, leading English language publications kept the topic alive: the *New York Times*, the *Washington Post*, the *Toronto Daily Star* and *Chicago Daily Tribune*, and *Time* magazine.

Some of the commentary concerned the manner of the divorce: the government decree divorce Mustafa Kemal resorted to was deemed quite bizarre, hardly flattering to the image of the new Turkey. The first lady of Turkey was referred to in political terms: 'Mustafa Kemal divorced his suffragette wife by decree.' The foreign press claimed politics had played a part in the divorce; an interview Latife gave soon after her return to Izmir must have played its part. She likened their divorce to that of Napoleon and Joséphine.

A period of suffering lay in wait for Latife. She was quick-tempered, quick to flare up and equally quick to calm down. Her fury had abated by the time she reached Izmir; all that remained was remorse. She blamed herself for this outcome and thought she'd been 'childish'.

The White Mansion was full of memories, every single room bringing back so much. She could not bear to step on to the veranda where she and Mustafa Kemal had first met or to look at his oil portrait hanging on the wall. The place where once sweet nothings had been whispered now appeared sepulchral. She could not believe what had happened. Latife, her mother and grandmother all wept together.

The English, French and German newspapers she could not bear to look at all spoke of her. The American press, in particular, heaped praises on her and kept the divorce constantly on the agenda.

She was still reeling with the shock when the doorbell rang one day: an American journalist had arrived. We do not know whether this was a previously arranged appointment or whether he'd simply turned up on spec. In any case, she admitted him and spoke at length. This riveting interview, never published in Turkey, reveals not a woman defeated, but one who is determined to live on. Let us all lend an ear to her frank views published first in the *Toronto Daily Star*, then in the *New York Times* and finally in *Time* magazine:

WIFE OF MUSTAFA KEMAL IS SACRIFICED TO AMBITION

Latife Hanım, the beautiful wife whom Mustafa Kemal, the ruler of Turkey, has by presidential decree set aside, declares in an exclusive interview that she is a modern Joséphine.

Her husband allowed himself to be persuaded, she declares, that she stood in the way of his career, and like Napoleon, he sacrificed his love to his ambition.

'It is terrible to have one's dream of happiness thus shattered; to have all the romance go out of one's life so suddenly.'

This was the passionate comment of Latife Hanım, the newly divorced wife of Kemal Paşa, the first president of Turkey, speaking of the decree, which has just dissolved her marriage.

She was visibly affected. Though she left Istanbul some time ago with a dread of impending shipwreck of her married happiness hanging over her, it was clear that she had always hoped that 'things would come right'[12]

The Canadian paper makes the assumption that she went to Istanbul before moving back to Izmir.

'It is a case of Napoleon and Joséphine over again. I loved my husband and did all in my power to help him realise his ambitions for himself and the country. Our union stands in the way of his further progress, and as in the case of Joséphine, it is the woman who must be sacrificed.'

'But I have no complaints. If by parting I can make for his happiness I will be proud, but just a little heartsore at the time when I think of what has been.'

Madam Kemal has all the presence one would expect in a woman who has played such a great part in the history of Turkey and in the advancement of her husband's political fortunes. A beautiful woman, and sturdily built, she has a masterful manner about her, and an evident mastery of the methods of public business.

Time magazine added on 24 August 1925:

'It's a pity, isn't it, this parting of two whom Allah seemed to have brought together to work His will by a harmonious, happy association?'

'Ours was a love match even in the sense in which you understand the term in the West. My husband and I were as happy as a man and woman could be in our Garden of Eden until the serpent entered.'

'Who was the serpent? I can see the question shaping in your mind, but I cannot answer it. That is my secret and it will die with me. Suffice it for the world that the point was reached where my husband was brought to the belief that he had to choose between his partner and his future. He chose.'

'There is one thing I must say,' she went on. 'This is not the end of my career. The days when women died of broken hearts are long since past.'

'There is no better balm for a bruised heart than hard work, and I shall throw myself into such work as I can do for my country and my sex from now on. I will show them that it takes much to break the spirit of a woman such as me.'

The *New York Times* journalist who went after the secret she had vowed to keep all her life comes to the conclusion that the divorce was the consequence of the greatest peril Turkey had faced since Gallipoli, as he comments on the political environment in Ankara:

Statesmen and publicists sought the secret which the Lady Latife carried locked in her breast from the Presidential Palace in Ankara to the home of her father in Izmir. Any attempt to solve this riddle is but guesswork, yet, despite her quoted reference to 'who was the serpent', gathering storms around Mosul and the borders of Iraq may possibly provide the answer.

32

Separation

Several people attempted to bring about a reconciliation in the early stages of the break-up. Vecihe comments on Latife immediately following the divorce:

> Latife Hanım was desperately heartbroken about having lost the one man she had found compatible. Her immediate environment was divided. One group wanted to bring Latife Hanım and Atatürk back together again. The other, to cement the separation. How many times have I heard with my own ears, Nuri Conker saying, 'C'mon, Paşam, who needs a nagging woman? Let's have a drink instead ...'?

Latife slowly began to visualise her new life after receiving the divorce document sent to her father's home. There was so much suffering ahead. One moment she stood at the zenith, the next, she was reduced to the status of the woman 'sent to her father's home' by the ruler of the country.

Her father was in Trieste at the time of the divorce; Latife had been reluctant to inform him. Hearing the news upon his return, he wrote a letter of farewell to Mustafa Kemal:

> I have been made aware of your command in respect of my daughter upon my return from Trieste on Thursday.
>
> Our – now dispossessed – esteem and fondness for your noble person, our Venerable Leader and the Great Saviour of the country and the people, has always grown and shall continue to do so. I should like to present my gratitude for gracious concessions in the past with our occasional requests and beg your

illustrious favour, Your Excellency.
 Uşşakizade Muammer
 16 August 1925[1]

Two highly complimentary letters sent by an American congressman that arrived around then, inviting Latife to lecture in Paris and New York, perked her up a little: 'You have attracted the attention of the entire world with your intelligence, grace, courage and sparkle; what you have achieved for your country at such a young age has conferred an unforgettable status upon you.'

Her films were shown in cinemas across America; hundreds of news items appeared about her; and were she to accept, she would do enormous service to her country as one of the leading women in the world. Latife would earn $100,000 from these paid lectures, and she would attract as much attention as Marie Curie. The topic was already determined: Turkey, women and the world, yesterday, today and tomorrow.

The letters waxed lyrical, but Latife was of two minds. As the divorced former first lady of Turkey, she had to weigh up all foreign trips and lecture invitations.

The letter she sent Mustafa Kemal

Mustafa Kemal visited Izmir in October 1925. This trip tormented Latife beyond description, and unable to control herself, she wrote at some length of her feelings for her former husband. Let us read some passages from this letter dated 12 October:

> My Great Leader,
> Kastamonu, Bursa, Balıkesir, Akhisar, Manisa and finally my beautiful hometown, virtuous Izmir, redolent of perennial roses. An eternally vanquished and devoted lover, dedicated to you with all her emotions, ideas and whole existence!
> [...] you entered Izmir at the head of the army. Do you remember? The Turkish maiden weeping, enslaved in black chains. You made

straight for her. You made her the 'victory girl', the symbol of Izmir whom you'd liberated.

Yet you, who unshackled the chains on her wrists and ankles ... you locked her heart up for ever.

Yes, victory is in love with you, great man.

[...] and yes, I hereby repeat the sentence I had originally written, sitting at the feet of that noble lady: 'No power can drive me away from your blue eyes. So long as all Izmir swears allegiance to you, and you return this affection, I consider myself a member of this flock.'

[...] No other woman in history or anywhere in the world has enjoyed such ecstasy as I have with you. Rest assured of this fact! I write not to beg compassion. Passion, not compassion. Isn't that so, my great leader?

[...] Let no one be bereft of you. It is so dreadful ... Please allow me. Allow me to repeat my favourite habit, the one I desperately miss, let me kiss your sacred hand ...

Let me raise it to my pure and honest forehead.

From Latif

She turned down Mustafa Kemal's offers of financial assistance, claiming she did not need it. At first, she thought she could get a job. Sadly, this was a dream. She informed Mustafa Kemal of her trials in a series of notes.

These were conveyed to Mustafa Kemal by their mutual friend Rıza Bey in October 1925. She was asking for a position as a teacher in a school or a secretarial job in an embassy or other similar civil servant's job. We do not know if the letter and the notes were all sent together.

General Fahrettin Altay, a guest at Çankaya around that time, writes in his diary:

She dared not go out lest she face insults, and was offended by how some acquaintances she met by chance turned their faces away. A job would keep her occupied. Atatürk related all this quite calmly and equivocally, but refrained from announcing his decision. He turned to Afet Hanım [İnan] and told her to start teaching now; he would send her back to Paris later to complete her education.[2]

He adds that Mustafa Kemal changed the subject after the letter was read.

Latife evidently never received a response to her requests for a job. Would all doors now shut on the face of this young woman who was so well educated and who was so willing to do so much? Would she be left to her own devices, alone with her experience, skills and energy?

Let us go back once more to the world press of the time. A news item with the headline 'Kemal Pasha's Divorce' appeared in the *Washington Post* on 16 November 1925; it advances yet another angle:

> It is said now that Latife Hanım, former wife of Kemal, will contest her divorce by the paşa in the Turkish courts. She was the first really emancipated woman of Turkey, and inspired her husband to abolish the Mohammedan divorce and put into effect the existing marriage law of Turkey.
>
> The decree of divorce was issued not by a Turkish court, but by Kemal's own declaration, permissible only under the old Mohammedan law, which had been nullified. Reports from Turkey say his former wife and her friends are preparing to make her effort to set aside her divorce a real test of validity of the marriage law that was enacted largely because of her great personal influence.

We do not know whether she ever appealed, although it is not hard to imagine the thought must have occurred. The *Washington Post* also commends the hat reform, as it criticises the practice of unilateral divorce by men in Turkey.

> Now the hitherto undisputed privilege of putting aside his wife at will is challenged. The wheels of progress do move in the confines beyond the Bosphorus.

With the Civil Code still in feverish consultation, as yet to appear before the assembly, there was little Latife could actually do just then. But a presumption of common law must have been the starting point for the newspapers: by interpreting the reforms already implemented, they might have assumed Islamic laws to have been superseded, thus opening up the way for her to contest the divorce. A draft bill – one that would relieve Latife and all women in Turkey – was in fact presented to the assembly on 20 December, one month after the publication of this item.

Suppose Martha Washington were like Latife ...

The *New York Times* revisited Latife and Mustafa Kemal's divorce nearly a year later, on 6 June 1926, in an article by S. T. Williamson:

STRANGER THAN FICTION

He is called the George Washington of his country. The foremost military genius of his compatriots, he raised and led an army of embattled farmers, expelled the invader from the land, freed the country of European domination and then became the first president of a young, rough, struggling republic.

But no one ever likened his wife to Martha Washington. Suppose Washington had seen Martha Custis for the first time when he entered Yorktown at the head of his ragged Continentals. Suppose they had been united in marriage a few weeks later, not by a clergyman, but by the Town Clerk, hastily summoned from his records to the Custis home. Furthermore, suppose President Washington's wife, the first lady of the land, had discarded the voluminous, conventional costume of her sex and appeared publicly in riding breeches upon such occasions as when the president inspected New York's militia.

Then, if this is not enough, imagine George Washington not only sanctioning his wife's advanced ideas, but even echoing them in messages to Congress. Finally, suppose a Congress and nation largely made up of farmers, a people for centuries hostile to progress, had placidly accepted the modern ways of George and Martha Washington.

All of this is evidence that, although history repeats itself, it is dangerous to draw historic parallels.

[...]

In fact, to continue the Washington parallel would hamper the telling of the story of the wife of a man who is still the leader of his country. She was born in a villa at the head of a flight of a thousand steps, high above the city where the figs come from. Her father was a powerful merchant, a man who knew the outside world and declined to bring up his daughter according to strict Muslim customs. As a girl she learned French in Paris and English in London. In intellect she was a cosmopolite, but in spirit she remained Turkish.

[...] Theirs was a modern wedding, but their divorce was according to good old Muslim custom. The only formality was for the man to announce that he had put aside his wife. Thus the exponents of New Turkey and of the emancipation of Turkish women separated in the manner sanctioned by the past they so earnestly sought to overthrow.

Even now the former wife of the President of Turkey declines to look upon her experiences in a modern light, for she has refused to write a book about them. Yet, perhaps because she is a woman, she would speak of them, for –

The Ankara Government has refused a passport to enable Latife Hanım, divorced wife of Mustafa Kemal, to visit Europe and America on a lecture tour.

A letter Latife wrote to her former husband on 22 March 1926 reveals a woman on the brink of suicide. It reflects the plaintive unhappiness of a woman left to flounder amid a maelstrom of gossip, and reminds Mustafa Kemal of his duty. ... Latife tells him that he's turned a blind eye to the belittlement of a woman who views herself as an integral part of him.

My great leader, irreplaceable Paşa,

If only you knew just how much I miss you. How I thirst for the might and warmth of the pensive light emanating from your eyes.

For your attractive, enchanting voice, that stentorian voice that overwhelms the listener, kindles the greatest of nationalist passion and directs towards the hardest of objectives ...

If only you knew just how bereft I am, [...] how desolate.

Being left without you ... What utter destitution ... What a great disaster. I am living this with all my being.

Paşam. The abyss beside me is deep and dangerous enough to make the most robust of people of the highest character reel with dizziness. Have no doubt. I am fearful of this abyss. I stare at it. My soul is hungry, I am devastated, but I look upon you though you are so far away.

Oh my handsome Paşa. Are you well? How is your health? Are you looking after yourself? Are they looking after you well? Oh, would that I could see you but once, I would rest easy. There exists a poor 'rose' that you plucked from the victorious fields of Izmir, a Turkish girl you appreciated for one day, respected, shed tears for once and loved, albeit for a brief moment. She belongs to you alone. I beg of you! You've faded her smiling face. You've left her homeless and destitute ...

You've flung her into the maelstrom of gossip.

Please pay respect to her memory, if you do nothing else. Don't let her suffer insults or contempt whilst you protect the children left to your patronage from a different era! Because ... She belongs to you, whatever may have happened! You possess superhuman faculties that sense and express others' wishes before even they themselves know them!

My despair and grief are bottomless. Please give me permission ... Let me go and declare to the entire universe this fact: 'My tiny heart is a temple. Therein burns a flame. A flame called the love of Mustafa Kemal. I am a creature who lives with and for this love alone. My only path is the one he will indicate!'

From Latif

Reşat Kaynar, whose duty as an archive expert entailed reading Latife's private letters, does remember Mustafa Kemal issuing a permit for her to travel to Europe for treatment. 'He gave his permission under the strict proviso that she wasn't to talk to anyone.'[3]

Foreign papers frequently published references to restrictions placed on Latife's ability to travel abroad in June 1926, claiming she was prevented from accepting offers of lectures and books.

Latife Hanım is reluctant to apply for a passport that would enable her to attend lectures planned to take place in the USA in an effort to avoid any allegations of criticising her former husband or the régime.[4]

Whether she genuinely applied for a passport just then or whether this was pure speculation on the part of the foreign press, we do not know. Ankara's attitude must have exacerbated her own doubts. Her niece Dilek Bebe says, 'She received lecture invitations from around the world, proposals for her to write and lecture at universities. But they wouldn't let her.'[4]

Latife was considering applying for a passport just before an incident that would shake the political life of Turkey to the core.

June 1926: Assassination plot in Izmir

As Mustafa Kemal was preparing to set off for Izmir on 14 June 1926, crushing news arrived by telegram. Kâzım Dirik, governor of Izmir, related the discovery of an assassination plot and was asking the Paşa to delay his trip.

The alleged leaders of the plot were captured in Izmir later that day: Ziya Hurşit, an impassioned orator of the Second Group who had led the opposition in the previous parliament, and three hitmen. The plan, it was claimed, was that as the hitmen attacked Mustafa Kemal, Ziya Hurşit would create a panic, thus enabling the killers to get away. Universal outrage paved the way for the decision to try the conspirators at the Independence Tribunal, which lost no time in rounding up the alleged suspects. The targets were the MPs of the dissolved Progressive Republican Party and leading names in the pre-republican era

Committee of Union and Progress. Former ministers, MPs and even
some of Mustafa Kemal's brothers-in-arms were arrested, all accused of
involvement with the plot.

Amongst those arrested were Ali Fuat Cebesoy and Kâzım
Karabekir, celebrated commanders of the National Struggle. Rauf
Orbay was nowhere to be found. Halide Edib and her husband, Adnan
Adıvar, had gone abroad in 1925.

The Izmir Independence Tribunal convicted thirteen people as conspirators, and they were hanged early in the morning on the streets and
squares in which the assassination would have been staged. It was only
thanks to the intervention of İsmet Paşa that the generals were acquitted.

The Ankara Independence Tribunal opened on 2 August and
tried former Committee of Union and Progress leaders who were
charged with attempting to change the constitution and disband the
Grand National Assembly of Turkey. The verdict was announced on
26 August: four Unionists, former minister of finance Cavit included,
were sentenced to death.

MPs, former ministers, governors and bureaucrats were accused,
were given no access to defence counsel, were tried by a council that
was not made up of lawmen and were sent to their deaths in Izmir and
Ankara.

Latife in Istanbul

It is thanks to an American newspaper that we learn of Latife's move
from Izmir to Istanbul in June 1926, in those heavily charged times:

> Latife Hanım's return to Istanbul has revived speculation as to
> why Mustafa Kemal divorced her. Her mouth is sealed, and the
> president of New Turkey has never seen fit to discuss the reason.
>
> Older Turkish women are inclined to believe it was because she
> was childless. All Turks want children, especially sons, and Latife
> lived with Kemal two years without giving him an heir.
>
> But younger women, especially women who know more about
> modern politics, advance other reasons. Latife was not on good

terms with most of the politicians who surrounded her husband; she worshipped him and was so jealous of his entourage that she is alleged to have opened telegrams and letters addressed to Kemal.[5]

Mustafa Kemal was no emperor, and the reason for the divorce was not the lack of an heir, but such speculation would not have been a major surprise.

Latife was an important 'celebrity', whom the entire world expected to act as the spokeswoman for the process of change in Turkey. This is the reason she commanded international media attention and continued to receive invitations well into the 1930s. Turkey might have dismissed her in one fell swoop, but the world press viewed her as a woman wronged and stood by her side.

Did she have visitors?

Who, if anyone, called upon her in those days? Rıza Nur, a cabinet minister, suggests that Chief Private Secretary Tevfik and Mahmut Soydan, MP for Siirt, were amongst those who did call on her, although his view is that these were hardly friendly calls. Rather, they were made with the express aim of 'cautioning her not to speak out'.

He himself tried very hard to break through her guard:

I approached the subject from so many angles, but she never said a thing. I stayed deliberately for hours. Her father didn't leave us alone for a moment, cautious man. Not everyone dared go visit her. I went back for a second visit. I tried once more to elicit something from her. Again, I failed. Poor thing saw no one. She was unable even to go out. So hard. Only yesterday she enjoyed absolute authority, basking in ceremony and applause. Now she's no more than an ordinary individual ... The Dual Schools used to be called Latife Hanım Schools. They carved the name out the day after the divorce. She was so offended when she heard this. I told her she needs a change of air, but she wouldn't listen. She's lost weight, grown sallow; she looked nearly on the verge of TB.[6]

All that we ever knew of Latife's second life was this: the recluse, the deserted, devastated woman! Long discussions with her great-nephew Muammer Erboy revealed a completely different Latife Hanım: a lady who was determined to transcend her pain, who spent her time with her nearest and dearest, and enjoyed a lifestyle well beyond the reach of many of us. A Latife Hanım who constantly followed the problems of Turkey and the world, who retired to her library to read avidly, who wrote, who might have outwardly erased Mustafa Kemal from her soul, but who always cherished him on the inside.

A new home for the Uşşakizades

Her family purchased a four-storey wooden mansion overlooking the Bosphorus in Ayaspaşa: this was one of the finest houses in Istanbul, right in the heart of the city. They clearly had no intention of withdrawing from the city or from people.

Three of Latife's siblings had all married whilst she lived at Çankaya: Ömer, İsmail and Vecihe.

Latife lived on the top floor of her father's home in Ayaspaşa, with her close circle of family and friends and with her memories. She spent many hours in her room and took long walks in the garden overlooking the Bosphorus and shaded by magnolia trees. Looking out of her window, she could see Mustafa Kemal arriving at, and departing from, Dolmabahçe Palace. There were rumours that as she looked out for her former husband, the state kept a close eye on *her*.

Letters to Vasıf Çınar

We know well Latife's state of mind in the couple of years following the divorce. In the first letter she wrote to Vasıf Çınar, a former cabinet minister and a close friend, she refers to herself as Izmir's heartbroken daughter wasting away in heartache and anguish in a corner of Istanbul.

In this letter dated 21 August 1926, Latife describes herself as a creature on the verge of returning to the earth like an autumn leaf. She is obviously thinking of death. She also writes of her ailments physical and mental. She says she is ill disposed to part from all things Turkish, the language or the country. It appears therefore that the days of the unobtainable passport are well past. All the same, she vacillates between going and staying.

Expressing her grief in an elegant, profound and literary language, she summarises her tragedy, 'What a governess heartache is! If only you knew how much it continues to teach me ...' She then mentions how, although she once nearly succumbed to the clutches of that accursed sense of sorrow, she rose again and dreams of the day when she can disregard all worldly pain.

She addresses him in the formal 'you' throughout this letter.

Who was Vasıf Çınar and why did they correspond?

Like Latife, Vasıf Çınar was also an Izmir native. His father was from the Bedirhan family; his mother originally came from Crete, where he was born in 1896. He grew up in Izmir and joined the resistance. He, too, had read law, and he and Latife were nearly the same age. He had been elected in August 1923 and served as minister of education when Latife was in Çankaya. He was, in fact, the author and champion of the Unity in Education Bill, a reform that was close to Latife's heart.

The second letter she wrote to him is dated 10 December 1926. This letter heralds the emergence of a new Latife determined to live on, come what may:

> I appear before you today with renewed courage. This is because I have decided to follow the advice of those who concern themselves with me, and who want me to survive and seek serious treatment. I have been gravely ill of late. I have finally accepted the need to travel and undergo therapy abroad. I shall stay incognito to avoid any hassle. [...]
> Latife[7]

Latife's stay at the sanatorium appears to have coincided with Vasıf Çınar's tenure as the Turkish ambassador to Prague between June 1925

and December 1927. The letters she sent him from Tatra are signed
'Fatma Sadık'. Vecihe says, 'Atatürk preferred her to travel under an
assumed name so she could preserve her anonymity. It was on his wish
that her passport be made out to the name Fatma Sadık.'

Latife knew Europe well. Why, then, had she picked a sanatorium
in Tatra, close to Prague, and not somewhere else? Kafka, who died
in 1924, had stayed at a sanatorium in Tatra between 1921 and 1922.
His famous work *The Castle* was written during that stay, and he and
Milena had met up one last time when he was at the sanatorium. The
publication in 1925 of *The Trial* brought the writer to prominence, and
The Castle followed the following year. Latife might well have felt an
affinity with the author.

The letter she sent Vasıf Çınar on 26 January 1927 refers to a book
for children she was writing:

> I've been lying down for a week. I'm suffering with a mild case of
> Spanish flu. A second radiogram was taken this morning. They
> confirm that five weeks of concentrated therapy did indeed prove
> to be of benefit to me. All I wish for now is to distance myself from
> this place. I have read of Minister of Education Necati Bey's trip in
> the papers. Should I recover my health, I would present him with a
> teeny piece of work I have been working on for a long time and that I
> would hope to be of great service to the country. Naturally, my work
> is as diminutive as I am. But it will help nannies so much in teach-
> ing our beloved children the love of land and nation. So long as the
> ministry finds some value in indulging our feelings, that is.
> Fatma Sadık

If the Turkish History Institute had disclosed the 'Latife Hanım
Documents' in February 2005, we might all have had the opportunity
to read this 'teeny piece of work' that contained her views on the
Turkish education system.

A fourth letter, again signed 'Fatma Sadık', was dated 4 February
1927 and again posted from Tatra:

My Esteemed, Noble Brother,

[...] If a disaster victim such as me, floundering in an endless and exhausting abyss, were to manifest an excess of grief or excitement as she battles life unaided, it would behove refined, noble spirited persons to indulge her.

Fatma Sadık[8]

In her fifth letter, dated 25 February 1927, she wrote that she had gained four kilos and was tired of staying in a hospital. She was ready to return to life.

33

Tears in Mustafa Kemal's Blue Eyes

Latife felt very sorry for herself in the days immediately following the divorce: she called herself a disaster victim or a woman devastated. Mustafa Kemal, on the other hand, had been the petitioner: now a bachelor, a free man, he was released from the ties of marriage that had, on occasion, cramped his style. True, he had many a reform in the works, he had power, brothers-in-arms who did all he asked at once and countless admirers, but he was a man alone.

Was he happy with the decision he had taken? Most memoirs appear to avoid the subject.

The cavalry general Fahrettin Altay Paşa was the first Turkish commander to enter Izmir on 9 September 1922; he might well be the only person to have commented on Mustafa Kemal's life immediately after the divorce. He kept a diary throughout his eleven-day stay as a house guest at Çankaya. He emphasises how grief-stricken Mustafa Kemal was:

The saddest event of this year was the break-up of Atatürk and Latife Hanım. How this broke his heart and how he tried to put on a brave face were all too evident. He was heard crying in his room as he listened to a sad folk song, 'I've Turned into a Heartbroken Nightingale'.[1]

Mustafa Kemal's sister Makbule Atadan disagrees.

He wasn't one to cry easily. He kept his composure even in the most tragic moments. I remember he cried when our mother died. I've not known him to cry since then.[2]

Latife had people she could share her grief with, but Mustafa Kemal was not as fortunate.

Mustafa Kemal went to Izmir a few months after the divorce, and he took Fahrettin Altay along. The first officially recorded ball of the republican era was given in Izmir, almost as a taunt to Latife. This trip must have caused both parties enormous pain.

'We all feared he might have a breakdown!'

Fahrettin Altay candidly notes the general air of concern for Mustafa Kemal's mental health as he describes the remorseful husband who had just divorced his wife. He also credits Afet İnan, a young girl then sixteen, whom they met on the Izmir trip, with possibly preventing a mental breakdown. This newly qualified teacher was seated between Mustafa Kemal and Kâzım Özalp during the afternoon tea offered to the statesmen as they visited her school. Her family originally came from somewhere in the vicinity of Salonica, a fact of sufficient interest for Mustafa Kemal to introduce her to Fahrettin Altay:

> He introduced her to me with a 'Madam Teacher', and I greeted her with courtesy. He then began to speak of this very young, blonde and blue-eyed and polite young lady: 'Her family are very close to ours in Salonica, close enough to be relations. I'm delighted to have met her here. Her mother died, and her father married a young girl; so this lady had to start teaching to earn a living. She would love to continue her studies, but has not had the opportunity. She has accepted to become my daughter and come to Ankara. She will continue to teach and I will make sure she has the opportunity for further education.' We were all relieved that he had found a companion; to be honest, we all feared he might have a breakdown. This young lady, who prevented it, has done the country a great service.[3]

Fahrettin Altay started this diary on Friday 22 October 1925. Mme Baver, a tall and elegant fifty-five-year-old Swiss lady who moved in soon after Latife's departure, earned the rank of 'Office Manageress' from the general. She was apparently entrusted 'with raising Atatürk's daughters as European ladies'. Mustafa Kemal adopted four daughters, who also moved in around the same time.

The general writes of the times he accompanied Mustafa Kemal to parliament and when they ate together, and he offers insight into the parties at the residence, where there were new faces every night. He describes in great detail the dances, the guests, the food and even the pets in the garden. The dinner on his first night at the residence found its way into his diary:

> Atatürk himself fetched me to supper at eight thirty. There was music in the drawing room. He was sitting with the Swiss Madam and the four young girls he had adopted, chatting happily. There was a tumbler of rakı before him and some roasted chickpeas.

İsmet and Tevfik Rüştü Aras were also invited to supper that night. Tevfik Rüştü, accompanied by his wife and daughter, was in white tie and carried a collapsible silk top hat. Fahrettin Altay laments, 'So few of us knew about white ties and such hats at the time!' İsmet Paşa had come alone, as usual; Mevhibe had not accompanied her husband. Afet was also at the table, seated to the right of İsmet. Mme Baver and the little girls had all taken their places.

The menu consisted of soup, lamb steaks, gratin, aubergines, a creamy pudding and melon. Wine was offered with the meal and champagne at the end; evidently, Latife's housekeeping style had survived. After the meal, Mustafa Kemal danced the foxtrot with Mme Baver and then urged the cavalryman, who had never learned to dance, to ask Mme Baver to the floor. 'My youth had been spent in the East; so I was fated to dance my very first with this fifty-five-year-old lady,' Fahrettin Altay notes, before describing the breathtaking waltz Mustafa Kemal danced with Mme Baver.

Emel, Tevfik Rüştü's daughter, had long hair. Mustafa Kemal found it old-fashioned and insisted someone bob her hair then and there, after which he paid her a compliment: 'Look, much prettier now! You should never ignore fashion.'

İsmet was the first to beg his leave at midnight.

The void left behind by Latife Hanım was filled by the arrival of four daughters, Afet and Mme Baver ... One of the daughters was Sabiha of Bursa. The others' names are not noted. Rukiye and Nebile were adopted much later.

On 23 October, Fahrettin Paşa noted a walk in the garden with Muzaffer ADC to look at the rabbits, two bear cubs, two gazelles, one small monkey, peacocks and hens. Many fine types of pigeons flew in large wire coops. He writes of a few horses and some foals, and when he notes how he kissed and patted Sakarya, sadness permeates his tone:

> As Atatürk no longer had the time to look after them, these fine horses lacked the attention they deserved. They hadn't even left the stables in a long time.

Reading between the lines, he means no one looks after the horses since Latife's departure. Everyone knew Sakarya was Mustafa Kemal's engagement gift to Latife; no one was more likely to be sensitive to this purebred's plight than the cavalryman.

Vecihe says Latife despatched Sakarya back to Mustafa Kemal in a freight car with the explanation, 'The only person who deserves to ride him is you.'

Other changes were also taking place in Çankaya: Salih Bozok's wife and daughters had adopted European-style clothes and trendy hats. And as a stroll around town proved, they were only a minute proportion of Ankara people who had exchanged Ottoman-style headwear for hats; Fahrettin Altay struggled to recognise once familiar faces. Mustafa Kemal's appearance in a panama hat on 25 August on a trip to İnebolu had kindled a love of modern hats in men and women. The Hat Law would be passed on 25 November 1925.

White tie and evening dress for supper at Çankaya

Fahrettin Altay writes of the men who attended Çankaya suppers in white tie and of the ladies in evening dresses. These parties certainly disprove any earlier suggestion that Latife's attempts at introducing a formal protocol at Çankaya had somehow annoyed Mustafa Kemal.

The 23 October entry continues:

> Atatürk's daughters had surrounded him like a ring of flowers in their colourful silk frocks. Madam Baver also was very stylish, in a low-cut black evening gown with a fringed hem; she wore make-up and powder. Afet Hanım, also, looked very good in a black silk evening gown with gold embroidery.

The orchestra in the hall played waltzes and *zeybek*s, and everyone joined in the folk dances. The yawning madam was also relieved once the younger girls had gone up to bed.

Mustafa Kemal spoke to Fahrettin in an aside, and in French, referring to the sullen Afet: 'This girl is very bright, and she'll go far. I will give her a perfect education; I know she struggles to cope with my moods, but she'll get used to them.'

Mustafa Kemal pointed to Salih ADC dozing in a corner. The following act entertained them all. 'A handsome youth, waiter Saib, turned up in women's clothing and did a turn. It was like a modern version of the old street theatre, where men played women's parts, and it was received well,' writes the general.

Mustafa Kemal, who had been on his feet most of the time, sat down beside Afet on the sofa and repeated what he had said to Fahrettin earlier, albeit in a different tone:

'My daughter Afet loves me well and loves to learn. Some of my moods cause her concern, and she has every right. I, too, love her very much. I have noticed her aptitude, so I'll see to it that she has the best education possible, and will learn languages, too. She will be a leading lady in the future. The little ones, too, are my diamonds.'[4]

The party ended at 3 am.

The entry for 24 October refers to housekeeping standards slipping. The cheese offered at breakfast was of poor quality; Fahrettin Altay did not find it appropriate for Çankaya.

There was a supper party that night, too. İsmet Paşa was invited, but had pleaded to be excused as his wife was poorly. The guests were again in white tie and evening dress. There was wine but no champagne, and dancing and Turkish shows entertained the guests.

On 25 October, a plump little orphan named Ayşe joined the children in the residence.

On 26 October, someone mentioned Latife, who had asked Rıza Bey to convey some requests to her former husband. Mustafa Kemal remained mostly silent, but ordered Mahmut Bey to help his former father-in-law with his debts in Izmir.

Afet took Fahrettin Altay on a tour of the residence that day. The diary entry reveals that Mustafa Kemal had not changed the bedroom he had shared with Latife.

Facing us was Atatürk's largish bedroom, with extraordinarily ornate and valuable furniture. Two beds side by side, an en-suite bathroom, fully tiled, largish and spacious ...[5]

The young girls had rooms in the attic, and Afet had been allocated the bedroom on the right on the first floor landing, the room that faced Mustafa Kemal's.

That night, the younger girls were not invited to the table, and a young artist entertained the guests with Turkish and European acts. Mme Baver had been conspicuous by her absence for the last two days. Mustafa Kemal grumbled to Tevfik Rüştü, 'My former wife never found dusting beneath her; this one just gives herself airs and orders people about. Find some pretext and send her packing.'

The İnönü family had invited Fahrettin Altay to supper on the evening of 27 October. Mevhibe Hanım wore a dark dress with long sleeves and buttons all the way down with a tight black headscarf. The general found this outfit eminently suitable at a time of transition when the *çarşaf* was being discarded.

This diary comes to an end on 1 November 1925.

Latife had brought the family cook and a couple of servants to Çankaya. They, too, must have left when she did. Vedad, Halit Ziya's son, appears to have continued as secretary at Çankaya for a little longer.

I now turn to Halit Ziya, who relates a Çankaya evening without
Latife.

Vedad was playing the *Cavalliera Rusticana* as he 'had been ordered
to', when his father's pencilled note was handed out to Vedad during the
distribution of letters from Istanbul. Vedad stopped playing and began
to read. Mustafa Kemal was intrigued:

'Vedad! Is that a letter from your father? Let me see what he says!'

Mustafa Kemal carefully scanned these sheets, little graced by
literary style or merit – in Halit Ziya's words – and then kept them.
'Leave these with me!'

Halit Ziya continues:

Mustafa Kemal must have been highly impressed by the
instructions I had given my son and, deciding that the divorce did
not impinge upon the favour I had found with him, took special
pains to be nice to me whenever our paths crossed and always made
sure I was aware of his patronage of Vedad. He began manifesting
his favour by sending me a portrait immediately after the divorce,
and he showed his patronage of Vedad by appointing him to third
secretary at the embassy in London, deeming his further stay in
Ankara inappropriate.

Halit Ziya adds that he does not remember precisely what he had
written:

Strangely, news of that letter I wrote such a long time ago was so
distorted by the time it reached Latife's ears that it had quite the
opposite effect, creating animosity against Vedad and me. We've
never discussed this openly. Sometimes such problems arise in life
that any debate only makes things much worse.

Indeed, this letter would create a rift between Latife and Halit Ziya that
lasted many years.

Was there any talk against Latife in Çankaya?

The interview I had with Suna Güler, granddaughter of Ahmet

Ağaoğlu – and daughter of Tezer Taşkıran – revealed that Mustafa Kemal did not tolerate any criticism of Latife. She says:

> Just around the time he was going to finalise the divorce, someone in his close circle was heard denouncing Latife Hanım, referring to her as 'that bitch'. Mustafa Kemal went incandescent. 'She is a lady, and will always remain a lady.' My grandfather was present at the time.[6]

Süreyya, the older of the Ağaoğlu girls, is amongst the many to have remarked upon the changes that took place in Çankaya after the divorce. Latife and Mustafa Kemal had spent a good deal of time with this family, and the women were particularly good friends.

She adds, 'After he divorced his wife, we, too, found ourselves relegated to seeing him at formal receptions and balls,' and adds, 'Our friendship continued. Even if *we* no longer did, our father spent time with him frequently.'[7]

Mustafa Kemal moved into the new Çankaya residence in 1932, and the entire household was rearranged. The celebrated Istanbul furniture maker Psalti was commissioned to make his bedroom furniture. A green suite replaced Latife Hanım's blue in the drawing room.[8] The old residence still stands in the garden, its furnishings intact, a monument to old memories.

Vecihe refuses to shake Kılıç Ali's hand

A formal ball was given in Dolmabahçe Palace on the occasion of Mustafa Kemal's first visit to Istanbul in 1927. Mustafa Kemal expressly asked Vecihe and Hayri İlmen to attend. Vecihe had just arisen from her confinement and begged to be excused. Mustafa Kemal would not take no for an answer, so they had little choice but to go. This would be the first contact between the two families since the divorce.

Vecihe came face to face with Mustafa Kemal as she was entering the ballroom. He was accompanied, as ever, by Kılıç Ali, who held out his hand to her. She refused to extend hers, prompting Mustafa Kemal to remark, 'Birds of a feather, these two sisters ... You honour her because she stands here beside me, but she puts *you* in your place.'

They began to talk. When Mustafa Kemal complained, 'Vecihe, just look at the state of me!' she asked, 'But what is wrong, Paşam?'

'Look at me; no one to care for me ...'

Latife was living in Ayaspaşa at the time. Mustafa Kemal asked, meaning the Ayaspaşa house, 'She's there, isn't she?'

'Yes, Paşam, she is,' replied Vecihe.

'What a pity, huh, Vecihe?' he continued.

'Paşam,' she replied, 'this was your desire. No one is to blame.'

He berated himself in no uncertain terms, using some choice language.

Vecihe Hanım later related this exchange to her nearest and dearest.

Filling Latife's place in the protocol

Afet was sent to the Rochemont School in Lausanne to learn French. Upon her return in 1927, she enrolled at the Notre Dame de Sion in Istanbul and later started teaching in Ankara.

It was 1929. Afet placed a ballot box in the class she was teaching and asked the pupils to cast their votes. Her world was shattered when one of the boys pointed out 'that girls can't vote, Miss!' 'I had no idea. It was never something that had occurred to me,' she says. She thought, *Well, if I don't have this right, but my pupils do, then I can no longer teach them*, and left the school in tears.

Mustafa Kemal laughed at her streaked face and suggested she research how it was in other countries. So the books arrived, and she began. An amendment enabled women to vote in local elections in time for the following April's International Congress of Women to be held in Istanbul. Afet gave a lecture at the Turkish Hearth on women's rights to vote and to stand in public elections. She had taken oration lessons from Hamdullah Suphi, on Mustafa Kemal's advice, prior to the lecture and practised before the mirror.[9]

Those who once cast aspersions on Latife's speech rehearsals in the garden had done her a great injustice, claiming she intended to outshine the commander. The wheel had turned full circle.

Afet went to Switzerland to earn a degree, but whenever she was in Turkey, she accompanied Mustafa Kemal on trips and important occasions, and assisted with his work. Another woman he had met in Izmir had filled Latife's place in the photographs and protocol.

34

Latife Supports the Second Party

Latife maintained a low profile during her travels abroad, introducing herself by a pseudonym: Fatma Sadık, the name on her passport. Keeping quiet about her real identity – the former first lady of Turkey – enabled her to relax a bit, and she felt a little better each time she went abroad.

She returned in August 1930 after a long sojourn in Europe. Democracy in Turkey still seemed a long way off. Although the gallows had long been dismantled after the assassination attempt in Izmir, the terror created by the tribunals had yet to dissipate. Not a single voice dared to rise in opposition, either in the assembly or in the press.

Latife spent the first five years after the divorce nursing her broken spirit and exhausted body. Now she returned to her father's home, a woman matured in pain and ready to put her life in order.

Fethi Okyar, the Turkish ambassador to France, and his family – his wife, Galibe, and their children – had come back in July 1930 for his two-month annual holiday. They were staying at the seafront mansion of Necmeddin Molla, a leading academician of law and a close friend of Muammer's. Fethi Okyar went to Yalova to pay his respects to Mustafa Kemal and to convey the views of the French government on Turkey. Mustafa Kemal summarised the situation at home:

Our current political landscape is more or less one of a dictatorship ... True, there is an assembly, but I am considered to be a dictator both within and without the country. Emil Ludwig, a German writer, visited Ankara last year; after asking some bizarre questions about the form of our government and, returning to his country, convinced of our dictatorship, he then wrote of this conviction.

I, on the other hand, have no desire to bequeath a tyranny as my legacy, nor do I wish history to remember me as such.[1]

He then continued:

I've found the solution. The country needs an opposition party. Such a party will enable free debate in the chamber. And you, for instance, could head such a party, and speak freely in parliament.

Fethi's first reaction was to decline. 'Please do excuse me.'

Mustafa Kemal accompanied Fethi on his return from Yalova that day, telling him he would join them for dinner. When he arrived at the seafront mansion by motorboat, his mind was made up:

'I've found the name for your party.' And then, turning to Galibe, he added, 'It looks unlikely you'll return to Paris now.'

Galibe replied, 'I'd hoped we would stay another year and that you might postpone these plans.'

'No, no, not another year; this has to happen immediately, tomorrow even,' said Mustafa Kemal. As these words came out of his mouth, everyone present knew: the time to galvanise politics had arrived.

Fethi had some concerns, and he asked Mustafa Kemal to resign the leadership of the People's Party to demonstrate his impartiality. Mustafa Kemal, on the other hand, avoided giving him a definitive answer.

The second opposition party of the republican era was founded on 12 August 1930. *Serbest Cumhuriyet Fırkası* (the Free Republican Party, more commonly known as the Free Party) was led by Fethi Okyar, who agreed with İsmet Paşa that the new party would set off with seventy MPs.[2] Mustafa Kemal reportedly expressed a desire for the new party to be more liberal, and therefore more left-leaning, than the People's Party.[3]

Latife was thrilled to hear of the FRP on her return, and although she believed it an essential development, she was not sure of its immediate future. Politics had got under her skin, and she followed events through any means possible: the daily papers as well as close friends.

The Free Party and women

The women's movement that Latife had supported whilst in Çankaya had been conspicuous in its silence for some time. The Women's Union of Turkey had replaced Nezihe Muhiddin with Latife Bekir, who dismissed her predecessor's aspirations of political rights as mere dreams. All the same, women did begin to join the People's Party after the amendment to the Local Government Law.

The Free Party went one step further and included women's political rights on their programme, this one issue being added by Mustafa Kemal himself. He even asked his sister Makbule to join, consulting Fethi:

'Would you like me to send my own sister to join your party?'

It was uncertainty about Mustafa Kemal's attitude that had prevented politicians from joining the Free Party. Makbule's enrolment would indicate a stamp of approval, relieving Fethi to a degree.

Latife followed every step of the formation of the Free Party that was clearly Mustafa Kemal's brainchild. The opportunity to catch up with Galibe coincided with this time when politics was getting really interesting.

'Well done, my hometown ...'

Latife went to Altınkum beach in Sarıyer one day with her sister Vecihe and Vecihe's husband, Hayri, to spend the day with the Okyars. They were chatting, stretched out on the sand after a swim. Fethi sought Latife's opinion on the Free Party:

'What do you reckon? How do you interpret the situation?'

Latife replied:

'I'm delighted to be consulted: the entire nation has placed its hopes on you. Everyone's hurting; everyone's desperate for a bit of fresh air.'

Fethi began his propaganda tour in Izmir, Latife's hometown. A large crowd greeted him in the square outside his hotel on 5 September. But the People's Party organised a counter-rally of their own. The building of a printer known for their publications against the Free Party was stoned in the tense atmosphere; the police opened fire on the crowds, and a young boy was killed.

Fethi Okyar wanted to wire Mustafa Kemal at the Post Office, and when the operatives refused to cooperate, he had to pull rank and remind the governor of his duty. The telegram finally reached its destination and received an encouraging reply:

'I understand they want to prevent you from making your speech ... But deliver it you will!'

On 7 September, despite all the obstacles that had been thrown in his way, Fethi did address a crowd of 50,000.

Latife kept newspaper reports of Fethi's Izmir trip and noted on one: 'Well done, my hometown!'

Minister of Education Vasıf Çınar, who was in Istanbul just then, telephoned Latife:

'I've learned, quite by chance, that you were here. I'd like to pay you a visit before setting off with the president, to absolve myself ...'

Latife reassured him, 'You have no need to seek absolution.' She was still glowing after all she'd read in the morning papers. She might have kept a low profile herself, but she could not give up the habit.

Vasıf arrived at Ayaspaşa within the hour:

'We're returning to Ankara this evening with him.' Vasıf had politely refused Mustafa Kemal's insistence that he, too, enrol in the new party.

'Your true duty yet lies ahead,' offered Latife.

Vasıf was thoughtful; they discussed İsmet Paşa's disquiet. Latife concurred: 'In the long run, Fethi Bey will not prevail, but his sacrifice will still serve the nation. We all owe him our gratitude.'

Vasıf nodded. 'Fethi Bey is deeply concerned.'

Yakup Kadri had lambasted Izmir in a newspaper article that had incensed Latife. The two Izmir people had a heart-to-heart, and Latife explained her fury.

'The locals must have been deliberately provoked; someone wanted them to hurt. Izmir's people are neither lowly nor common, as Yakup Kadri alleges. The second thing that really offends me is how newspapers personalise everything. I understand freedom of the press, but this freedom is only assured if it's adopted by all.'

Vasıf took his leave when they finished chatting; he was due to accompany the president on the way back to Ankara on 19 September.

An anti–Free Party campaign started after the events in Izmir; both the party and the city's residents came under attack. Latife argued with those who criticised Izmir, fuming at the flak her hometown faced.

'These riots should never have happened, I grant you. But they were provoked. No one should condemn Izmir people on the basis of these events. The people are hungry, dressed in rags, and what little they've saved is going to the pockets of goodness knows who. These people are hurting, and what they need is support.'[4]

Mustafa Kemal may have wanted to end one-party rule, but the disturbances in Izmir did not bode well for the long-term prospects of the People's Party. The growth of the Free Party forced his hand: 'I'll have to show a little partiality as of now. Otherwise, the People's Party will disappear, and we'll be left with a single party once more, and this simply will not do.'[5]

Makbule Atadan – Mustafa Kemal's sister, and one of the founders of the Free Party – visited the Okyars soon after Fethi's Izmir trip. The former sisters-in-law suddenly came face to face one day. Makbule expressed her sadness at the break-up and later visited Latife in her Ayaspaşa home.

'You can't live this quietly for ever …'

Latife found herself in the thick of things once more: every time Mustafa Kemal stayed at Dolmabahçe, his visitors made their way up the hill to see her after they'd paid him their respects. This makes it highly likely that news between the two was carried both ways.

Latife and Galibe were chatting one day in the Büyükdere mansion. As they talked of the past and the future, the conversation turned to Mustafa Kemal. Galibe thought the two could get together again:

'I'm so hopeful. I really wish this would happen.'

But Latife had moved on.

'There is no way; I've already made my mind up. I've cried for five years, and now am finally able to see the delights of the world. As for marriage, if it is essential – and I'm not in the least bit convinced – I would prefer a new life. What would be the point if I couldn't enjoy family life?'

Galibe referred to the encounter of the former sisters-in-law: 'Makbule Hanım cried so much after you. She sang your praises, saying this would never have happened if she had been around.'

Latife broke her silence. 'Such encounters are normal. I've never bidden goodbye to the position I held in society. If I had felt such a need, I would have said farewell to the country.'

'You can't live this quietly for ever, you know. You will have to serve the country in one way or another ... You've done the right thing all these years, never given anyone cause to criticise you,' replied Galibe.

Latife said, 'I'm doing my duty. I will always respect him. Now I want to work. I just haven't made my mind up quite how.'

Galibe was inviting her friend to join the Free Party. Latife, on the other hand, had to assess the consequences of any political activity on her part. She could see the Free Party exercise was not destined to be long-lived, but was loath to upset her friend by saying it out loud.[6]

The Free Party in the elections

Fethi Okyar had also come to the conclusion that dissolving the party might be the best course of action, as Mustafa Kemal had now revealed his hand. But the FRP had one more political experiment to participate in: local government elections were coming up. Direct elections would take place for the first time in the history of the republic.

The elections were held in August 1930. There were a total of nine women candidates for the first time; both the People's Party and the Free Republican Party had placed their women candidates at the top of their lists. The name at the top of the Beyoğlu list was Makbule Atadan, closely followed by the former head of the Women's Union of Turkey, Nezihe Muhiddin.[7]

The Free Party outdid all expectations, winning thirty-one of the 502 districts according to official results. In Istanbul, the Free Party polled 13,000 out of a total of 36,000. In Izmir, the People's Party polled 14,600, and the Free Party, 10,000.[8]

This time, the Free Party faced allegations of religious reactionism.[9]

More importantly, state officials at all levels had intervened in the elections: the Home Office, police and *jandarma* all worked to make sure the Free Party lost. Fethi therefore proposed a motion of censure against the home secretary. The motion came to the floor on 15 November, by which time Fethi found himself left high and dry in the assembly. He announced the decision to dissolve the Free Party on 17 November.

Turkey had returned to one-party rule, and any opposition was crushed once more. Latife, who had not quite made her mind up how to come out, decided the most prudent course of action just then was to stay out of the public arena.

Armstrong publishes Grey Wolf

In the early 1930s Latife used one of the rooms on the fourth floor of the Ayaspaşa house for her translations.

The Turkish Touring and Automobile Club had been founded to promote the country; its president, Reşit Saffet, was a close relation of the Uşşakizade family. The club began to publish a magazine in August 1930, and notable writers of the time contributed articles to encourage tourism. Latife is known to have written and translated for this magazine under an assumed name. Her niece Dilek Bebe tells us that Latife wrote novels and short stories, as well as newspaper articles, all under noms de plume, to earn some money.

She had a distinctive literary style, which might help us to discover what she wrote, even if we do not know what pen names she used.

It is also said that each time an important book on Turkey was published abroad, Latife translated it and sent it to Mustafa Kemal through mutual friends. She did, in a manner of speaking, continue her duty of translator to Çankaya.

In October 1932, Harold Courtenay Armstrong published the controversial *Grey Wolf*, in which he drew a lupine portrait of Mustafa Kemal, sparing no detail of his personal life. Although the book was banned in Turkey, Latife translated and sent it through the usual channels, believing Mustafa Kemal ought to read it.

One evening at supper in Çankaya, Mustafa Kemal said, 'Bring this book then. Let's read it.' *Grey Wolf* was read at the table that night as everyone listened.

'What have you done with this book?' asked Mustafa Kemal.

'We've forbidden its import.'

'Why?'

'Because of the libels on yourself ...'

'What, drinking and so on?'

'Yes, sir.'

'Nooo. He's even pulled his punches. Let it in, so people can read it.'[10]

Kılıç Ali was also at the table that evening; in his account Mustafa Kemal joked, 'The government was wrong to ban this book. The poor man hasn't given enough credit to our dissipation. Perhaps I ought to fill in the blanks, and *then* we'll let the book come in, so people can read it.'[11]

The ban remained in place, however.

Mustafa Kemal's corrections were published in *Akşam* on 7 December 1932, in an article compiled by Necmettin Sadak.[12]

Mustafa Kemal refuted Armstrong's assertion that he had fallen head over heels in love with Latife; no, the article stated, he had married her out of compassion. Latife's exclamation as the great fire of Izmir raged was repeated: 'All our family's fortune is burned to the ground; we are ruined, but no matter. You have arrived, delivered us and our land; this will suffice.'

There was worse to come:

It was these words, and the values Mustafa Kemal assumed to be inherent in Latife Hanım, that gave rise to his feelings of protectiveness and compassion towards her and her family. He did not marry her out of an emotional attachment, but acted out of compassion and gallantry instead, and lived with her for a few years despite the incongruity.

Seven years after their divorce, Mustafa Kemal was humiliating Latife in public, using the press to do so. The ruthless style of the *Akşam* article asserted there had been no love between the two.

Latife wrote to İsmet Paşa after reading it, and he replied. She then sent the paper two separate letters, laying out her objections to the article. Her corrections were never published.

Mustafa Kemal might have suspected Latife's contribution to some of the more personal details in *Grey Wolf*, or she might simply have irritated him by presuming to send him the translation. He might have even suspected her of an ulterior motive, and so deliberately set out to hurt her.

Münci's death

Another blow came in late 1932: Latife's beloved brother Münci died after a love affair. No one has been able to discover whether this was an accident or suicide, but his death compounded Latife's grief.

Münci had started working at the Turkish Touring and Automobile Club after obtaining a degree in law. He and Latife had been very close, and the two had corresponded regularly.

Latife and Halit Ziya meet again

After the divorce, Latife had fallen out with her beloved uncle.

One day his phone rang:

'Hallo? Hallo? Uncle, it is I!'

He recognised her voice and manner of speech immediately, but he made her sweat it out. This was the first time he was hearing her voice since the divorce.

She had, on a number of occasions, mentioned the rift between them to mutual friends. And here she was on the phone, saying, 'Uncle, it is I, Latife. I miss you so much I couldn't bear it any longer.'

Although Halit Ziya did not quite know what tone of voice to adopt, it was obvious that, 'Well, one had to use the same tone, naturally ...' And he also had to admit, however reluctantly, 'I, too, miss you.' There would be more: Latife was asking when they might meet.

'I somewhat mischievously invited her to Yeşilköy, but she declined.

She didn't want to get anywhere near the mansion she'd lived in for such a long time. We never knew why. So we agreed on a place and time. She thanked me profusely. I accepted on condition that there would be no explanations asked or given between us.'

They did meet, and they followed the rules they had set. They would chat 'of this, that and Vedad, after the kissing and the hugging was done!'

Halit Ziya had come to the conclusion that Latife had only the warmest concern for her cousin, undiminished and genuine.

They would 'part closer and warmer than ever before, uncle and niece, after this sweet reunion,' but they were not destined to meet again until Münci's death.[13] So this meeting must have taken place before 1932.

His granddaughter Zeynep Lange refers to how close Halit Ziya and Latife had been:

Latife Hanım loved Halit Ziya Uşaklıgil, whom she held in great esteem. I remember the numerous letters she'd written him; they were kept in my father's home, tied up with a blue ribbon. My father called her one day, asking, 'What should I do with these letters?' She requested, 'Bülend, please burn them, lest they fall into the wrong hands.' Sadly, no one ever read them out to us. But I do know she had written in one, just after she had met Atatürk: 'I met a pair of beautiful blue eyes.'[14]

35

A Unique Surname from Atatürk

The Surname Law came into force in 1934, compelling every citizen to adopt a formal family name. For centuries people had been known by their given names, patronymics and frequently cognomens designating place of origin, family trade or personality trait; in true Ottoman fashion, these cognomens had been devised with elements from a variety of languages. As the new law restricted some of these older suffixes, *Uşakizade* ('son of the family from Uşak' but effectively implying nobility) could no longer qualify.

Halit Ziya sent Muammer Bey word: he would adopt *Uşaklıgil* ('of those from Uşak'). Muammer had not warmed to the *-gil* suffix, possibly also because he did not wish to share his surname with Halit Ziya; so he applied for *Uşşaklı* ('of Uşak'). Latife would have to adopt her father's surname. For some reason, however, the application was stuck at the register office in Istanbul. Something was holding it up. They tried one thing after another, and the matter finally went all the way up to Çankaya. Muammer and his family did adopt *Uşşaklı*. But Latife was given a different surname.

Rumour has it that Mustafa Kemal asked for the application papers to be brought up and then approved Muammer's surname. But when he came to Latife's application, he crossed out *Uşşaklı* and wrote in his own hand *Uşşaki*. Turning to those around him, he asked, 'Do you know what that means?' It was a refined, subtle, multilayered pun: *âşık* means 'lover', but also 'wandering minstrel' and 'Sufi dervish'. In Ottoman Turkish, *uşşak* is the plural of *âşık*, as well as being the name of the county the family originally hailed from.

Muammer Erboy verifies the tale: 'Look it up in the dictionary; it means "of the lovers". The year was 1934.'

Mustafa Kemal sends roses

Muammer Erboy continues: 'Whenever Atatürk came to Istanbul, he invited Latife to Dolmabahçe Palace. He'd send cars and aides to fetch her. He'd send roses. My grandparents accepted every invitation they received, but Latife Hanım must have declined each time.'

Although she put up framed individual photos of her and of Mustafa Kemal, too, she never displayed a single photo of them together. To all intents and purposes, she had erased him from her life.

She had only one request for Mustafa Kemal after their divorce. Muammer Erboy says, 'She was incredibly proud. She asked for neither alimony nor compensation.' He adds:

> She contracted TB, but couldn't get a passport. Someone around him must have objected, 'Paşam, she'll go talk to foreign journalists. Don't let her go!' This was the only thing she ever asked for. She sent word again, saying she was sick and had to go. Eventually she was granted a passport in the name of Fatma Sadık.

Did they ever meet again? Vecihe says they did, at Göksu in Istanbul:

> Latife Hanım was in a skiff at Göksu one day. Atatürk had a motorboat, whose name escapes me now. When they spotted each other, Atatürk got to his feet and saluted her. Latife cried her eyes out afterwards; that was the only time they met after the divorce. She loved him from the moment she set eyes on him, through to her last breath ...

Did Latife and Mustafa Kemal ever talk after the divorce? We do know they kept themselves apprised of each other's doings. But there is more: journalist Niyazi Ahmet Banoğlu mentions a telephone conversation between the two, something he heard about personally from Latife. She told him:

> I rarely went out on visits. I did notice, however, that whenever I did, I was tailed by a plainclothesman. On a rainy day, this officer

– whom I had recognised by then – followed me all the way to the
gate of the mansion. It was raining very heavily indeed. I signalled
him over and said:

'Son, I recognise you now. You've been following me. You're
drenched; get into the hut and dry yourself off.' And then, once I
was inside the mansion, it occurred to me what to do. Atatürk was
in Dolmabahçe Palace. I called him on the phone and asked:

'Paşam, am I suspected of posing such a threat to your safety that
the police follow me?' We chatted for a while. It wasn't half an hour
before Şükrü Kaya turned up. He'd been around at the time I called,
and Atatürk had despatched him at once to beg my forgiveness.
Şükrü Kaya said, 'He tore a strip off me. "Who's ordered you to tail
my wife? This is a disgrace!" I'd never seen him so enraged.'[1]

A suicide

Vedad was appointed as the third secretary at the Turkish embassy in
London soon after Latife left Ankara. Halit Ziya wired his thanks to
Mustafa Kemal when his son took up his new job, and noted down the
date: 17 August 1342 [AD 1926].

Vedad served as a diplomat for over a decade, although he
increasingly grew listless in the latter half of this period. He was inclined
to be depressive and, despite being a virtuoso, he no longer cared to
play the piano. He was convinced someone at the ministry was on his
case, recalling him at unexpected times. The Turkish embassy in Tirana
would be his final stop.

One day in December 1937, as the embassy was getting ready for a
special occasion party, he froze after deciphering an order recalling him
with no further explanation. He finished the preparations for the party
and retired to his room, leaving strict instructions not to be awakened.
'I'm a little tired; I'll take a rest.' He hung up his jacket, put his pyjamas
on, tidied up his files and then took four packs of Luminal and lay down
to die.

Halit Ziya learned later that Atatürk had ordered funds to be sent
to repatriate the body.

1938: The year of pain

News of Atatürk's illness had spread by 1938. He must have felt the approach of death. The love of Latife's life was gravely ill, but she did not know it: she herself had been in hospital in Berne, Switzerland, undergoing treatment for months.

A 'shock to the core' confronted her on the morning of 11 November. Splashed across the front pages of papers were stories of the death of the man she loved. Evidently not even her nearest and dearest had undertaken the dreaded task of telling her.

In a letter she wrote İsmet Paşa on the same day, Latife poured out her grief:

To the President of the Republic General İsmet İnönü, Ankara

My Very Dear and Honourable Leader,

I was shocked to the core in the hospital room I'd been lying in for months when I read the papers that arrived as usual this morning.

I have no doubt of Your Excellency's capacity to guess just how shaken I am by this great disaster, you, who have appreciated my suffering for these thirteen years and who have always protected me.

The only consolation I have, for myself, and for the nation, is that you have shouldered the heavy burden he once bore.

The degree of sincerity I address you with is well known to yourself. As I extend my wishes for constant success, health and a long life, I offer my complete allegiance. I ask you not to deny this sick girl with the broken wings your mercy or protection, and I kiss your fortunate hands.

Latife

Address: F. Sadık, Lindenhospital, Berne, Suisse[2]

Her mourning was as heavy as death: she had not been on hand to look after him on his last days.

We do not know quite who was courteous enough to extend his or her condolences to Latife. The entire country cried after him, but her pain was different. She had not even been able to bid him goodbye.

Atatürk was carried to Anıtkabir, his mausoleum, in November 1953. Jale, the young wife of General Refik Tulga, the chief of staff, was visiting Latife one day. When she learned Jale was due to go to Ankara soon, Latife had a request to make.

How different Ankara must be now! I'm so curious. And you ask if there's anything you could do for me. Here you are then, a secret, more like a charge, really ... Something I've been wanting to do for years but never had the courage to carry out. Go and buy a single red rose from a florist in Ankara. Only a single one. Take it to Anıtkabir and lay it down at the ground in his sacred tomb. At his feet. He'll know who sent it, but tell him anyway, 'This is from Latife!' Would you please be so kind?

Jale Tulga did not disappoint; she went to Anıtkabir with a single red rose early the following morning. Daunted by the official crowds and huge wreaths she spotted as she ascended the stairs, she drew aside and waited for them to finish.

She asked an officer who was inside: it was the president. So it was some official occasion when a visit to Atatürk's mausoleum was on the agenda. The young woman briefly considered turning back, but then Latife's voice echoed in her mind. She pressed on, mingled with the protocol and went in. She laid the rose at the foot of the tomb, murmuring, 'This is from Latife Hanım,' and followed the crowd out.

That night she could not sleep. Had the single rose been crushed under those grandiose wreaths? She made her way back to Anıtkabir early in the morning once more. Huge wreaths were lined up outside; evidently, they were taken out in the night. But no one had noticed the single rose: it was still where she had laid it down the day before. Latife's salute had not been disturbed.[3]

Muammer Uşşakizade, who never denied his daughter compassion and financial support, died at the age of seventy-nine of a heart attack in 1951.

Her father had said years ago, on that day when she insisted she would marry Mustafa Kemal: 'Should this marriage ever come to an end and you return to my home, never talk to me of him, or of marriage!' Latife kept her word for twenty-six years. She never once mentioned her marriage, divorce or Mustafa Kemal within his hearing in all that time. Adeviye Hanım survived her husband until 1956, although her final years were spent battling Alzheimer's.

The White Mansion

Latife's love of children was well known. The house in Izmir where Latife Hanım and Mustafa Kemal first met, and later married, had been abandoned since the family had moved to Istanbul. One day she received Bahattin Tatış, who had founded the Izmir Independent Turkish College earlier; the educator was looking for new premises. Latife agreed to lease it in 1951 with the hope that 'This school might raise little Mustafa Kemals.'

The White Mansion was home to the school for four decades, before being transformed, this time into a museum, a role it still serves today.

Always dignified, head held high ...

Latife was the iconic woman who had made women visible, although she herself lived the rest of her life as the invisible woman. Despite all that she could have done in Turkey, she had been relegated to a life of obscurity, without function, without a voice. Still, although she had withdrawn from the limelight, she certainly monitored things closely from the wings. She had, in her own words, 'never bidden goodbye to the position she'd held in society'. According to those in her close circles, she said, 'If I had felt such a need, I would have said farewell to the country.'

There is a tendency, specifically amongst those who did not know her, to depict Latife Hanım as a woman crushed, devastated beyond help. Those who did know her, on the other hand, paint an entirely different picture. Şehvar Çağlayan, a close friend, is one who brooks no suggestion of a disconsolate Latife. 'Absolutely not. She was always dignified and authoritative; she never compromised her integrity, and she held her head high. You felt the force of her personality when you met her.' She adds, 'I loved her dearly, and respected her, too. She was truly European in her manners and mind. I don't much care for all these so-called disclosures and reminiscences about her.'[4]

Şen Sılan comments, 'She might have been unhappy, but she most certainly was not beaten. She simply didn't talk of her marriage. Her eyes and smile always looked sad. The pain of being left alone was visible in her eyes. Those eyes affected me hugely.'[5] Sılan's portrait comes from the 1960s, and strangely resembles one drawn decades earlier by Berthe Georges-Gaulis in 1923:

> She had a terrifically imposing personality. One felt the need to collect oneself in her presence. It was impossible not to be impressed by the elegance and character of this well brought up young lady. I used to feel myself bowing before her. You benefited from being in her company.
>
> When you gained her approval, you found something within yourself.
>
> She descended the stairs in a way that was impossible not to admire. Being with her was a big deal. If she hadn't married Atatürk? She would indisputably have become an important person.

Latife was very fond of her blonde, blue-eyed great-niece Füsun İşcan, who says, 'For me, she wasn't Atatürk's wife, she was my aunt. She was very forceful. She was like a state in her own right. She wasn't one to stay in the shadows.'[6]

Meral Bebe, another niece, believes Latife kept her troubles to herself. 'She wouldn't share it, in any case. Some things are best unsaid. My aunt was like that. She did make a remark when the occasion called for it, though.'[7]

Dilek Bebe stresses the solitude. 'It must have been like being buried alive. My aunt was very lonely. Although, I must confess, in my view, all great people are lonely. And of course she was sad, too. However frequently we might visit her, there was a deep loneliness inside, not just because of him, but because she was misunderstood.'

Did Latife regret marrying? According to Meral, she did not: 'She used to say she'd do exactly the same if she were born again.'

Did she never consider marrying again? Meral dismisses the suggestion out of hand, 'She never once thought about it.' Her daughter Dilek adds, 'My aunt rejected every single suitor.'[8]

Professor Yurdakul Yurdakul writes, 'Latife Hanım rejected numerous proposals of marriage after breaking up with Atatürk; she was a lady whose devotion to him was apparent in every action throughout the rest of her life even after his death.'[9]

Şehvar Çağlayan disagrees. 'I can't imagine anyone having the courage to propose to her ...'

Latife's position on remarriage was unequivocal. She was heard to comment, upon hearing about the marriage of US president Kennedy's widow, Jacqueline, to Aristotle Onassis, 'What was it that she needed so much: money or a man? Who'd ride a donkey after coming off a horse?'

From the mansion to a flat

After the death of her parents, Latife lived on her own in the mansion in Ayaspaşa for quite a while. She surprised the family in the late 1960s with an announcement: she'd purchased a flat on the seventh floor of an apartment block in Harbiye.

'You could have purchased a seafront villa! How can you squeeze five-metre ceilings into two?'

'I've had the bookcases cut down!'

When she moved to her top-floor flat in Safir Apartment, she left her grand piano behind.

Muammer Erboy describes her life in the flat: 'She was perched, virtually on one cheek, on a tiny footstool upholstered in Chinese silk, watching the road. She asked what we thought. She insisted we look out, right opposite. The flat faced the officers' club. She then pointed: Atatürk's statue. "The one that most closely resembles him, the truest depiction," she said, and added, "Why would I have moved to such a flat otherwise?"'

'That love never died,' says Erboy.

Her niece Meral also mentions the love Latife had for Mustafa Kemal, 'It never was all pink and lovely, but the love and respect never disappeared. And that love stayed with her all her life.' She then adds, 'To the extent that it used to irritate me, I'd ask what sort of person she was. I mean, there's a limit to everything. "Did you have no pride?" I'd ask.'[10]

Reşat Kaynar, who read Latife's documents, concurs. 'She was very much in love with Atatürk.'[11]

A considerable number of people kept up with Latife. Did this ever bother Mustafa Kemal? Apparently not.

The İnönü family stayed friends with Latife: their daughter Özden Toker indicates that the friendship was sanctioned by Atatürk. The İnönüs must have sought it on such a delicate matter.

Muammer Erboy confirms that Mevhibe İnönü held a special place in Latife's heart: 'Mevhibe Hanım frequently called my aunt Latife. She was friendly with my grandmother, too, and İsmet Paşa himself visited, always much more than simply returning a courtesy visit.'

The Latife–İnönü family friendship outlasted Mustafa Kemal's lifespan. Vecihe's son Erdem married İsmet İnönü's niece, thus forging a further tie between the families.

Latife received lunch invitations each time İnönü stayed at Dolmabahçe Palace. Her visits reportedly animated the palace; she even stayed overnight occasionally.

Those who did not know her would ask who the woman kissing İsmet on the forehead was: this was none other than Latife Hanım.

Did she ever comment on other first ladies in Çankaya? Muammer Erboy says no. 'She felt no need to say a thing. She rarely spoke of other first ladies.'

27 May 1960

Latife Uşşaki always followed the political events in Turkey very closely. Although she had criticised Adnan Menderes – 'He made some huge mistakes, so reactionary' – she was not amongst those who welcomed the 27 May coup.

Berrin Menderes, the wife of the imprisoned former prime minister, called on Latife each time she returned from Yassıada, the island where her husband was on trial.

She is reported to have telephoned İsmet İnönü when the trial returned a sentence of death:

'Paşam, no one could deny you if you were to stand up in the middle of Kızılay Square. Please go to the square. Countless people will follow you; no one can stop you. It was you who brought democracy to this country; this coup targeted you equally.'

36

The Campaign of Vilification

As Mustafa Kemal's wife-cum-aide, Latife had enjoyed considerable political clout on numerous matters. As soon as she came down, she became vulnerable. She simply had to be brought down to size. Latife had detractors in Mustafa Kemal's close circles who now mobilised: it was time to denigrate her.

Society finds fault with the woman sent back to her father's home by her husband. And the husband who had sent his wife away was no less than Mustafa Kemal Paşa himself, so Latife had to be not only at fault but declared to be the 'bad party'.

First, she was styled as a woman hostile to Mustafa Kemal. Then this fake image came under relentless attack. The same attrition tactics used against the opposition now targeted Latife.

As the former first lady, she posed a potential threat with the power to undermine the leader. She had to be ostracised by society, and to a degree she was. All too soon, life became suffocating for Latife.

Another reason for the campaign of vilification was all that she had witnessed throughout her time in Çankaya. There was no secret she did not know about anyone. She had been Mustafa Kemal's confidante, the person he had entrusted with all his important papers.[1] The dramatis personæ of the Turkish political scene had not changed much since she had left. She could so easily create utter chaos, if she wanted to: all she had to do was to pronounce a few sentences attributed to Mustafa Kemal. Marginalising her would not only ensure she stayed in the background but also cast aspersions on anything she might say.

A deliberate insulating ring surrounded her. Disparaging her became all the rage. News reports published in foreign papers indicate she was under constant surveillance. On the orders of the governor of Istanbul, a police hut had been erected opposite her home.[2]

Latife preserved her silence, refusing all interview requests.

'We gave each other our word as we were divorcing; I'll never break it!'

So Mustafa Kemal must also have given her his word. He certainly stood up for her publicly, castigating the person who had dared to insult Latife behind her back soon after her departure. Ahmet Ağaoğlu was a personal witness to Mustafa Kemal's furious retort: 'She is a lady, and will always remain a lady.'

Each new book that was published about him after *Grey Wolf* was met with trepidation. 'What if Latife had spoken?' Ankara's cauldron never stopped bubbling. But local pens were unable to write of the contents, and in any case, no one dared publish any reminiscences about Atatürk's life during his lifetime. It was only after November 1938 that such books appeared.

Apprehension of Latife grew after Mustafa Kemal's death, partly over the concern that she might one day embark upon a political career. A Lady Latife, seasoned in politics and having played a major part in the change of women's status, could easily become a leading name in the new two-party politics and would certainly pull votes. As the once marginalised political personalities re-emerged one by one, her name remained conspicuous in its absence. Would a party that invited Latife to join increase its credibility in the 1950s? This is such a difficult question to answer. Certain circles might well have wanted to block just such a contingency.

Nearly all the books that relate Mustafa Kemal's life story were written after the divorce, and Latife was declared to be 'bad'. The gossip pot kept boiling, and everyone took a shot at her. All the authors were male, and they all had a firmly male viewpoint. This explains the unsympathetic choice of adjectives. It might also explain the disparity between the two irreconcilable characters described by all these writers: a unanimously admired young lady, highly educated, well brought up and the domineering shrew who enervated her husband.

Latife had to contend with the adjectives 'spoiled' and 'capricious' for the rest of her life.

Şen Sılan dismisses these allegations: 'Look: a twenty-two-year-old girl marries the man adored by the entire world; she might have teased him playfully. A young wife flirts with her husband, and this they call spoiled.'[3]

Kinross and Şevket Süreyya

Lord Kinross, in the first comprehensive biography of Atatürk, draws the portrait of a wonderful young lady and then makes an about face as he carves Latife into history as 'the spoiled child of her father'.[4]

Latife refused to receive him, despite his persistent messages and requests for an interview. He might have been less hostile if she had agreed to speak to him. Who knows?

Şevket Süreyya, the first Turkish biographer of Atatürk, does not even mention her once in the account of events, relegating her to the notes on Atatürk's personal life at the end. Şevket Süreyya was not exactly sympathetic either.

These tales found favour; no attempt was made to reverse this fiction.

37

Latife Hides Her Illness

'I was a pupil at the Austrian Lycée in 1975; I went to visit my aunt, report card in hand. An acrid smell of burning greeted me. My aunt Latife had cancer. I don't know whether she'd burned her memoirs or something else she'd written. This was on the thirty-first of May. We lost her in July.'

That is the account of her great-nephew Muammer Erboy remembering a visit with Latife two months prior to her death.

Latife Uşşaki learned in Switzerland that she had cancer. The doctors had seen something in the lungs and informed her. It is believed the illness had begun in 1969.

She returned and refused to go to a doctor or even tell anyone other than her confidante Kalyopi. But not before she made her lifelong companion swear on the Holy Cross and Iesous Christos, too, that she would not reveal this to anyone.

Professor Dr Nevzat Öke, her niece Gülümser's husband, thought he'd pop upstairs one day; he'd been at a friend's birthday party in the flat below. It was this chance visit that led to her family's discovery of the illness.

Kalyopi opened the door, but she was not herself. 'Latife Hanım is sick, she won't be able to receive you today.' Nevzat Öke insisted, went in and caught Latife trying to pull her sleeve over her arm. The long-sleeved outfits that she had recently adopted had hidden the sores on her arms. He spotted a large, seeping lesion. He would not take no for an answer, and she eventually admitted she had been suffering with cancer for a long time. The state of the lesions told him it was too late for treatment.

Latife insisted Nevzat Öke refrain from telling anyone, but he felt compelled to as a doctor.

'Then give me three days; I will tell everyone myself. I just have a few things to see to first.'

Nevzat Öke broke his promise by telling his wife:

'This will upset you, but you need to know. The Lady Auntie is in a bad way.'

He was an expert who knew every moment was crucial in cancer treatment, and she had refused to seek treatment for years.

Latife used this three-day grace period to burn some documents; that was the smell that had assailed Muammer Erboy's nostrils. He comments on her determination to hide her disease: 'She didn't seek treatment for her cancer, because she'd always said, "I was a living corpse throughout my life; living a few days longer is only going to torment me."' Close friends had heard her say, 'I've died twice, once in 1925 and again in 1938.'

Her niece Dilek Bebe believes Latife effectively committed suicide.

Latife continued to refuse treatment, even after her illness came out into the open. She was hospitalised at Güzelbahçe Clinic during her final two months.

Dilek visited her two days before Latife died; her aunt wore an Atatürk portrait tiepin on her chest.[1]

Latife Hanım died around six in the morning on 12 July 1975. She had asked of her nearest and dearest that her body be taken back to the flat, and they complied. She went to her home prior to the funeral.

Her family placed quarter-page death notices in *Milliyet* and *Cumhuriyet* but not in *Hürriyet*, out of respect for her wishes: that paper had repeatedly offended Latife in the past.[2] One intriguing aspect of these notices that began 'Our beloved and precious Latife Uşşaki ...' was that, although she was named as the daughter of Muammer Bey and Adeviye Hanım, there was absolutely no reference to Mustafa Kemal. The family might have thought that is what she would have wanted; it is also possible they wished to avoid altering the nature of the funeral.

The news of her death and reports on the funeral, all illustrated with photos, made the front pages of newspapers. They treated her with respect on the occasion of her death. But no two papers managed to agree on her age, education, or even surname.

Latife Hanım was laid to rest with a funeral held at Teşvikiye Mosque on 13 July. There was no state ceremony. Namık Kemal Şentürk, the governor of Istanbul, knew the family from Izmir. He pulled rank and organised an honour guard of army, navy and air force units. Someone noticed at the last minute that there was no flag. Gültekin Ağaoğlu says, 'There wasn't a Turkish flag over the coffin. My elder sister and I insisted, and one was found and draped over her.'[3]

Indeed, the flag had been missing from the first, and Governor Şentürk was one of those people who strove to procure one.

No official from Ankara participated in the funeral.

The prayer leader at the funeral, Hacı Hafız Nusret Yeşilçay, is reported to have said, 'The lack of interest shown by so-called followers of Atatürk in the funeral of Atatürk's wife is a disgrace.'

Latife had asked of her only surviving sibling, Vecihe, to stay in her flat for forty days and keep the bedroom light on. Vecihe managed a fortnight. Pots full of lamb shanks and other delicacies were carried to Safir Apartment day in, day out, feeding visitors who had come to offer condolences.

There was nothing left to keep Kalyopi, Latife's lifelong companion, in Turkey. Her relations moved her to Athens, where she died after a while.

With the exception of *Milliyet* columnist Burhan Felek, no one wrote about Latife Hanım. Neither historians nor philosophers offered much. The mindset that for years preferred to smear or ignore her altogether persevered even after her death.

Waxing lyrical about the dead is a Turkish tradition. Latife herself had expressed her own revulsion at this practice in a piece after the death of Ahmet Ağaoğlu. Signed 'An Old Friend', it says:

We like the dead because they have just resigned all their causes, needs, benefits, claims, passions and desires; that is why we lament over the body of someone whom we'd reviled in life.

Once we think upon this fact, it isn't hard to understand why we transform the 'blind into an almond-eyed beauty'! [...]

There are so many precious assets and well-known people who, in life, suffered untold hardships under general neglect, ignorance and ingratitude, whose graves now provide the stage for such bright commemorations that might endear death to us.[4]

The Turkey of 1975 wasted absolutely no effort to remake her into an 'almond-eyed beauty'. Latife Hanım was spared this ghastly indignity after her death.

38

Guarding the History
of the Republic in Her Safe

People suddenly noted a crucial fact after Latife's death: she had left this world without saying a single word about her years with Mustafa Kemal. Surprised, her detractors then went about restoring Latife to her former 'noble lady' status. All at once it was fashionable to begin, 'In a thoroughly dignified manner, she refrained from ever speaking ...' For some reason everyone dreaded she might denigrate Mustafa Kemal. But Latife was not his foe; she was his former wife. Those who had somehow moulded her into an enemy had ended up living in fear of their own creation.

Latife Hanım died misunderstood, and she had lamented this lack of appreciation. Yet she diligently guarded numerous papers that might one day help us understand her, keeping these in two bank safes in Istanbul. The letters she left behind sparked the imagination of the entire country, not to mention the press; so-called scoops abounded, reporting the discovery of her diaries in Switzerland, for instance.

Her family came to the conclusion that sharing these documents out amongst themselves would be the wrong thing to do. These were valuable documents on the history of the republic and had to be kept together. Just when they were debating what to do, Professor Enver Ziya Karal – then president of the Turkish History Society – contacted the family on 17 March 1976 with a proposal that they entrust Latife's documents with the THS. Her family accepted.

Latife had witnessed the birth of the Turkish Republic; she had kept notes, other documents and diaries. These documents – the mere possibility of whose eventual disclosure still fills so many hearts with dread – are much more than her personal history: they attest to the history of modern-day Turkey. Latife had worked like a one-person history society, a chronicler who safeguarded so much.

With the possibility of declassification and even publication on the agenda thirty years on, debates began to rage once more in early 2005. Some people created so much tension by claiming the publication of these documents would cast aspersions on Atatürk's life that Latife Hanım's family approached the THS to request the extension of the secret status. These documents were thus sentenced to obscurity once more. Professor Reşat Kaynar, after inspecting and reading through the entire collection, had written his evaluation on 10 April 1979:

> These documents are of a calibre high enough to serve as major documentary evidence in bolstering both the history of our reforms and the republic itself. Writing an accurate history of the reforms, and more importantly, of the republic, would be impossible until these documents have been inspected thoroughly. However much they might, in places, include personal expressions by Latife Hanım, this can never diminish their value as a crucial resource in the study of our history.

Latife's documents, logged as 219 separate items, still await the time they might see the light of day.

The wedding rings in the safes

Latife had died a rich woman. She had jewellery. She had property – a flat in Istanbul and more property in Izmir: a house, a commercial block and two plots, as well as shares in thirty-five plots and a building.

During the inventory of her private possessions, a wedding band turned up. Inscribed inside was 'Latife 1339 [AD 1923]' in old script. The ring had been kept together with the ten silver coins Mustafa Kemal had given her as immediate settlement at the wedding. Latife had wrapped these items she regarded as valuable in pink tissue, placed them in a jewellery box and wrapped the box in muslin. Also inside the box was a gold seal engraved with the names 'Mustafa Kemal' on one face and on the second, 'Latife Mustafa Kemal' (a present from the people of Adana during an official tour). These mementos were listed as 'historic items' before being wrapped again, placed in the box and finally wrapped in muslin once more. The muslin pouch opened at Osmanlı Bank Beyoğlu Branch on 10 April 1979 was sealed by court order.

Years earlier an 'engagement ring evidently made for a slender finger' had been found amongst Atatürk's personal possessions that emerged from his safe. Engraved inside the ring were the words 'Gazi M. Kemal 1339'.[1]

They had evidently exchanged their rings after they broke up.

Both Latife and Mustafa Kemal Atatürk kept the rings İsmet Paşa had bought for them in Lausanne as their wedding present until the end of their days, as mementos of their short-lived marriage.

Appendix I

Two Obituaries in the Foreign Press

LATİFE UŞŞAKI, WIFE OF ATATÜRK

Latife Uşşaki, once the wife of Kemal Atatürk, the late founder of the Turkish Republic, died Saturday after surviving her divorced husband by 37 years. Death was caused by heart trouble.

Latife Hanım, as she was called under a title given to distinguished women in the early years of the republic, was buried in a simple ceremony before a small crowd including a few officials today.

She and Atatürk married in 1923 but the marriage lasted only two and a half years.

14 July 1975, *The Washington Post*

LATİFE HANIM: A SYMBOLIC ROLE FOR TURKISH WOMEN

Latife Hanım, who was married for two years to Mustafa Kemal Atatürk, founder of modern Turkey, and played a symbolic role in the emancipation of Turkish womanhood, has died in Istanbul at the age of 76.

Born in 1898, the daughter of a wealthy family in Izmir (then Smyrna), Latife Hanım met the conquering Turkish commander after he rode triumphantly into Izmir following the Turkish rout of invading Greek troops in 1922. When a fire burnt much of Izmir, she invited Atatürk to stay at her family's villa in suburban Bornova [sic] while he directed negotiations with the First World War allies on Turkey's independence and new frontiers. Educated in France, she served as secretary and translator of French and English diplomatic correspondence for Atatürk. He stayed there for 20 days and then returned to Ankara, Turkey's new capital.

She wrote to him a (recently published) letter in October 1922 in which she said: 'My whole happiness lies in serving your excellency. My only wish is that my loyalty be a weapon at your side. How many people are there actually who love your excellency and are free from every sort of personal ambition?'

Latife proved her loyalty later, even though their marriage ended in divorce by refusing ever, as one Turkish writer put it, 'to exploit that great name for sensation or politics'.

Atatürk came to Izmir in January 1923, and married Latife. She was 24 and he was 42. Atatürk used Latife to show Turkish women how he expected them to act after the republic was declared in 1923. As President, he took her unveiled around the country with him to the discomfort of local officials who had to break tradition and bring their own wives into public. She was a symbol of the new Turkish women to be freed from the muslim restrictions of the harem and veil, under Atatürk's reforms.

Friction between Atatürk and Latife developed over his late nights and heavy drinking on top of a crushing work schedule. She attempted to put a rein on him to conserve his energy. Atatürk grew restive as she tried to order his regime and on August 5, 1925, he divorced her by the simple declaration, which was all that was necessary. Shortly thereafter the Turkish laws were changed including civil divorce giving women equal rights.

In her later years Latife Hanım lived a secluded life in a house in Istanbul's Ayaspaşa district overlooking the Bosphorus. She refused to the end to give press interviews or relate her memoirs, which would have been a blockbusting sensation in view of the idolisation of Atatürk in Turkey. Şevket Süreyya Aydemir, a close associate of Atatürk's, wrote recently that her seclusion and silence 'showed the signs of a dignity, sensitive and touching character'.

17 July 1975, *The Times*

Appendix II

An Obituary in the Turkish Press

LATİFE HANIM

With great regret, we have learned, from the most trusted sources of the press, of the passing of Atatürk's former wife, Latife Hanım.

A number of noteworthy women have commanded respect in the history of Turkey. Despite her self-imposed seclusion and the sad weight of a broken happiness, honourable yet short-lived, Latife Hanım has attained eternity through the medium of history as one of these women.

How thought-provoking and sad a coincidence it is that Latife Hanım closed her eyes as the World Conference of the International Women's Year (1975) comprising female delegates from 132 nations came to an end in Mexico City, without appointing a woman president or taking any resolutions concerning women – a total fiasco, in other words. The irony hasn't escaped our notice.

Fifty-two years ago in the days immediately following decisive victory, Latife Hanım found in herself the courage to marry one of the greatest military commanders and geniuses of all time, Gazi Mustafa Kemal Paşa, the saviour of Turkey, clearly proving her confidence in her own personality and femininity. This was praiseworthy indeed.

As an exceptional daughter of the Uşşaki [sic] family, who had raised remarkable children in their virtues and failings, Latife Hanım took more than her fair share of the attributes of her lineage, in my view. She was a cultured Turkish lady, an intellectual with vast knowledge who spoke several languages.

I had the opportunity to meet her on a boat trip some twenty to twenty-five years ago. She impressed me hugely with her knowledge, her demeanour and gravitas. Her knowledge was vast enough to enable her to make authoritative comments on whatever subject one might choose to discuss. To the extent that this knowledge at times overshadowed her femininity. I never had the opportunity to see her again after that journey. Today, as her abandoned, though above reproach, life has ended, I have come to the conclusion that she successfully carried out to the very end the requirements of the honourable status she once bore as Atatürk's wife.

What fate has decreed is foreknown to no one. The first lady of Turkey, from the moment she married Gazi Paşa in January 1923 to their break-up in August 1925, never relinquished this status. Whilst the whole world has watched countless merry first widows living it up, Latife Hanım never once considered marrying again, nor did the Gazi ever take up with another woman ...

And what was this incompatibility, in any case? I humbly hazard a guess that the cause might lie in a combination of external factors: Mustafa Kemal Paşa, just back from having vanquished an entire world of enemies, and thus having rescued Turkey, the dust of the battlefield still on his boots, about to embark upon a series of reforms intended to launch Turkey into the world of western civilisation, was surrounded by an Ottoman-style male-dominated entourage wherein his wife, eager to undertake as much work as she could bear, stood out, magnifying the slightest marital clash. Fate might have so decided.

I didn't know Latife Hanım that well. All I wished to do was to express in these lines the respect I felt for her determination to maintain her sad silence despite persistent requests, her composure as she nurtured the dignified liberty of happiness cut short, a happiness denied all others, as she refused to share even a single word of her reminiscences.

She had, a few years earlier, specifically asked for my intervention to stop the publication of yet another series of 'unofficial memoirs' that sought neither her knowledge nor her consent. I was president of the Journalists' Society at the time. I cannot recollect having been of any use. In an atmosphere where a plethora of interpretations of freedom of the press prevails, whose strings can you pull?

In summary, Gazi Mustafa Kemal would never become sultan, nor would Latife Hanım become an empress ... And the murky waters of the period, clouded by the dregs of Ottomanism, would never allow them to unite as two citizens of Turkey.

This is what we call fate.

I call upon God to grant Latife Hanım peace eternal.

Burhan Felek, 16 July 1975, *Milliyet*

Biographical Notes

Some of the principal persons mentioned in the text are arranged by given name, since surnames were adopted later. All the officers were veterans of the Balkan Wars and the Great War before joining the Nationalists.

AFET INAN (SALONICA 1908–1985)
A teacher who accompanied Mustafa Kemal after his divorce. Under his patronage, she studied in Geneva, became a historian and carried out research into Turks as a race. Served as deputy president of the Turkish History Society for many years. Contributed to the promotion of the Piri Reis map of the world.

AHMET (BEY AĞAYEV) AĞAOĞLU (SHUSHA 1869–1939)
Prominent Azeri and Turkish publicist, a pan-Turkist, secularist and defender of women's emancipation. A multilingual journalist, graduate of the universities of St Petersburg and the Sorbonne, exiled by the British to Malta in 1919. After his release, served as the director of the press bureau, editor-in-chief of the official newspaper and advisor and close friend of Atatürk. He, his wife, Sitare, and their daughters were very close to Latife and Mustafa Kemal during their marriage. His daughters were pioneers of their era: Süreyya, the first female lawyer; Tezer Taşkıran, a philosopher, educator and MP; and Gültekin, a doctor.

ALI FUAT CEBESOY (ISTANBUL 1882–1968)
Officer and politician, Mustafa Kemal's classmate from War College, War of Independence commander, MP, diplomat, deputy speaker. One of the founders of the PRP, tried for involvement in an assassination plot against Mustafa Kemal and acquitted, he later returned to parliament. Speaker in 1948, and Democrat Party MP for ten years from 1950.

(MEHMET) CEVAT ABBAS GÜRER (NIŞ 1887–1943)

Officer, politician, diplomat and chief aide-de-camp to Mustafa Kemal. Elected from Bolu county to the last Ottoman parliament, he then served in the Nationalist parliament in the same capacity. Founded the Turkish Aviation Society and was amongst the founders of İş Bank. His wife, Memduha, introduced Latife to the women of Ankara; the two women's friendship survived their divorces. (Memduha and Cevat Abbas also divorced later.)

FAHRETTIN ALTAY (SHKODËR 1880–1974)

Officer and statesman; the Turkish commander who led the cavalry liberating Izmir on 9 September 1922. Although born in today's Albania, he came from an Izmir family. Joined the Nationalists after organising resistance against the occupying Greeks. Resigned his seat in parliament, preferring to continue to serve as a soldier. Later served as commander of the First Army Corps and patron of equestrian sports. Escorted Edward VIII in Gallipoli in 1936. Commanded Atatürk's funeral and served as Burdur MP.

(ALI) FETHI OKYAR (PRILEP 1880–1943)

Officer and statesman, member of the CUP, exiled to Malta after the Mudros armistice. Served as home secretary, prime minister and speaker during the War of Independence and later in the republic. Generally viewed as more liberal and conciliatory than İsmet, had to resign in the wake of the Şeyh Said revolt and go to Paris as ambassador. Commissioned by Mustafa Kemal to form the FRP in 1930, which he soon had to abolish in the face of growing opposition to Mustafa Kemal. He and his wife, Galibe, were very close to Latife and Mustafa Kemal during their marriage, and their friendship with Latife continued.

(MUSTAFA) FEVZI ÇAKMAK (ISTANBUL 1876–1950)

Officer and statesman, one of the only two marshals in the Turkish Republic (the other was Atatürk). Chief of the general staff after Mudros, later Ottoman war minister. He joined the Nationalists in 1920. MP, defence and deputy prime minister and deputy chief-of-staff, later prime minister and substantive chief of the General Staff. Promoted to marshal after Dumplupınar, he stayed in charge of the armed forces until retirement. Joined the opposition to President İnönü in 1946.

HALIDE EDIB ADIVAR (ISTANBUL 1882–1964)

Feminist, writer, educator and political activist. An outspoken opponent of Allied occupation of Turkey, she is famous for her public speeches decrying the partition. Joined the Nationalists and served in the army as sergeant. Their critical stance on Mustafa Kemal attracted accusations of treason, and she and her husband, Dr Adnan Adıvar, deputy speaker and a cabinet minister, had to leave Turkey for a long exile in London and Paris until 1939. Founded the School of English Philology at Istanbul University upon her return. Later served as MP and columnist. Wrote many novels, as well as her memoirs and works on the foundation and prospects of the Turkish Republic.

(MEHMED) HALIT ZIYA UŞAKLIGIL (ISTANBUL 1867–1945)

Writer, cousin to Muammer Uşşakizade and father of Vedad. Chamberlain to Sultan Abdülhamid, later chief chancery clerk to Mehmed Reşad and MP in the Ottoman parliament. Published a newspaper and contributed to others, writing novels in instalments, short stories, essays, poems and travel journals, and tutored his niece Latife in Turkish literature. Overhauled and simplified his own work after the adoption of Latin script. His novels that examine complex personalities and relationships still inspire highly popular adaptations.

(MUSTAFA) ISMET INÖNÜ (IZMIR 1884–1973)

Top graduate of Staff College in 1906, he joined the CUP and later served under Mustafa Kemal throughout the Great War. Joined the Nationalists in 1920, serving as chief-of-staff, MP, cabinet member, deputy war minister and western front commander during the War of Independence. Victorious commander of the two İnönü battles and planner of the final offensive. As foreign minister, he led the Turkish delegation in Lausanne and signed the treaty in 1923. Served as prime minister on a number of occasions. Fell out with Atatürk in 1937 and was elected president upon Atatürk's death. Kept Turkey out of the Second World War. Presided over the introduction of multiparty democracy, alternately serving as prime minister and leader of the opposition. His wife, Mevhibe, was a close friend of Latife Hanım's.

(MUSA) KÂZIM KARABEKIR (ISTANBUL 1882–1948)
Top graduate of Staff College in 1905 and a former colleague of Enver Paşa in the CUP. Recaptured Erzurum and Kars after the Great War, sponsoring the eastern Anatolia congress and helping Mustafa Kemal assume leadership of the Nationalists. Known as the Father of Orphans for taking thousands of war orphans under his wing. Founded the PRP after disagreements with Mustafa Kemal. Accused of involvement in an assassination plot, he withdrew from politics until after Atatürk's death. Elected an MP in 1939.

(EMRULLAHZADE ASAF) KILIÇ ALI (GAZIANTEP 1888–1971)
Officer, politician and aide-de-camp to Mustafa Kemal. One of Mustafa Kemal's inseparable companions, member of the Independence Tribunal in 1926 and MP for Gaziantep. Married Füreya Koral, Turkey's first woman ceramicist.

NEZIHE MUHIDDIN TEPEDENGIL (ISTANBUL 1889–1958)
Women's rights activist, journalist, writer, teacher and political leader. Educated privately. Founded *The Turkish Women's Path* magazine in 1924, financing it personally for eighteen issues. Founded the Women's People's Party, the first women's political party in the history of the republic. In the face of official refusal of recognition – on the pretext that women had no rights of political representation – she led the formation of the Union of the Women of Turkey. Later sidelined and even falsely charged with corruption, she withdrew from politics and focused on her writing. She died in an asylum.

(HÜSEYIN) RAUF ORBAY (ISTANBUL 1881–1964)
Naval commander, Great War hero, leader of the resistance and later a politician. The famed commander of the battleship *Hamidiye*, leader of

the Ottoman delegation that signed the Mudros armistice, arrested and exiled by the British to Malta in 1920. Joined the government in Ankara after his release and served as prime minister. Resigned and founded the PRP. Accused of being involved in an assassination plot, he returned from exile but did not make peace with Atatürk, after whose death he served as MP and later ambassador.

RIZA NUR (SINOP 1878–1942)

An army doctor, he moved to the opposition from the CUP and had to flee abroad until 1918. Joined the Nationalists and served as minister of health and education until he fell out with Mustafa Kemal; lived in Paris until 1939. Wrote his memoirs concerning Atatürk and entrusted them to the British Museum on the proviso that they would not be opened until 1960. Known as a Turkist and a leading detractor of Atatürk. His wife and Latife were related.

SALIH BOZOK (SALONICA 1881–1941)

Distant relative and inseparable companion of Mustafa Kemal. A CUP member, he joined Mustafa Kemal's staff in 1917. Chief aide-de-camp and later MP, Bozok survived a suicide attempt on the day Atatürk died.

(MEHMED) ZIYA GÖKALP (ÇERNIK 1876–1924)

Sociologist, writer, poet and political activist. Dropped out of veterinary school to focus on politics, and joined the CUP. Principal proponent of Turkism, an ideology he based not on ethnic, racial, geographic, political or volitional groups, but one composed of individuals who share a common language, religion, morality and aesthetics. Known as the father of Turkish nationalism.

Acknowledgements

When *Latife Hanım* was first published I got into trouble, facing criminal charges. PEN supported me at the time, and five years later, they have extended a helping hand once again. Sara Whyatt, my friend from PEN International, provided the first inspiration. She'd been wishing she could read *Latife Hanım*, and suggested last year that PEN might recommend this book, 'and then we could all read it'. Just then I received some good news: Feyza Howell wanted to translate *Latife Hanım* into English, and Nermin Mollaoğlu of the Kalem Agency added her own encouragement. Their combined tenacity stimulated me. Translation was no simple matter: the text had to be edited for a new readership, necessitating additions and deletions, and material published outside of Turkey had to be sourced. Feyza's energy proved equal to this exhausting task: she not only translated the book, but worked miracles in sourcing the quotes in their original languages. The original book ran to 500 pages so I, too, had my orders. I deleted sections originally written to convince a potentially sceptical readership in Turkey, and I abbreviated the text.

We then applied to English PEN, contacting Emma Cleave, manager of the Writers in Translation Programme. A professional reader's report was needed to complete the application process. The reader proposed was inspiring: Moris Farhi, writer and vice president of PEN International. He wrote a wonderful analysis I shall always treasure. Five women – that is, Sara, Emma, Nermin, Feyza and I – combined our efforts, and Moris championed us all to bring *Madam Atatürk* to the attention of international readers.

So many friends offered their assistance as I was writing Latife Hanım's biography. I have had the opportunity to thank them all repeatedly, and so will refrain from presenting you with a very long list here. There are some people, however, without whose support this book would have been much poorer, and I hereby thank members of Latife's family once more: Muammer Erboy, Mehmet Öke and – sadly – the late Gülümser Öke.

And as ever, heartfelt thanks to our own families, who affectionately supported us through the numerous hours of work.

Notes

Chapter 1

1. S. Pekşen, 'Atatürk'ün Özel Yaşamı, Vecihe İlmen Anlatıyor', *Cumhuriyet* (10 November 1984). All further quotes from Vecihe İlmen – Latife's sister – are taken from this interview.
2. M. Dobkin, *Smyrna 1922*, p. 103
3. Dobkin, pp. 107–108
4. From an interview with Feyza İplikçi Howell, great-granddaughter of Hacı İsmail İplikçizade; this was the house commandeered by Venizelos and King Constantine during the Greek occupation.
5. H. Adıvar, *The Turkish Ordeal*, pp. 384–85
6. Adıvar, p. 387
7. From an interview with Zeynep Lange, granddaughter of Halit Ziya
8. I. Marcosson, *The Turbulent Years*, p. 171

Chapter 2

1. H. Uşaklıgil, *Kırk Yıl*, p. 21
2. S. Yücel, 'Uşşakizadeler', *Izmir Life*, (24 August 2003)
3. N. Moralı, *Mütarekede Izmir, Önceleri ve Sonraları*, p. 129
4. Y. Aksoy, *Bir Kent Bir İnsan*, p. 43
5. Nationalised by the Karşıyaka Council in 2005 and restored, this house serves as a cultural centre. The street itself was renamed after Latife Hanım on International Women's Day (8 March) in 1998.
6. Uşaklıgil, pp. 303–306
7. I. Grosser-Rilke, *Nie Verwehte Klänge*, p. 198
8. The date on Latife's wedding certificate is 1315 AH (1899 AD), but her tombstone states 1900. I took the certificate as my basis.
9. Yücel
10. R. Beyru, *On Dokuzuncu Yüzyılda Izmir'de Yaşam*, pp. 300, 308
11. 'Dilimiz', *Türk Yurdu* (September 1917), p. 213
12. Uşaklıgil, p. 111
13. H. Armstrong, *Grey Wolf: The Life of Kemal Atatürk*, p. 200
14. Grosser-Rilke, p. 198

Chapter 3

1. B. Umar, *Izmir'de Yunanlıların Son Günleri*, p. 13
2. T. Baran, *Bir Kentin Yeniden Yapılanması, Izmir 1923–1938*, p. 25

3.   S. Kurnaz, *Cumhuriyet Öncesinde Türk Kadını*, p. 125
4.   Quoted by Beyru, p. 206, from Karal, p. 274
5.   Quoted by Beyru, p. 207, from *Hizmet*, 7 January 1890
6.   Aksoy, p. 43
7.   "Long live Venizelos!" Venizelos was the prime minister of Greece at the time.
8.   Adıvar, p. 23
9.   Dobkin, p. 84

Chapter 4
1.   C. Snowden, *Tudor Hall: The First Hundred Years 1850–1949*, pp. 22–41
2.   N. Özgentürk, 'Halam Hep Yalnızdı', *Sabah* (1 November 2003)
3.   Adıvar, p. 385
4.   Adıvar, p. 386
5.   I. Bozdağ, *Atatürk'ün Başyaveri Salih Bozok anlatıyor, Latife ve Fikriye, İki Aşk Arasında Atatürk*, p. 79
6.   Z. Oranlı, *Atatürk'ün Şimdiye Kadar Yayınlanmamış Anıları: Anlatan Ali Metin, Emir Çavuşu*, p. 139
7.   Bozdağ, pp. 81–82
8.   F. Atay, *Çankaya*, p. 325
9.   T. Özalp and K. Özalp, *Atatürk'ten Anılar*, p. 300
10.   Quoted by Akay, p. 87, from Külçe, p. 236
11.   I. İnönü, *Hatıralar*, p. 300
12.   B. Şimşir, *Atatürk ile Yazışmalar*, p. 274
13.   D. von Mikusch, *Mustapha Kemal: Between Europe and Asia*, pp. 331–32
14.   B. Georges-Gaulis, *La Nouvelle Turquie*, p. 219
15.   Ibid.
16.   Adıvar, p. 387
17.   Adıvar, p. 389
18.   Quoted by Akay, p. 87, from Külçe, p. 236
19.   C. Sheridan, *Nuda Veritas*, p. 276
20.   Sheridan, pp. 277–78
21.   M. Baler, *Baldan Damlalar 3 ve Hatıralarım*, pp. 59–60

Chapter 5
1.   P. Kinross, *Atatürk: The Rebirth of a Nation*, p. 329
2.   V. Volkan and N. Itkowitz, *The Immortal Atatürk: A Psychobiography*, p. 203
3.   Bozdağ, *Atatürk'ün Başyaveri Salih Bozok anlatıyor*, pp. 86–87
4.   Georges-Gaulis, p. 219
5.   F. Bayhan and M. Sadık Öke, *Teyzem Latife*, pp. 130–31
6.   Y. Süsoy, 'Latife Hanım'ın Öyküsünü Sıfırcı Baha'dan Dinleyin', *Hürriyet* (16 June 2003)
7.   Bozdağ, p. 92
8.   Bozdağ, pp. 91–92

Chapter 6
1.   Bozdağ, *Atatürk'ün Başyaveri Salih Bozok anlatıyor*, p. 98
2.   Bozdağ, p. 98

3. B. Bozok and C. Bozok, *Hep Atatürk'ün Yanında,* p. 215
4. Bozdağ, *Atatürk ve Eşi Latife Hanım,* p. 66
5. Bozdağ, p. 66
6. Bozdağ, *Atatürk'ün Başyaveri Salih Bozok anlatıyor,* p. 55
7. Adıvar, p. 398
8. A. Gündüz, *Hatıratlarım,* p. 208
9. Bozok, p. 95
10. Letter to Salih Bozok from Latife Hanım, 26 October 1922
11. C. Dündar, 'Söz Kız Tarafında', *Milliyet* (10 November 2004)
12. Bozdağ, p. 122

Chapter 7
1. Volkan and Itkowitz, p. 73
2. C. Sönmez, *Atatürk'ün Annesi Zübeyde Hanım,* pp. 13–20
3. A. Yalman, *Atatürk'ün Söylev ve Demeçleri,* p. 39
4. Sönmez, p. 31
5. C. Gürer, *Ebedi Şef Kurtarıcı Atatürk'ün Zengin Tarihinden Birkaç Yaprak,* pp. 88–89
6. Sönmez, p. 38
7. M. Atatürk, *Atatürk'ün Söylev ve Demeçleri,* p. 40
8. Today's Bitola in FYR Macedonia.
9. S. Belli, *Fikriye,* p. 83
10. Sönmez, p. 86

Chapter 8
1. Oranlı, pp. 141–42
2. Bozdağ, 2005, pp. 122–23
3. Gündüz, p. 208
4. Z. Oranlı, *Atatürk'ün Şimdiye Kadar Yayınlanmamış Anıları: Anlatan Ali Metin, Emir Çavuşu,* pp. 140–41
5. Bozdağ, *Atatürk'ün Başyaveri Salih Bozok anlatıyor,* pp. 123–24
6. Bozdağ, *Gazi ve Latife,* p. 87
7. G. Ellison, *An Englishwoman in Angora,* pp. 189–90
8. İ. Sevük, *Atatürk İçin,* pp. 20–23
9. U. Kocatürk, *Kaynakçalı Atatürk Günlüğü,* p. 317
10. Ellison, pp. 185–86
11. Kocatürk, *Atatürk Çizgisinde Geçmişten Geleceğe,* p. 373
12. Sönmez, p. 105
13. Kocatürk, p. 373

Chapter 9
1. Bozok and Bozok, p. 211
2. Bozdağ, *Atatürk'ün Başyaveri Salih Bozok anlatıyor,* pp. 132–33
3. 'Mme. Kemal Tells of Her Romantic Marriage to the Turkish President', *Current Opinion* (January 1924), p. 80.
4. Volkan and Itkowitz, p. 220

5.   Ellison, p. 186
6.   Dündar, 'Yüzyılın Aşkları – Latife Hanım', CNN (10 November 2004)
7.   F. Ahmad, 'The Development of Capitalism in Turkey', *Journal of Third World Studies* (Autumn 1998)
8.   Yalman [II], *Yakın Tarihte Gördüklerim ve Geçirdiklerim*, p. 830

Chapter 10

1.   Atatürk, vol. II, p. 91
2.   von Mikusch, p. 333
3.   N. Kal, *Atatürk'le Yaşayanlar*, p. 115
4.   Volkan and Itkowitz, p. 228
5.   G. Ökçün, *Türkiye İktisat Kongresi, Izmir 1923*, pp. 194, 326
6.   L. Lue, 'Kemal and Wife Pledge Liberty of Turk Women', *Chicago Daily Tribune* (28 February 1923), p. 6
7.   G. Price, *Extra-Special Correspondent*, p. 140

Chapter 11

1.   Armstrong, p. 201
2.   Adıvar, p. 388
3.   I. Marcosson, 'Kemal Pasha', *Saturday Evening Post* (20 October 1923)
4.   Marcosson, *The Turbulent Years*, pp. 169–70
5.   Bozdağ, *Atatürk ve Eşi Latife Hanım*, p. 137
6.   Quoted by Orhan Koloğlu, 'İki Şehrin Hikâyesi' ('A Tale of Two Cities'), *The Times*, 28 December 1923, ed. Seyfi Öngider, Aykırı, Istanbul 2003, p. 18
7.   Atay, p. 355
8.   Ibid.
9.   Atay, p. 350
10. N. Yiğit, *Atatürk'le 30 Yıl*, p. 180
11. Atay, p. 353

Chapter 12

1.   Bozdağ, *Atatürk ve Eşi Latife Hanım*, p. 66
2.   G. Bilgehan, 'Çankaya'nın Hanımefendileri', *Milliyet* (11–12 October 1982)
3.   Yiğit, p. 181
4.   Bozdağ, p. 154
5.   Bozdağ, *Atatürk ve Eşi Latife Hanım*, pp. 156–57
6.   Banoğlu, 'Atatürk ve Latife Hanım', *AAMD* (July 1991), p. 530

Chapter 13

1.   Price, p. 141
2.   Ibid.
3.   Georges-Gaulis, pp. 213–21

Chapter 14

1.   Arıkoğlu, *Hatıralarım*, p. 306
2.   Atatürk, vol. II, pp. 151–57

3.   Sevük, p. 100
4.   Sevük, p. 57
5.   Çankaya, p. 196
6.   Bozdağ, *Atatürk ve Eşi Latife Hanım*, p. 174

Chapter 15
1.   M. Perinçek, *Atatürk'ün Sovyetlerle Görüşmeleri*, p. 397
2.   P. Gentizon, *Mustapha Kemal, ou, L'Orient en Marche*, p. 163
3.   G. Bilgehan, *Mevhibe*, p. 117
4.   Bilgehan, pp. 139–40
5.   Sevük, pp. 53–54
6.   Atay, p. 412
7 . *Yakın Tarihimiz*, vol. II, issue 16, pp. 87–88

Chapter 16
1.   A. Demirel, *Birinci Meclis'te Muhalefet İkinci Grup*, p. 508
2.   Kılıç Ali, *Kılıç Ali'nin Anıları*, p. 188
3.   Demirel, p. 392
4.   Bozdağ, *Gazi ve Latife*, p. 139
5.   R. Nur, *Hayat ve Hatıratım*, vol. II, p. 380
6.   Şener, p. 103
7.   Nur, vol. II, p. 389
8.   Mehmet Sadık Öke was originally reluctant to be cited. After the book ran to several editions and I was charged with insulting Atatürk, however, he issued a detailed statement to the press, which I then used in my defence. I was acquitted in December 2006.
9.   Kılıç Ali, p. 60
10. Nur, vol. II, p. 385
11. Kılıç Ali, *Kılıç Ali'nin Anıları*, p. 193
12. Şener, p. 115

Chapter 17
1.   Bozdağ, *Atatürk'ün Başyaveri Salih Bozok anlatıyor*, p. 148
2.   T. Taşkıran, *Cumhuriyetin 50. Yılında Türk Kadın Hakları*, pp. 97–99
3.   Zihnioğlu, p. 122
4.   Bozdağ, *Atatürk ve Eşi Latife Hanım*, pp. 177–78
5.   Y. Zihnioğlu, *Kadınsız İnkılap*, p. 123
6.   Bozdağ, pp. 177–78
7.   Zihnioğlu, p. 139
8.   Bozdağ, pp. 178–80
9.   Bozdağ, p. 179
10. From the Women's Status Directorate General of the Ministry of Family and Social Policies web site.
11. Zihnioğlu, p. 56
12. Marcosson, 'Kemal Pasha', *Saturday Evening Post* (20 October 1923)
13. Cebesoy, *Siyasi Hatıralar, Lozan'dan Cumhuriyete*, p. 4

Chapter 18

1. Marcosson, 'Kemal Pasha', *Saturday Evening Post* (20 October 1923)
2. Bozdağ, *Atatürk ve Eşi Latife Hanım*, p. 212
3. Mevlüt Baysal was a landscape architect and agriculturalist who was in charge of the Çankaya grounds and gardens.
4. K. Karabekir, *Paşaların Kavgası*, p. 273
5. Marcosson
6. M. Baysal, *Çankaya'da Gazi'nin Hizmetinde*, pp. 95–100
7. Bilgehan, 'Çankaya'nın Hanımefendileri', *Milliyet* (11–12 October 1982)
8. Pekşen, 'Atatürk'ün Özel Yaşamı, Vecihe İlmen Anlatıyor', *Cumhuriyet* (10 November 1984)
9. Bilgehan
10. Uşaklıgil, *Bir Acı Hikâye*, pp. 112–14 (Vedad committed suicide in 1937)
11. S. Selçuker, 'Kadın Gözü ile Atatürk, Süreyya Ağaoğlu'yla Görüşme', *Güneş*, date unknown.

Chapter 19

1. Cebesoy, vol. I, p. 143
2. Marcosson, 'Kemal Pasha', *Saturday Evening Post* (20 October 1923)
3. Bilgehan, 'Çankaya'nın Hanımefendileri', *Milliyet* (11–12 October 1982)
4. Bozdağ, *Atatürk ve Eşi Latife Hanım*, pp. 215–16

Chapter 20

1. H. Soyak, *Atatürk'ten Hatıralar*, pp. 36, 684
2. Cebesoy, vol. II, pp. 59–60
3. Soyak, p. 684
4. Bozdağ, *Atatürk ve Eşi Latife Hanım*, pp. 222, 223

Chapter 21

1. E. Ülger, *Latife Gazi Mustafa Kemal*, pp. 20–21
2. Bozdağ, *Atatürk ve Eşi Latife Hanım*, p. 223
3. Bozdağ, p. 224
4. Banoğlu, pp. 524–26
5. Bilgehan, *Mevhibe*, pp. 101, 168–69
6. Dündar, 'Latife Hanım'ın Atatürk'süz Hayatı', *Milliyet* (28 October 2003)
7. Tunçay, *Türkiye Cumhuriyetinde Tek Parti Yönetimi*, p. 90
8. Yalman, vol. I, pp. 916–18
9. Ülger, p. 127
10. Marcosson, 'Kemal Pasha', *Saturday Evening Post* (20 October 1923)
11. Baltacıoğlu, pp. 107–10
12. Bozdağ, *Atatürk ve Eşi Latife Hanım*, pp. 225–26
13. Cebesoy, *Siyasi Hatıralar, Lozan'dan Cumhuriyete*, p. 67
14. Tunçay, p. 228

Chapter 22

1. Bozdağ, *Atatürk ve Eşi Latife Hanım*, pp. 148–50
2. Kinross, p. 389
3. T. Çavuşoğlu, *Çocuk Esirgeme Kurumu*, p. 10
4. Zihnioğlu, p. 222 (Zihnioğlu personally gave me the transcription of the speech that was not included in the book.)

Chapter 23

1. Oranlı, p. 88
2. Yiğit, p. 231
3. Bilgehan, *Mevhibe*, p. 206
4. Bilgehan, 'Çankaya'nın Hanımefendileri', *Milliyet* (11–12 October 1982)
5. Ibid.
6. Bilgehan, *Mevhibe*
7. Ağaoğlu, pp. 40–42
8. Atay, p. 412
9. Bozdağ, *Atatürk'ün Başyaveri Salih Bozok anlatıyor*, pp. 143, 144
10. Bozdağ, p. 144
11. Bozdağ *Atatürk ve Eşi Latife Hanım*, p. 211
12. Volkan and Itkowitz, p. 244
13. Kinross, pp. 389–90

Chapter 24

1. Beni Hasan, 'Kemal Pasha at Home – The New Master of Turkey', *The Mentor* (May 1927)
2. Ağaoğlu, p. 185
3. B. Aslan, pp. 270–71 (Abilov died following a coronary during the congress.)
4. 'Mme. Kemal Tells of Her Romantic Marriage to the Turkish President', *Current Opinion* (January 1924), p. 80
5. Kinross, p. 389
6. H. Öz, *Atatürk Tarsus'ta*, p. 21
7. J. Glasneck, *Kemal Atatürk ve Çağdaş Türkiye*, p. 34
8. H. Gerede, *Hüsrev Gerede's Memoirs*, p. 247
9. B. Ötüş-Baskett, *Nezihe Muhiddin ve Türk Kadını*, pp. 156–59
10. Ötüş-Baskett, p. 161
11. H. Cin, *İslam ve Osmanlı Hukukunda Evlenme*, p. 288
12. Cin, p. 291
13. Şimşir [II], p. 814
14. Tunçay, 'Latife Hanım–Kameneva Mektuplaşması', *Toplumsal Tarih* (March 2003)
15. Zihnioğlu, p. 7
16. Fatma Aliye Hanım Archive, envelope number 12, document number 29, cited by Zehra Toska, *Cumhuriyet'in Kadın İdeali, Eşiği Aşanlar ve Aşmayanlar, 75 Yılda Kadınlar ve Erkekler* (The Feminine Ideal of the Republic, The Glass Ceiling, Women and Men on the 75th Anniversary), Istanbul: Tarih Vakfı, 1998, p. 76
17. von Mikusch, pp. 333, 369
18. J. Villalta, *Atatürk*, p. 362

Chapter 25

1. Bozdağ, *Atatürk ve Eşi Latife Hanım*, p. 190; Bozdağ, *Atatürk'ün Başyaveri Salih Bozok anlatıyor*, p. 150
2. Belli, p. 96
3. Belli, p. 98
4. Yiğit, p. 232
5. Dündar, 11 November 2004
6. Kılıç Ali, *Kılıç Ali'nin Anıları*, pp. 545–46
7. Kılıç Ali, p. 547
8. Belli, p. 103
9. Dündar, 'Fikriye', Milliyet (1992), p. 34
10. Belli, p. 99
11. Oranlı, pp. 146–47
12. Ülger, pp. 113–19
13. Bozdağ, *Atatürk'ün Başyaveri Salih Bozok anlatıyor*, p. 154
14. Ülger, pp. 113–19
15. Bozdağ, *Atatürk ve Eşi Latife Hanım*, pp. 206–208
16. Bozdağ, pp. 210–11

Chapter 26

1. Glasneck, p. 43
2. D. Avcıoğlu, *Türkiye'nin Düzeni*, p. 207
3. Tunçay, *Türkiye Cumhuriyetinde Tek Parti Yönetimi*, p. 206
4. Glasneck, p. 52
5. F. Alpkaya, *Türkiye Cumhuriyet'nin Kuruluşu*, p. 190
6. U. Kocabaşoğlu, *İş Bankası Tarihi*, p. 85
7. Kocabaşoğlu, p. 626

Chapter 27

1. Bozdağ, *Atatürk ve Eşi Latife Hanım*, p. 249
2. S. Aydemir, *Tek Adam: Mustafa Kemal*, p. 295
3. Bozdağ, *Atatürk ve Eşi Latife Hanım*, pp. 249–50
4. *Cumhuriyet*, 18 September 1924
5. Aydemir, pp. 487–88
6. N. Onat, *Cumhurbaşkanı Gazi M. Kemal Paşa'nın Sonbahar Gezileri*, p. 117
7. M. Önder, *Atatürk'ün Yurt Gezileri*, p. 149
8. Bozdağ, p. 255
9. Gündüz, p. 210
10. Kılıç Ali, *Kılıç Ali'nin Anıları*, p. 540
11. Bozok and Bozok, p. 223
12. E. Çölaşan, 'Leman Karaosmanoğlu ile Sohbet, Atatürk'ü İki Kadın Deli Gibi Severdi', *Hürriyet* (10 November 1985)
13. Bozdağ, p. 209

Chapter 28

1. Armstrong, p. 252
2. E. Zürcher, *Political Opposition in the Early Turkish Republic: The Progressive Republican Party (1924–1925)*, p. 46; Cebesoy [II], pp. 225–33
3. Zürcher, pp. 47–48
4. Tunçay, *Türkiye Cumhuriyetinde Tek Parti Yönetimi*, p. 104
5. Zürcher, pp. 48–49
6. Y. Karaosmanoğlu, *Politikada 45 Yıl*, pp. 66–70
7. Tunçay, p. 105
8. Tunaya, p. 477
9. Z. Sertel, *Türkiye'de Siyasal Partiler*, pp. 128–33
10. Tunçay, p. 110
11. H. Uyar, *Tek Parti Dönemi ve CHP*, p. 104
12. Zürcher, p. 58
13. Zihnioğlu, p. 177
14. Tunçay, p. 110
15. Zürcher, p. 72
16. Zürcher, p. 81
17. Ibid.
18. Zürcher, p. 85
19. Tunçay, p. 149
20. Kinross, p. 400
21. Tunçay, p. 136
22. *Cumhuriyet*, 24 May 1925, p. 3
23. Cebesoy, vol. II, p. 170
24. Yalman, vol. II, p. 922
25. Tunçay, p. 164
26. Kinross, p. 402
27. Kinross, p. 390; Price, p. 141
28. Bozdağ, 1991, pp. 182–83
29. Villalta, p. 361
30. Armstrong, pp. 252–53

Chapter 29

1. Volkan and Itkowitz, p. 223
2. Aydemir, p. 486
3. Adıvar, p. 387
4. Armstrong, p. 202
5. Kinross, p. 389
6. M. Atadan, *Ağabeyim Mustafa Kemal*, p. 58
7. L. Bryant, 'A Turkish Divorce', *The Nation* (26 August 1925)
8. Georges-Gaulis, p. 215
9. von Mikusch, pp. 369; Vamık Volkan's talk on the TRT on 10 November.
10. Volkan and Itkowitz, p. 223
11. Armstrong, p. 253
12. Aydemir, p. 486

13. Selçuker, 'Kadın Gözü ile Atatürk, Süreyya Ağaoğlu'yla Görüşme', Güneş, date unknown.
14. Kinross, p. 390
15. Külçe, quoted by Akay, p. 87
16. H. Gerede, *Hüsrev Gerede's Memoirs*, p. 270
17. Kinross, p. 422
18. Selçuker
19. Volkan and Itkowitz, p. 244
20. Lengyel, p. 299
21. Interview with Aydan Eralp, April 2005
22. Kinross, p. 391
23. Gerede, p. 247

Chapter 30
1. Kinross, p. 423
2. Pekşen
3. M. Barlas, *Latife Hanım'ın Sırları ve Türk Sosyetesi*
4. Bozdağ, *Atatürk ve Eşi Latife Hanım*, p. 266
5. Soyak, p. 10
6. 'Atatürk'ün Boşanma Mektubu Göz Yaşartacak' ('Atatürk's Divorce Letter Will Bring You to Tears'), Yeni Şafak, 6 December 2004.
7. Uşaklıgil, *Bir Acı Hikâye*, pp. 116–18
8. Bilgehan, *Mevhibe*, p. 186
9. Akay, p. 179
10. Bozok and Bozok, p. 219
11. Kinross, p. 423

Chapter 31
1. Barlas,
2. '61. Yıldönümünde Atatürk'ün Boşanma Öyküsü' ('Atatürk and the Tale of His Divorce on Its 61st Anniversary'), trans. Tanıl Bora, Tarih ve Toplum, August 1986, issue 32.
3. Dündar, 28 October 2003
4. T. Sorgun, *İmparatorluktan Cumhuriyete: Fahrettin Altay Paşa Anlatıyor*, pp. 389–90
5. Akay, p. 184
6. Belli, p. 105
7. Uşaklıgil, *Bir Acı Hikâye*, p. 116
8. Interview with Şehvar Çağlayan
9. Kinross, p. 423
10. Villalta, p. 361
11. von Mikusch, p. 369
12. *Toronto Daily Star*, 28 August 1925

Chapter 32
1. Kocatürk, 2005, p. 375
2. Sorgun, p. 403

3. S. Kaplan, 'Latife Hanım'ın Günlüğünü Bir Bilim Kurulu İncelesin', *Hürriyet* (3 January 2005)
4. *Toronto Daily Star*, 10 June 1926
5. *Washington Post*, 14 June 1926
6. Nur, vol. III, p. 316
7. Barlas, p. 27
8. Barlas, p. 47

Chapter 33
1. Sorgun, pp. 389–415; Altay, p. 30
2. Atadan, p. 50
3. Sorgun, p. 390
4. Sorgun, p. 399
5. Sorgun, p. 405
6. Interview with Suna Güler
7. Selçuker
8. Bilgehan, *Mevhibe*
9. A. İnan, pp. 269–71

Chapter 34
1. F. Okyar, *Üç Devirde Bir Adam*, p. 378; Okyar *Fethi Okyar'ın Anıları*, p. 98
2. Okyar, *Serbest Cumhuriyet Fırkası Nasıl Doğdu, Nasıl Feshedildi?*, pp. 7–37
3. Okyar, p. 66
4. This section is a fictionalised account based on numerous interviews.
5. Okyar, p. 73
6. This section is a fictionalised account, based on numerous interviews.
7. Tunçay, pp. 280–82
8. Yetkin, pp. 194–95
9. Karaosmanoğlu, p. 96
10. Borak, p. 29
11. Kılıç Ali, *Atatürk'ün Hususiyetleri*, p. 96
12. S. Borak, *Atatürk'ün Armstrong'a Cevabı*, p. 30
13. Uşaklıgil, *Bir Acı Hikâye*, pp. 135–3
14. From an interview with Zeynep Lange

Chapter 35
1. Banoğlu, p. 526
2. 'What did Latife Hanım Feel on 10 November?' *Milliyet* (8 May 2006)
4. Interview with Şehvar Çağlayan, 2005
5. Interview with Şen Sılan
6. Interview with Füsun İşcan
7. Özgentürk, 'Gazi'den Sonra', *Sabah*
8. Özgentürk, 'Halam Hep Yalnızdı', *Sabah*
9. Y. Yurdakul, *Atatürk'ün Hiç Yayınlanmamış Anıları*, pp. 172–76
10. Özgentürk, 19 August 2000
11. Günal

Chapter 36
1. Nur, p. 315
2. 'Beş N Bir K', 2 June 2005
3. Interview with Şen Sahir Sılan
4. Kinross, pp. 389–90

Chapter 37
1. Dündar, 'Ata'nın Resmiyle Öldü', *Milliyet* (11 November 2004).
2. Özgentürk, 'Bir Başka Latife', *Sabah* (2 December 2000)

3. Interview with Gültekin Ağaoğlu
4. Latife Uşşaki, 'Ölmek' ('Dying')

Chapter 38
1. M. Leventoğlu, *Atatürk'ün Vasiyeti*, p. 107

Bibliography

Books

Adıvar, Halide Edib, *The Turkish Ordeal*, New York and London: The Century Co., 1928.

Ağaoğlu, Süreyya, *Bir Ömür Böyle Geçti* (A Whole Lifetime), Istanbul: İsak, 1975.

Akay, Oğuz, *Gazi*, Istanbul: Truva, 2005.

Aksoy, Yaşar, *Bir Kent Bir İnsan* (A City, A Person), Istanbul: Dr Nejat Eczacıbaşı Foundation, 1986.

Alpkaya, Faruk, *Türkiye Cumhuriyet'nin Kuruluşu* (The Foundation of the Turkish Republic), Istanbul: İletişim, 1998.

Altay, Fahrettin, *On Yıl Savaş ve Sonrası* (Ten Years of War and Afterwards), Istanbul: İnsel, 1970.

Araz, Nezihe, *Mustafa Kemal ile 1000 Gün* (1000 Days with Mustafa Kemal), Istanbul: Dünya, 2002.

Arıkoğlu, Damar, *Hatıralarım* (Memoirs), Istanbul: Tan, 1961.

Armstrong, Harold Courtenay, *Grey Wolf: The Life of Kemal Atatürk*, London: A. Barker Ltd, 1932.

Aslan, Betül, *Türkiye-Azerbaycan İlişkileri* (Turkish-Azeri Relations), Istanbul: Kaynak, 2004.

Atadan, Makbule, *Ağabeyim Mustafa Kemal* (My Elder Brother Mustafa Kemal), ed. Şemsi Belli, Ankara: Ayyıldız, 1959.

Atatürk, Gazi Mustafa Kemal, *Atatürk'ün Söylev ve Demeçleri* (Atatürk's Speeches and Declarations), vol. III, Ankara: Türk İnkılap Tarihi Enstitüsü, 1997.

Atay, Falih Rıfkı, *Çankaya*, Istanbul: Doğan Kardeş, 1969.

Avcıoğlu, Doğan, *Türkiye'nin Düzeni* (Turkey's System), Ankara: Bilgi, 1973.

Aydemir, Şevket Süreyya, *Tek Adam: Mustafa Kemal* (The Only Man: Mustafa Kemal), vol. III, Istanbul: Remzi, 1965.

Baler, Mahmut, *Baldan Damlalar 3 ve Hatıralarım* (Honey Drops III and Memoirs), Istanbul: Kervan, 1982.

Baltacıoğlu, İsmail Hakkı, *Atatürk*, Erzurum: Atatürk University, 1973.

Banoğlu, Niyazi Ahmet, 'Atatürk ve Latife Hanım', AAMD, July 1991, issue 21.

Baran, Tülay Alim, *Bir Kentin Yeniden Yapılanması, Izmir 1923–1938* (Restructuring a City, Izmir 1923–1938), Istanbul: Arma, 2003.

Barlas, Mehmet, *Latife Hanım'ın Sırları ve Türk Sosyetesi* (Latife Hanım's Secrets and the Turkish Upper Classes), Istanbul: Birey, 2005.

Bayhan, Fatih and Mehmet Sadik Öke, *Teyzem Latife* (My Aunt Latife), Instanbul: Pegasus, 2011

Baysal, Mevlüt, *Çankaya'da Gazi'nin Hizmetinde* (At the Gazi's Service in Çankaya), Istanbul: Ercan, 1954.

Belli, Şemsi, *Fikriye*, Ankara: Bilgi, 1995.

Beyru, Rauf, *On Dokuzuncu Yüzyılda Izmir'de Yaşam* (Life in Nineteenth-Century Izmir), Istanbul: Literatür, 2000.

Bilgehan, Gülsün Toker, *Mevhibe*, Ankara: Bilgi, 1994.

Borak, Sadi, *Atatürk'ün Armstrong'a Cevabı* (Atatürk's Response to Armstrong), Istanbul: Kaynak, 1997.

Bozdağ, İsmet, *Atatürk'ün Başyaveri Salih Bozok anlatıyor, Latife ve Fikriye, İki Aşk Arasında Atatürk* (Atatürk's Aide-de-Camp's Tale: Latife and Fikriye, Atatürk Between Two Loves), Istanbul: Truva, 2005.

Bozdağ, İsmet, *Atatürk ve Eşi Latife Hanım* (Atatürk and his Wife Latife Hanım), Istanbul: Kervan, 1975.

Bozdağ, İsmet, *Gazi ve Latife*, Istanbul: Tekin, 2001.

Bozok, Salih, *Yaveri Atatürk'ü Anlatıyor* (Atatürk by his Aide-de-Camp), ed. Can Dündar, Istanbul: Doğan, 2003.

Bozok, Salih, and Cemil Sait, *Hep Atatürk'ün Yanında* (Always by Atatürk's Side), Istanbul: Çağdaş, 1985.

Çankaya, Necati, *Atatürk'ün Hayatı, Konuşmaları ve Yurt Gezileri* (Atatürk's Life, Speeches and Country Tours), Tifdruk, Istanbul 1985.

Çavuşoğlu, Turgay, *Çocuk Esirgeme Kurumu* (Society for the Protection of Children), Istanbul: Beyaz Gemi, 2001.

Cebesoy, Ali Fuat, *Siyasi Hatıralar, Lozan'dan Cumhuriyete* (Political Memoirs, from Lausanne to the Republic), Istanbul: Temel, 2002.

Cin, Halil, *İslam ve Osmanlı Hukukunda Evlenme* (Marriage in Islamic and Ottoman Law), Ankara: Ankara University, 1974.

Demirel, Ahmet, *Birinci Meclis'te Muhalefet İkinci Grup* (Opposition in the First Assembly: The Second Group), Istanbul: İletişim, 2003.

'Dilimiz' ('Our Language'), *Türk Yurdu*, issue 143, September 1917.

Dobkin, Marjorie Housepian, *Smyrna 1922*, New York: Newmark, 1988.

Ellison, Grace, *An Englishwoman in Angora*, London: Hutchison, 1923.

Gentizon, Paul, *Mustapha Kemal, ou, L'Orient en Marche* (Mustafa Kemal, or The Orient on the March), Paris: Éditions Bossard, 1929.

Georges-Gaulis, Berthe, *La Nouvelle Turquie* (The New Turkey), Paris: Armand Colin, 1924.

Gerede, Hüsrev, *Hüsrev Gerede's Memoirs* (in Turkish), ed. Sami Önal, Istanbul: Literatür, 2002.

Glasneck, Johannes, *Kemal Atatürk ve Çağdaş Türkiye* (Kemal Atatürk and Contemporary Turkey), Istanbul: Cumhuriyet, 1998.

Grosser-Rilke, Anna, *Nie Verwehte Klänge* (Never Forgotten Melodies), Leipzig and Berlin: Verlag Otto Beyer, 1937.

Gündüz, Asım, *Hatıratlarım* (Memoirs), Istanbul: Kervan, 1973.

Gürer, Cevat Abbas, *Ebedi Şef Kurtarıcı Atatürk'ün Zengin Tarihinden Birkaç Yaprak*

(A Few Leaves from the Wealth of History That Is the Eternal Chief and Liberator Atatürk), Istanbul: Halka, 1939.

İnönü, İsmet, *Hatıralar* (Memoirs), vol. I, ed. Sabahattin Selek, Istanbul: Bilgi, 1985.

İnan, Arı, *Prof. Dr. Afet İnan*, Istanbul: Remzi, 2005.

Kal, Nazmi, *Atatürk'le Yaşayanlar* (They Lived with Atatürk), TC Ziraat Bankası Kültür, Ankara 2003.

Karabekir, Kâzım, *Paşaların Kavgası* (The Generals Fall Out), Istanbul: Emre, 2000.

Karal, Enver Ziya, *Osmanlı Tarihi* (Ottoman History), vol. 5, Ankara: Çağdaş, 1976.

Karaosmanoğlu, Yakup Kadri, *Politikada 45 Yıl* (Forty-five Years in Politics), Istanbul: İletişim, 2002.

Kinross, Lord Patrick, *Atatürk: The Rebirth of a Nation*, London: Phoenix, 1995.

Kılıç Ali, *Atatürk'ün Hususiyetleri* (Atatürk's Characteristics), Istanbul: Cumhuriyet, 1988.

Kılıç Ali, *Kılıç Ali'nin Anıları* (Kılıç Ali's Memoirs), Istanbul: İş Bankası, 2005.

Kocabaşoğlu, Uygur, *İş Bankası Tarihi* (History of İş Bank), Istanbul: Tarih Vakfı, 2001.

Kocatürk, Utkan, *Kaynakçalı Atatürk Günlüğü* (A Documented Atatürk Diary), Ankara: AAMD, 1999.

Kocatürk, Utkan, *Atatürk Çizgisinde Geçmişten Geleceğe* (From the Past to the Future Following Atatürk), Ankara: AAMD, 2005.

Kurnaz, Şefika, *Cumhuriyet Öncesinde Türk Kadını* (Turkish Women Before the Republic), Istanbul: Ministry of Education, 1992.

Külçe, Süleyman, *Mareşal Fevzi Çakmak, Askerî Hususi Hayatı* (Marshal Fevzi Çakmak: The Man and the Military Commander), vol. I, Istanbul: Cumhuriyet, 1953.

Lengyel, Emil, 'Epilogue,' as ed. of H. C. Armstrong's *Grey Wolf: The Life of Kemal Atatürk*, New York: Capricorn Books, 1961.

Leventoğlu, Mazhar, *Atatürk'ün Vasiyeti* (*Atatürk's Will*), Istanbul: Leventoğlu, 1968.

Marcosson, Isaac, *The Turbulent Years*, New York: Dodd, Mead and Co., 1938.

Moralı, Nail, *Mütarekede Izmir, Önceleri ve Sonraları* (Izmir During the Armistice, Before and After), Istanbul: Tekin, 1976.

Nur, Rıza, *Hayat ve Hatıratım* (My Life and Memoirs), vols. II and III, Istanbul: İşaret, 1992.

Okyar, Fethi, *Üç Devirde Bir Adam* (A Man in Three Eras), ed. Cemal Kutay, Istanbul: Tercüman, 1980.

Okyar, Fethi, *Serbest Cumhuriyet Fırkası Nasıl Doğdu, Nasıl Feshedildi?* (How the Free Republican Party Was Born, and How It Was Dissolved), Tercüman, Istanbul, 1987.

Okyar, Fethi, *Fethi Okyar'ın Anıları* (Fethi Okyar's Reminiscences), ed. Osman Okyar, Mehmet Seyitdanlığoğlu, Istanbul: Türkiye İş Bankası, 1997.

Onat, Nuri, *Cumhurbaşkanı Gazi M. Kemal Paşa'nın Sonbahar Gezileri* (President Gazi Mustafa Kemal Paşa's Autumn Tours), Istanbul: Çağdaş, 1984.

Oranlı, Ziya, *Atatürk'ün Şimdiye Kadar Yayınlanmamış Anıları: Anlatan Ali Metin, Emir Çavuşu* (Atatürk's Unpublished Memoirs, as Told by Ali Metin, Batman), Ankara: Alkan, 1967.

Ökçün, Gündüz, *Türkiye İktisat Kongresi, Izmir 1923* (Turkish Economy Congress: Izmir 1923), Ankara: AÜSBF, 1971.

Önder, Mehmet, *Atatürk Konya'da* (Atatürk in Konya), Ankara: AAMD, 1989.
Önder, Mehmet, *Atatürk'ün Yurt Gezileri* (Atatürk's Tours of the Country), Istanbul: İş Bank, 1998.
Ötüş-Baskett, Belma, *Nezihe Muhiddin ve Türk Kadını* (Nezihe Muhiddin and Turkish Women), Istanbul: İletişim, 1999.
Öz, Hikmet, *Atatürk Tarsus'ta* (Atatürk in Tarsus), Ankara: Ministry of Culture, 1986.
Özalp, Teoman and Kâzım, *Atatürk'ten Anılar* (Reminiscences of Atatürk), Ankara: İş Bankası Kültür, 1992.
Perinçek, Mehmet, *Atatürk'ün Sovyetlerle Görüşmeleri* (Atatürk's Meetings with the Soviets), Istanbul: Kaynak, 2005.
Price, George Ward, *Extra-Special Correspondent*, London: Harrap, 1957.
Sertel, Zekeriya, *Türkiye'de Siyasal Partiler* (Political Parties in Turkey), vol. I, Istanbul: Hürriyet Vakfı, 1988.
Sevük, İsmail Habib, *Atatürk İçin* (For Atatürk), Istanbul: Cumhuriyet, 1939.
Sheridan, Clare, *Nuda Veritas*, London: Thornton Butterworth, 1927.
Snowden, Charmian, *Tudor Hall: The First Hundred Years 1850–1949*.
Sorgun, Taylan, *İmparatorluktan Cumhuriyete: Fahrettin Altay Paşa Anlatıyor* (From the Empire to the Republic: Fahrettin Altay Paşa Speaks), 2nd ed., Istanbul: Kamer, 1998.
Soyak, Hasan Rıza, *Atatürk'ten Hatıralar* (Reminiscences of Atatürk), Istanbul: Yapı Kredi, 2005.
Sönmez, Cemil, *Atatürk'ün Annesi Zübeyde Hanım* (Zübeyde Hanım, Atatürk's Mother), Ankara: AKDTYK, 1998.
Şener, Cemal, *Topal Osman Olayı* (The Lame Osman Incident), Istanbul: Etik, 2004 (cited in Mahir İz).
Şimşir, Bilal [I], *Atatürk ile Yazışmalar* (Correspondence with Atatürk), Ankara: Ministry of Culture, 1981.
Şimşir, Bilal [II], Dış Basında Atatürk ve Türk Devrimi (Atatürk and the Turkish Revolution in the International Press), vol. I, Ankara: TTK, 1981.
Taşkıran, Tezer, *Cumhuriyetin 50. Yılında Türk Kadın Hakları* (Women's Rights on the 50th Anniversary of the Republic), Ankara: PM's Office, 1973.
Tunaya, Tarık Zafer, *Türkiye'de Siyasal Partiler* (Political Parties in Turkey), vol. I, Istanbul: Hürriyet Vakfı, 1988.
Tunçay, Mete, *Türkiye Cumhuriyetinde Tek Parti Yönetimi* (Single Party Rule in the History of the Turkish Republic) Istanbul: Tarih Vakfı Yurt, 2005.
Umar, Bilge, *Izmir'de Yunanlıların Son Günleri* (The Final Days of the Greeks in Izmir), Ankara: Bilgi, 1974.
Uşaklıgil, Halit Ziya, *Kırk Yıl* (Forty Years), Istanbul: İnkılâp, 1987.
Uşaklıgil, Halit Ziya, *Bir Acı Hikâye* (A Sad Story), Istanbul: İnkilâp, 1991.
Uyar, Hakkı, *Tek Parti Dönemi ve CHP* (The Single Party Period and the Republican People's Party), Istanbul: Boyut, 1999.
Ülger, Eriş, *Latife Gazi Mustafa Kemal*, Istanbul: İnkilap, 2005.
Villalta, Jorge Blanco, *Atatürk*, Ankara: TTK, 1979.
Volkan, Vamık D., and Itkowitz, Norman, *The Immortal Atatürk: A Psychobiography*, Chicago and London: University of Chicago Press, 1984.

von Mikusch, Dagobert, *Mustapha Kemal: Between Europe and Asia*, trans. John Linton, Garden City, NY: Doubleday, Doran & Co., Inc., 1931.

Yalman, Ahmet Emin [I], *Atatürk'ün Söylev ve Demeçleri* (Atatürk's Speeches and Statements), vol. III, Ankara: Turkish Reform History Institute, 1997.

Yalman, Ahmet Emin [II], *Yakın Tarihte Gördüklerim ve Geçirdiklerim* (What I've Seen and Experienced in Recent History), vol. 2, Istanbul: Pera, 1977.

Yetkin, Çetin, Atatürk'ün Başarısız Demokrasi Devrimi Serbest Cumhuriyet Fırkası (Atatürk's Failed Attempt at a Democratic Revolution: The Free Republican Party), Toplumsal Dönüşüm, 1997.

Yiğit, Nuyan, *Atatürk'le 30 Yıl* (Thirty Years with Atatürk), Istanbul: Remzi, 2005.

Yurdakul, Yurdakul, *Atatürk'ün Hiç Yayınlanmamış Anıları* (Never Before Published Reminiscences of Atatürk), Istanbul: Aksoy, 1999.

Zihnioğlu, Yaprak, *Kadınsız İnkılap* (Womanless Reform), Istanbul: Metis, 2003.

Zürcher, Eric Jan, *Political Opposition in the Early Turkish Republic: The Progressive Republican Party (1924–1925)*, Leiden: Brill, 1991.

Articles

Ahmad, Feroz, 'The Development of Capitalism in Turkey', *Journal of Third World Studies*, Autumn 1998.

'Atatürk'ün Boşanma Mektubu Göz Yaşartacak' ('Atatürk's Divorce Letter Will Bring You to Tears'), *Yeni Şafak,* 6 December 2004.

Barlas, Mehmet, 'Latife Hanım'ın Dramı' ('Latife Hanım's Tragedy'), *Güneş*, 10 November 1986.

Beni Hasan, 'Kemal Pasha at Home – The New Master of Turkey', *The Mentor*, May 1927.

Bilgehan, Gülsün Toker, 'Çankaya'nın Hanımefendileri' ('Çankaya's Ladies'), *Milliyet*, 11–12 October 1982.

Bryant, Louis, 'A Turkish Divorce', *The Nation,* 26 August 1925

Cebesoy, Ali Fuat [I], 'Hayalatla Uğraşmayalım Paşam' ('Let's Stop Wasting Time on Dreams, My Paşa'), *Yakın Tarihimiz*, Istanbul, 1962.

Cebesoy, Ali Fuat [II], 'Atatürk ile Milli Mücadele Arkadaşları' ('Atatürk and His Brothers-in-Arms in the National Struggle'), *Yakın Tarihimiz*, vol. IV, Istanbul, 1962.

Coşkunoğlu, Osman, 'Uşak Şeker Fabrikası'nın Kuruluşu' ('The Foundation of the Uşak Sugar Mill'), *Cumhuriyet*, 21 January 2004.

Çölaşan, Emin, 'Leman Karaosmanoğlu ile Sohbet, Atatürk'ü İki Kadın Deli Gibi Severdi' ('Chat with Leman Karaosmanoğlu: Two Women Loved Atatürk Madly'), *Hürriyet*, 10 November 1985.

Dündar, Can, 'Fikriye', *Milliyet*, 1992.

Dündar, Can, 'Latife Hanım'ın Atatürk'süz Hayatı' ('Latife Hanım's Life Without Atatürk'), *Milliyet*, 28 October 2003.

Dündar, Can, 'Söz Kız Tarafında' ('And the Bride's Side Speaks'), *Milliyet*, 10 November 2004.

Dündar, Can, 'Yüzyılın Aşkları – Latife Hanım' ('Great Love Stories of the Century –

Latife Hanım'), CNN, 10 November 2004.

Dündar, Can, 'Ata'nın Resmiyle Öldü' ('She Died Clutching Atatürk's Portrait'), *Milliyet*, 11 November 2004.

Günal, Bülent, 'Latife Hanım'ın Hatıra Defterini Okuyan Tek Adam' ('The Only Man to Have Read Latife Hanım's Diary'), *Vatan*, 7 August 2004.

Kaplan, Sefa, 'Latife Hanım'ın Günlüğünü Bir Bilim Kurulu İncelesin' ('A Committee of Experts Must Study Latife Hanım's Diary'), *Hürriyet*, 3 January 2005.

Kılıç, Ecevit, 'İşte Savcının Aradığı Tanık, Köşkü Bastık, Latife Yalnızdı' ('Here Is the Witness Sought by the Prosecutor, We Raided the Residence, Latife Was on Her Own'), *Yeni Aktüel*, issue 60, August 2006.

Lue, Larry, 'Kemal and Wife Pledge Liberty of Turk Women', *Chicago Daily Tribune*, 28 February 1923

Lue, Larry, 'Mrs Kemal Charms an American Visitor, *fe hanım*28 February 1923

Marcosson, Isaac, 'Kemal Pasha', *Saturday Evening Post*, 20 October 1923.

'Mme. Kemal Tells of Her Romantic Marriage to the Turkish President', *Current Opinion*, January 1924, p. 80.

Özgentürk, Nebil, 'Gazi'den Sonra' ('After the Gazi'), *Sabah*, 19 August 2000.

Özgentürk, Nebil, 'Bir Başka Latife' ('A Different Latife'), *Sabah*, 2 December 2000.

Özgentürk, Nebil, 'Halam Hep Yalnızdı' ('My Aunt Was Always Alone'), *Sabah*, 1 November 2003.

Pekşen, Yalçın, 'Atatürk'ün Özel Yaşamı, Vecihe İlmen Anlatıyor' ('Atatürk's Private Life, as Told by Vecihe İlmen'), *Cumhuriyet*, 10 November 1984.

Selçuker, Selma, 'Kadın Gözü ile Atatürk, Süreyya Ağaoğlu'yla Görüşme' ('Atatürk from a Female Viewpoint: Interview with Süreyya Ağaoğlu'), *Güneş*, date unknown.

Süsoy, Yener, 'Latife Hanım'ın Öyküsünü Sıfırcı Baha'dan Dinleyin' ('Hear Latife Hanım's Story from Baha, the Stingy Marker'), *Hürriyet*, 16 June 2003.

Tunçay, Mete, 'Latife Hanım–Kameneva Mektuplaşması' ('Latife Hanım–Kameneva Correspondence'), *Toplumsal Tarih*, March 2003 (cited in George Harris, *The Communists and the Kadro Movement*, Appendix 3, Istanbul: İsis, 2002, English translation from the original Russian in *Novyi Vostok*, issue 7, 1925, pp. 228–301).

'What did Latife Hanım Feel on 10 November?' *Milliyet*, 8 May 2006, Presidential History, Ankara 2006.

'Wife of Mustafa Kemal is Sacrificed to Ambition' *Toronto Daily Star*, 28 August 1925.

Williamson, S. T., 'Stranger Than Fiction-D etained by Order', *The New York Times*, 6 June 1926

Yalman, Ahmet Emin [I], 'Hayatına Ait Hatıralar' (Reminiscences), *Vakit*, 10 January 1922.

Yücel, Şükran, 'Uşşakizadeler' ('The Uşşakizade Family'), *Izmir Life*, issue 24, August 2003.

Index